SECOND EDITION

Development by Agreement

A TOOL KIT FOR LAND DEVELOPERS AND LOCAL GOVERNMENTS

AMERICAN BAR ASSOCIATION

State and Local
Government Law Section

Cover design by Sara Wadford/ABA Design

Printed in the United States of America.

28 27 26 25 24 5 4 3 2 1

A catalog record for this book is available from the Library of Congress.

CONTENTS

PREFACE AND ACKNOWLEDGMENTS

In 2003, David Callies, Julie Tappendorf, and the late Dan Curtin wrote *Bargaining for Development*, which analyzed laws pertaining to impact fees and exactions and suggested that most related legal issues could be avoided using development and annexation agreements. In 2012, soon after the Great Recession, David, Julie, and Cecily Barclay expanded upon that premise, and wrote the first edition of this book, focusing entirely on the development-by-agreement process. A decade later, Julie, Cecily, and Matt Gray decided to update this book, providing current legal and practical considerations affecting the drafting, negotiation, and interpretation of development agreements, annexation agreements, and numerous other agreements between developers and public agencies. As part of our "tool kit," we also have provided both new and updated appendixes for our readers' use that provide practical solutions for overcoming at least some of the development challenges facing developers, owners, and local governments today.

In the research and editing for this book, we are particularly indebted to Erin Monforti, an associate at Ancel Glink, P.C. in Chicago, and Kaela Shiigi, an associate at Perkins Coie LLP in San Francisco.

Julie A. Tappendorf
Cecily T. Barclay
Matthew S. Gray

ABOUT THE AUTHORS

Julie A. Tappendorf is an equity partner with Ancel Glink, P.C., in Chicago, where she represents local governments in transactional and litigation matters, including defending land use decisions; negotiating and drafting contracts; drafting zoning, annexation, and subdivision regulations; and advising clients on special service area (SSA) financing and tax increment financing (TIF) as well as other economic development matters. Ms. Tappendorf currently serves as city attorney for the cities of Lake Forest and Park Ridge, and village attorney for the villages of Glenview, Gilberts, and Lindenhurst. She was an original co-author of the first edition of *Development by Agreement*, is a co-author of *Handling the Land Use Case* (3d ed. 2023-2024), *Social Media and Local Governments* (1st ed. 2013, 2d ed. forthcoming), *Bargaining for Development* (with David L. Callies & Daniel J. Curtin, Jr., 2003), and has written numerous chapters and articles on architectural design, annexation and development agreements, annexation and subdivisions, and regulating distressed properties. Ms. Tappendorf is a frequent speaker at national and local conferences on a variety of land use topics and issues, including annexation and development agreements. Prior to her law career, she served for eight years as a Korean cryptologic-linguist in the Military Intelligence Branch of the U.S. Army. She earned her J.D. from the University of Hawaii School of Law and her B.A. from Illinois State University.

Cecily T. Barclay is a partner with Perkins Coie LLP in San Francisco, where she represents landowners, developers, and public agencies on matters involving complex land use and entitlements, real estate acquisition and development, redevelopment, and local government law for hotels and resorts, life science campuses, residential communities, and mixed-use and retail centers, as well as reuse of former military facilities and other infill and redevelopment sites. Ms. Barclay is co-author (with Matt Gray) of *California Land Use and Planning Law* (39th ed.) and has written and spoken extensively on land use law, including for programs sponsored by universities, city and county counsel associations, and state, local, and national law associations. Ms. Barclay has served on the Publication Oversight Board for the American Bar Association's State and Local Government Law Section for almost two decades. She received her J.D. from Harvard Law School and her B.A. from the University of California, Berkeley.

Matthew S. Gray is a partner with Perkins Coie LLP in San Francisco, where he focuses his practice on securing land use entitlements, environmental compliance, and real estate transactions. He negotiates and secures approval of development agreements, general plan amendments, specific plans, zoning, subdivision approvals, and annexations. He has worked on a variety of significant projects across California, including large urban redevelopment projects, military base reuse projects, and mixed-use waterfront developments. Mr. Gray is co-author (with Cecily Barclay) of *California Land Use & Planning Law* (39th ed.) and is the annual update author of *California Subdivision Map Act and the Development Process* (2d ed.). He earned his J.D. from Georgetown Law and his B.A. from University of California, Los Angeles.

1

Introduction and Background

Formal agreements between landowners and local governments governing the development and use of land have been on the rise over the past several decades. These agreements frequently change the nature of the relationship between landowner and government in the land development process from adversarial to cooperative and build on both parties' mutual interests in, and benefits that can arise from, the proposed development.

In this chapter, we begin with an introductory overview of the major problems faced by governments and landowners that can often be solved by agreements concerning the development of land. We touch on some of the constitutional issues that come up in the development context, including the Takings Clause of the Fifth Amendment. The introduction also includes a summary of common development conditions (exactions, dedications, and impact fees) and discusses the types of improvements and facilities necessitated by land development. It also discusses the doctrine of vested rights, from the perspective of a landowner who wants to ensure his or her rights have vested, as well as the government's desire to apply changed regulations.

In Chapters 2, 3, and 4, we discuss in detail how to negotiate and draft agreements that relate to the development and use of land. Chapter 2 focuses solely on the development agreement. In that chapter, we discuss in more detail constitutional issues encountered by governments and landowners in negotiating development agreements, including the "reserved powers" doctrine and the "contracts clause." Chapter 2 also discusses the importance of statutory authority for development agreements, the source of authority, and general requirements for approval and adoption of these agreements. The chapter concludes with a discussion of the limitations on the imposition of conditions, exactions, and dedications in development agreements.

Chapter 3 focuses on annexation agreements and is organized in a similar fashion to Chapter 2. The chapter begins with a discussion of some of the more common legal issues and the authority for entering into annexation agreements. It also includes a discussion of the process for approval and adoption, as well as a discussion of the type of conditions that can be imposed through an annexation agreement.

In Chapter 4, we analyze a number of other development-related agreements that governments and landowners might encounter. Each of the agreements, listed below, is discussed in a separate section to allow a more detailed and individualized treatment within the chapter:

- Affordable housing agreement
- Community benefits agreement
- Conservation agreement
- Disposition and development agreement
- Exclusive negotiating agreement
- Facilities improvement agreement
- Habitat mitigation agreement
- Memorandum of agreement/memorandum of understanding
- Parkland dedication and improvement agreement
- Reimbursement and processing agreement
- School mitigation agreement
- Public improvements agreement
- Tax increment financing agreement
- Transit occupancy tax agreement

We have ended our book with a number of sample agreements and checklists in a comprehensive set of appendices listed below (if you would like an electronic copy of one or more of these appendices, please contact the authors at jtappendorf@ancelglink.com, cbarclay@perkinscoie.com, or mgray@perkinscoie.com). The appendices are intended to provide the practitioner with samples of agreements and other documents that can be customized in drafting and negotiating a variety of agreements related to the development and use of land. They include:

- Checklist for drafting annexation agreements
- Simple annexation agreement
- Model annexation and development agreement
- Sample development agreement
- Checklist for drafting community benefits agreements
- Sample reimbursement and processing agreement
- Sample project school facilities agreement
- Sample subdivision improvement agreement
- Sample parkland dedication agreement
- Sample economic development and tax sharing agreement

The Constitutionality of Common Land Development Conditions

Land development of any size and substance requires a variety of public facilities to support it. The most common development needs include additional roads, public utilities, parks, and schools, as well as other community facilities such as police and fire stations. In the distant past, local government was obligated to bear the principal cost of development improvements and facilities. However, state and local financial resources became and continue to be inadequate to provide these facilities since the end of massive federal subsidies in the early 1980s. For decades now, local governments have been charging land developers for at least a portion of the cost of public facilities. These costs often take the form of conditions on development approval and subdivision dedications and fees. Initially, these fees were "charged" as the price of drawing and recording the simpler and cheaper subdivision plat in place of the lengthy, tedious, and easily flawed metes and bounds description for land development. Soon, however, these fees and dedications became part of the regulatory land use process, exercised by local government under the police power for the health, safety, and welfare of the people, often as a method to control or manage growth.[1]

1. Robert H. Freilich et al., From Sprawl to Sustainability (2d ed. 2010); Julian Conrad Juergensmeyer & Thomas E. Roberts, Land Use Planning and Control Law (2d ed. 2002); Exactions, Impact Fees, and Dedications: Shaping Land-Use Development and Funding Infrastructure in the Dolan Era (Robert H. Freilich & David W. Bushek eds., 1995); David L. Callies et al., Cases and Materials on Land Use (6th ed. 2012); Robert H. Freilich & Michael M. Shultz, National Model Subdivision Regulations, Planning, and Law (1994); Daniel R. Mandelker, Land Use

By justifying land development dedications and fees as police power regulations instead of as "voluntary" costs of using the subdivision process, local governments invited judicial scrutiny under the Takings Clause of the Fifth Amendment to the U.S. Constitution, which permits the taking of private property for public use only upon payment of just compensation. While early cases typically upheld intrinsic dedications and fees, the more recent charges of impact fees for the shared construction by several land developments of large and expensive public facilities (such as municipal wastewater treatment plants and sanitary landfills) extrinsic to the development upon which the fee is levied led courts to scrutinize the connection between these fees and the demand generated by the charged development for the particular facility in question.[2] Nevertheless, it is generally agreed that the constitutionality of laws applicable to impact fees, exactions, and in-lieu fees, as well as to compulsory land dedications, is the same since they all represent development conditions levied at some point in the land development process, including subdivision plat approval, shoreline management permit, building permit, occupancy permit, or utility connection.[3] Throughout this book, these terms will be used interchangeably.

The major legal issue with respect to fees, dedications, and exactions is the connection or "nexus" to land development. Without this nexus, land development regulations will generally be considered unconstitutional

LAW (5th ed. 2003); Susan P. Schoettle & David G. Richardson, *Nontraditional Uses of the Utility Concept to Fund Public Facilities*, 25 URB. LAW. 519, 519–22 (1993); Frona M. Powell, *Challenging Authority for Municipal Subdivision Exactions: The Ultra Vires Attack*, 39 DEPAUL L. REV. 635 (1990); Julian Conrad Juergensmeyer & Robert M. Blake, *Impact Fees: An Answer to Local Government's Capital Funding Dilemma*, 9 FLA. STATE U. L. REV. 415 (1981); Thomas M. Pavelko, *Subdivision Exactions: A Review of Judicial Standards*, 25 J. URB. & CONTEMP. L. 269 (1983); DEVELOPMENT EXACTIONS (James E. Frank & Robert M. Rhodes eds., 1987).

2. Ira M. Heyman & Thomas K. Gilhool, *The Constitutionality of Imposing Increased Community Costs on New Suburban Residents through Subdivision Exactions*, 73 YALE L.J. 1119 (1964). *See also* John D. Johnston, Jr., *Constitutionality of Subdivision Exactions: The Quest for a Rationale*, 52 CORNELL L.Q. 871 (1967); *but see* Carlos A. Ball & Laurie Reynolds, *Exactions and Burden Distribution in Takings Law*, 47 WM. & MARY L. REV. 1513 (2006) (arguing that the exactions analysis should be adjusted to consider burden distribution to conform with constitutional takings doctrine).

3. Bd. of Cnty. Comm'rs of Douglas Cnty., Colo. v. Bainbridge, 929 P.2d 691, 698 (Colo. 1996) (citing DONALD G. HAGMAN & JULIAN CONRAD JUERGENSMEYER, URBAN PLANNING AND LAND DEVELOPMENT CONTROL LAW § 9.8 (2d ed. 1986)); DEVELOPMENT EXACTIONS, *supra* note 1, at 3–4.

takings of property without compensation, particularly after the U.S. Supreme Court decisions in *Nollan v. California Coastal Commission*,[4] *Dolan v. City of Tigard*,[5] and *Koontz v. St. John's River Water Management District*.[6] In *Nollan*, the Court held that land use exactions require an "essential nexus" between the nature of the condition and a public need generated by the proposed development.[7] The Court again considered the constitutionality of land use exactions in *Dolan*, adding an additional requirement of "rough proportionality" between the exaction and the harms caused by the regulated activity.[8] In *Koontz*, the Supreme Court reaffirmed the nexus and proportionality requirements announced in *Nollan* and *Dolan* and confirmed that the principles undergirding those decisions "do not change depending on whether the government *approves* a permit on the condition that the applicant turns over property or *denies* a permit because the applicant refuses to do so."[9] In the following sections, we summarize the most common forms of fees, dedications, and exactions and the factors courts have considered in determining whether they are a legally permissible exercise of police power or instead constitute an unconstitutional regulatory taking of property without just compensation.[10]

In sum, government generally seeks some legal way to obtain a variety of public improvements and facilities. Some of these are arguably not connected to a need actually generated by a particular development, while

---

4. 483 U.S. 825 (1987).

5. 512 U.S. 374 (1994). For recent commentary, see J. David Breemer, *The Evolution of the Nexus Test*, 59 WASH. & LEE L. REV. 373 (2002).

6. 570 U.S. 595 (2013).

7. *Nollan*, 483 U.S. at 837.

8. *Dolan*, 512 U.S. at 391.

9. *Koontz*, 570 U.S. at 606–07 (holding there had been an extortionate demand for property in violation of the Takings Clause where the local water management district had not approved the requested permits due to the applicant's refusal to accept proposed conditions to further reduce the size of his development and to make improvements to district-owned wetlands several miles away).

10. There is little difference in the law pertaining to land development conditions based on the subject matter of the condition. While the *Nollan* and *Dolan* cases deal primarily with land dedications, there is a strong argument to be made that the rules of the case apply to all manner of land development conditions, including impact fees and exactions, as the California Supreme Court held in *Ehrlich v. Culver City*, 911 P.2d 429 (Cal. 1996). *See also* N. Ill. Home Builders Ass'n v. Cnty. of DuPage, 649 N.E.2d 384 (Ill. 1995); Home Builders Ass'n v. Beavercreek, 729 N.E.2d 349 (Ohio 2000); Town of Flower Mound v. Stafford Ests., L.P., 135 S.W.3d 630 (Tex. 2004).

others are particularly appropriate given the impacts the development is expected to generate on the surrounding community. The most common (and expensive) facilities include street and street improvements, water and sewer facilities, affordable housing, parks and recreation, and schools.

Streets and Street Improvements

Streets and street improvements are the most common types of land development conditions required for the approval of subdivision plats and permits. These streets and street improvements are necessary to address the impact of increased traffic the proposed land development is expected to generate. These conditions are generally upheld when the fee, exaction, or dedication is designed for additional street and road facilities that closely approximate the additional traffic resulting from the proposed development. Otherwise, the condition is generally regarded as an invalid taking under the general rules of *Nollan-Dolan* and/or a state decision or local ordinance following these rules.

Water and Sewer Facilities

Fees imposed to fund capital improvements to a local government's water or sewer systems have been upheld in a number of jurisdictions. In most cases, the fees are called "connection" fees, or "tap-on" fees. The fees are used to fund expansion or improvement of the water or sewer system that becomes necessary because of increases in population and new development. As with other types of impact fees, a court will first ask whether the local government has sufficient authority in its enabling legislation to impose a fee. If so, the court then addresses the issue of whether the impact fee is a valid regulatory measure rather than an illegal tax or a taking without compensation. Most jurisdictions apply the rational nexus test to determine the reasonableness of the fee. This test requires showing first that the fee is related to a real need created by the new development, and second that the funds collected are sufficiently "earmarked" for the benefit of the development paying the fee.[11]

11. *Ehrlich*, 911 P.2d 429.

Affordable Housing

There is increasing authority for the use of set-asides and other housing exactions and fees to provide needed low-income or affordable housing in the community in which commercial or market rate housing is proposed for development. The California Supreme Court held in 2015 that inclusionary housing regulations are constitutionally permissible as long as they are reasonably related to the public welfare.[12] The court held that inclusionary housing ordinances should be evaluated as zoning regulations, rather than exactions. As a zoning regulation, an inclusionary housing requirement is valid in California if it is reasonably related to the public welfare; it need not satisfy *Nollan* or *Dolan* requirements of reasonable relationship and rough proportionality to the impacts of new developments. Similarly, in-lieu housing fees a California local government imposes on developers must be reasonably related to the overall availability of affordable housing and need not be reasonably related to a development's impact on an agency's affordable housing need.[13]

Housing linkage fees imposed upon *commercial* development have also been upheld in California in *Commercial Builders of Northern California v. City of Sacramento.*[14] The City of Sacramento enacted an ordinance conditioning certain commercial building permits on the payment of a fee to offset the burdens caused by low-income workers who were likely to move to the city to work at the commercial development. Commercial Builders challenged the ordinance, claiming that the fee was an uncompensated taking. The court upheld the ordinance, holding that the city had satisfied the essential nexus test under *Nollan* because the fee was designed to further the city's legitimate interest in housing low-income workers. The dissent, however, argued that the fees had little relationship to the impact of commercial development. The dissent further noted that if the fee imposed was sufficiently connected to the development, other more tenuously connected fees will also be upheld (i.e., exactions to subsidize small businesses, child care centers, food services, and health care delivery systems).

12. Cal. Bldg. Indus. Ass'n v. City of San Jose, 351 P.3d 974 (Cal. 2015).
13. 616 Croft Ave. LLC v. City of W. Hollywood, 3 Cal. App. 5th 621 (Cal. Ct. App. 2016).
14. 941 F.2d 872 (9th Cir. 1991).

Parks and Recreation

Typically, requiring land dedications for open space, parks, and recreation is found to be a valid exercise of the police power. However, like other impact fees, the amount of land required from the landowner must be proportional to the need created by the subsequent development. As an alternative to requiring dedication of specific amounts of land, local governments also may require in-lieu fees that are earmarked in a special fund to be used to purchase parks, recreational facilities, and/or open space.

Today, the ways in which a community will use open space are much broader than they once were. Greenways along streams and rivers, passive open space, wildlife habitat and travel corridors, and a variety of other undeveloped lands may be significant parts of a community's overall plan for open space.[15] The focus of most of the case law and many of the local programs tested in these cases has been on achieving a "rational nexus" and "rough proportionality" between the dedication or fee requirements and the impacts of residential development. The need for greenways and general open space is one that relates to the entire community and to all types of development. There is little doubt that some communities will attempt to exact a share of the cost of general open space from nonresidential development. So long as the community can show a nexus and proportionality, the exaction is likely to be upheld.[16]

Schools

The use of impact fees and other exactions to fund the construction of schools is a relatively common practice and has been the subject of frequent litigation. School impact fees also must be necessitated by, and provide a specific service for, the development charged.[17] For example, a retirement community should not have to pay into a fund for a school

15. *See* James D. Mertes & James R. Hall, Park, Recreation, Open Space, and Greenway Guidelines (1996); Eric Damian Kelly & Barbara Becker, Community Planning: An Introduction to the Comprehensive Plan (1999).

16. Note that one of the critical issues in *Dolan v. City of Tigard*, 512 U.S. 374 (1994), was a requirement for the dedication and improvement of a greenway along a creek and a related trail.

17. *See, e.g.*, Tanimura & Antle Fresh Foods, Inc. v. Salinas Union High Sch. Dist., 34 Cal. App. 5th 775, 792–93 (Cal. Ct. App. 2019) (describing the California statutory scheme for establishing school impact fees for different "types" of development projects and the required connection between the project's impact and the exacted fee).

that its residents neither drove the need for nor benefit from.[18] Even a rapidly growing community's need for adequate school facilities to meet the demand of its burgeoning population does not always provide a basis for an impact fee. Sometimes existing, underutilized facilities in older neighborhoods may exist and be available for renovation or expansion at a much lower cost. In the absence of existing school facilities, local governments use a variety of methods to help finance the need for new facilities.

One of the most noteworthy cases is *St. Johns County v. Northeast Florida Builders Ass'n, Inc.*[19] There, the Supreme Court of Florida held that a fee of $448 per single-family dwelling met a rational nexus test when applied to a 100-unit subdivision. However, the exaction failed a pre-*Dolan* proportionality standard because it was not clear the money collected would necessarily benefit those who paid the fee. The same court later held that a school impact fee as applied to a retirement community, which had covenants prohibiting minors from residing in the development, failed both the nexus and proportionality test.[20] While a landowner may elect to fund new facilities within or near its proposed development, such facilities should not be required absent a showing of true need.

Other Considerations That Can Affect the Legality of Impact Fees, Dedications, and Conditions of Approval

Although the question of whether a regulatory imposition is constitutional is of paramount consideration, other legal requirements also must be met for local governments to legally attach conditions or exactions to approvals for development of land. Among these are the need for authority to levy dedications, fees, and other exactions, in the form of enabling legislation and local ordinances. In the absence of this authority, landowners may claim that these requirements are illegal, that they are "ad hoc," or that the need to subsequently expend the fee ("in lieu" of a dedication requirement

---

18. *See* Volusia Cnty. v. Aberdeen at Ormond Beach LLP, 760 So. 2d 126 (Fla. 2000).

19. 583 So. 2d 635 (Fla. 1991).

20. *Volusia Cnty.*, 760 So. 2d 126. After a lengthy discussion of the legal and factual issues, the court held simply: "In sum, Aberdeen neither contributes to the need for additional schools nor benefits from their construction. Accordingly, the imposition of impact fees as applied to Aberdeen does not satisfy the dual rational nexus test." *Id.* at 137.

or an impact fee) within a reasonable period of time after collection does not exist.[21] Courts uniformly strike down—often as an unauthorized tax—land development conditions that are not so connected. Generally, this includes attempts to remedy existing infrastructure deficiencies[22] or to provide for operation and maintenance of facilities.[23]

In a few states, local governments have the authority to impose excise taxes that may accomplish the same purpose as an impact fee. The key here is "authorization," almost always through a specific enabling statute. For example, the Colorado Supreme Court determined that a road impact fee levied by Cherry Hills Village was actually a tax, but it went on to hold that it was an excise tax that the city was authorized to impose.[24] In a later case, the Ohio Supreme Court upheld a local road impact fee after rejecting an appellate court's application of the tax/fee distinction; the Ohio high court found that the distinction was not critical in Ohio.[25] The Pennsylvania Supreme Court also upheld an excise tax imposed on gross receipts of a construction company, holding that it was a valid gross receipts tax and not an unauthorized tax on homebuilding.[26] In contrast, the Washington Supreme Court struck down a "residential development unit fee" imposed on rental dwelling units, in addition to a business licensing fee imposed on the entire business location after finding the fee was an unauthorized property tax and not an excise tax, which would have been allowed under the

---

21. James C. Nicholas, *Impact Exactions: Economic Theory, Practice, and Incidence*, 50 Law & Contemp. Probs. 85 (1987); James C. Nicholas et al., A Practitioner's Guide to Development Impact Fees 37–38 (1991); Takings: Land Development Conditions and Regulatory Takings after Dolan and Lucas (David L. Callies ed., 1996); Timothy M. Mulvaney, *Proposed Exactions*, 26 J. Land Use & Env't L. 277, 292–93 (2011); Glen Hansen, *Let's Be Reasonable: Why Neither* Nollan/Dolan *nor* Penn Central *Should Govern Generally-Applied Legislative Exactions after* Koontz, 34 Pace Env't L. Rev. 237, 245–46 (2017).

22. Marblehead v. City of San Clemente, 277 Cal. Rptr. 550 (Cal. Ct. App. 1991); *see also* Drees Co. v. Hamilton Twp., 132 Ohio St. 3d 186, 197 (Ohio 2012).

23. *See* First Baptist Church of St. Paul v. City of St. Paul, 884 N.W.2d 355, 361 (Minn. 2016); *but see* Bloom v. City of Fort Collins, 784 P.2d 304 (Colo. 1989).

24. Cherry Hills Farms, Inc. v. City of Cherry Hills, 670 P.2d 779 (Colo. 1983).

25. Home Builders Ass'n v. Beavercreek, 729 N.E.2d 349 (Ohio 2000).

26. Sch. Dist. of Scranton v. Dale & Dale Design & Dev., 741 A.2d 186 (Pa. 1999).

Washington constitution.[27] The Massachusetts Court of Appeals also held that a school impact fee was an unauthorized tax.[28]

How Vested Rights Can Protect a Landowner from Bearing the Burden of Unexpected New Land Development Regulations

The principles of law and equity that permit a landowner to continue with or complete a land development or land use activity even after a change in regulations that would otherwise prohibit or limit that development or activity are commonly referred to as "vested rights." The point at which a landowner may continue with a land development project despite new land development regulations that would prohibit that development triggers an analysis of whether vested rights and its close cousin, equitable estoppel, have been triggered. The two legal doctrines arise from very different principles.[29] A vested rights analysis focuses on whether a landowner has acquired sufficient real property rights to proceed with a development project, or some phase of the project, unaffected by a subsequent change to government regulation. Equitable estoppel, sometimes called zoning estoppel, focuses on the conduct of government and whether it would be equitable under the circumstances to permit government to repudiate some official action on which the landowner has relied to proceed with a land development project.[30] The doctrine of vested rights is based on common law and constitutional principles dealing with rights in property, while equitable estoppel is derived from equitable principles.

---

27. "The character of a tax is determined by its incidents, not by its name." Kunath v. City of Seattle, 10 Wash. App. 2d 205, 222 (Wash. Ct. App. 2019) (citing Harbour Village Apartments v. City of Mukilteo, 989 P.2d 542 (Wash. 1999)).

28. Greater Franklin Devs. Ass'n v. Town of Franklin, 730 N.E.2d 900 (Mass. App. Ct. 2000). Note that in Massachusetts, towns have no authority to impose any sort of tax. *Id.* at 901–02 (citing Mass. Const. art. 89, § 7).

29. Robert M. Rhodes & Cathy M. Sellers, *Vested Rights: Establishing Predictability in a Changing Regulatory System*, 20 Stetson L. Rev. 475, 476 (1991); Mandelker, *supra* note 1; Charles L. Siemon et al., Vested Rights: Balancing Public and Private Development Expectations 9 (1982); Kenneth A. Stahl, *Reliance in Land Use Law*, 2013 BYU L. Rev. 949 (2013).

30. Rhodes & Sellers, *supra* note 29, at 476; David G. Heeter, *Zoning Estoppel: Application of the Principles of Equitable Estoppel and Vested Rights to Zoning Disputes*, 1971 Urb. L. Ann. 65; Mandelker, *supra* note 1, § 6.13.

Of course, to the extent that the landowner and local government execute a development agreement or annexation agreement, as described in Chapters 2 and 3 of this book, the issue of vested rights should not arise. In fact, the primary purpose of these agreements is to vest the rights of a landowner to proceed with whatever development is the subject of the agreement, as many development agreement statutes clearly contemplate.[31] Similarly, the presence of a development agreement should render moot the question of the constitutionality of a bargained-for condition.[32]

In the absence of a development agreement, the principles of vested rights and equitable estoppel must be examined to determine whether changed government regulations may alter or prohibit an intended development or use. The results may often be the same, whichever doctrine is applied, leading most courts to treat the two doctrines as interchangeable.[33] However, there is a critical difference between the two doctrines that should significantly affect the pleading and trial of cases where either might apply, if not their outcomes—good faith. Obviously a landowner proceeding on the basis of equitable estoppel must be proceeding in "good faith." He who seeks equity must do equity. Pursuing an equitable remedy requires "clean hands," as every first-year law student knows. But what of vested property rights based upon common law and constitutional principles? Should the courts care whether a landowner who claims to hold vested rights has clean hands?[34] Does it matter, legally, what a landowner knows, or should have known, if his or her theory of the case rests on vested rights and not estoppel? After all, no less an authority than the U.S. Supreme Court held that the "notice" of a strict land use regulation does not prevent a purchaser of land so restricted from challenging the restriction as a regulatory taking of property without compensation.[35] It would seem reasonable,

---

31. *See, e.g.*, CAL. GOV'T CODE § 65864.

32. *See, e.g.*, David L. Callies & Julie A. Tappendorf, *Unconstitutional Land Development Conditions and the Development Agreement Solution: Bargaining for Public Facilities after* Nollan *and* Dolan, 51 CASE W. RSRV. L. REV. 663 (2001).

33. *Id.*

34. For a discussion of the distinction between equitable or zoning estoppel and vested rights, particularly the elimination of equitable principles, including reliance, from the latter, see Morgan R. Bentley, *Effects of Equitable Estoppel and Substantial Deviations to Vested Rights in DRI Projects: A New Approach*, 43 FLA. L. REV. 767, 774 (1991). *See also* MICHAEL A. ZIZKA ET AL., STATE & LOCAL GOVERNMENT LAND USE LIABILITY § 2:11 (2011).

35. Palazzolo v. Rhode Island, 533 U.S. 606 (2001); Ark. Game & Fish Comm'n v. United States, 568 U.S. 23 (2012) (citing the decision in *Palazzolo* for the proposition that "reasonable

therefore, to keep the theories separate. Yet, it is likely that case law has irrevocably joined the two, as appears in the sections below. Consequently, except where noted, the term "vested rights" will include, for all practical purposes, equitable estoppel for the remainder of this section.

There are essentially three elements to a vested rights claim against government interference with respect to a land development project,[36] which include

- a governmental act or omission;
- landowner change of position or reliance upon that governmental act or omission; and (in the case of estoppel)
- a landowner's good faith.

Governmental Act or Omission

Nearly all commentators and cases agree that there must be some governmental act or omission on which a landowner relies to his or her detriment in order for there to be a legitimate claim for vested rights.[37] The more recent that act or omission, the better. It is generally considered to be a matter of black-letter law that a landowner has no vested right to zoning. Therefore, an existing zoning classification is rarely the basis for establishing vested rights,[38] unless the classification is relatively recent, passed at the request of the landowner, or passed or created principally to frustrate a land development project.[39] However, a variety of other acts or omissions by government often serve to vest rights in a landowner with respect to a particular land development project. There are significant differences among the states concerning the kind of governmental action upon which reliance will result in vesting. Therefore, it is important to check your own state law to determine when a right might vest for purposes of a vested

investment-backed expectations" may be hindered by a lack of foreseeability in a restrictive land-based regulation). See, for comment, David L. Callies & Calvert G. Chipchase, Palazzolo v. Rhode Island*: Ripeness and "Notice" Rule Clarified and Statutory "Background Principles" Narrowed*, 33 URB. LAW. 907 (2001).

36. MANDELKER, *supra* note 1, § 6.13; Rhodes & Sellers, *supra* note 29, at 478.

37. MANDELKER, *supra* note 1, § 6.14; Rhodes & Sellers, *supra* note 29, at 482–86.

38. MANDELKER, *supra* note 1, § 6.14.

39. *Id.* § 6.16. *See* W. Land Equities, Inc. v. City of Logan, 617 P.2d 388 (Utah 1980). In a very few jurisdictions, some measure of vested rights results from a "new" zoning classification, particularly if sought by the landowner now claiming such rights.

rights argument. The actions that may trigger a vested right range from the issuance of a building permit[40] to a letter from a city official.[41] In some states, a zone classification has been deemed sufficient.[42] The types of governmental action that may result in vested rights, from most to least secure, include the following:[43]

- Building permit
- Final subdivision plat approval
- Preliminary subdivision plat approval
- Final planned development plan approval
- Preliminary planned development plan approval
- Submission of one of the above
- Special use or conditional use permit
- Site plan approval
- Grading or other site preparation, by itself
- Newly enacted zoning classification, particularly if upon application or request of landowner claiming vested rights

Detrimental Reliance

Virtually all commentators and cases also agree that a landowner must change position or rely on an act or omission of government, however weak, in order to claim vested rights, and that the reliance or change in position must have economic consequences for the landowner—usually the expenditure of money. Indeed, the amount spent in reliance on a governmental act or omission is often a major factor in deciding whether there has been sufficient reliance to justify a finding of vested rights.[44] For example, Florida courts have found expenditures in amounts from $8,000 to

40. Mandelker, *supra* note 1, § 6.21.

41. Rhodes & Sellers, *supra* note 29, at 482.

42. *See* Tex. Co. v. Town of Miami Springs, 44 So. 2d 808 (Fla. 1950); Hough v. Amato, 212 So. 2d 662 (Fla. 1968).

43. For thorough discussions of these and other land development condition issues, see Robert H. Freilich et al., 21st Century Land Development Code (2008); David L. Callies et al., Bargaining for Development (2003).

44. Mandelker, *supra* note 1, § 6.20; Rhodes & Sellers, *supra* note 29, at 486–88; Siemon et al., *supra* note 29, at 32.

$600,000 sufficient for equitable estoppel to apply, even where the expenditures were made before the landowner has made any physical changes to the land.[45]

Not all states are willing to recognize vested rights solely on the basis of vast expenditures of money. Instead, many require the landowner to actually commence vertical construction of the development project. The most egregious example of such jurisdictions is California. In *Oceanic California, Inc. v. North Central Coast Regional Commission,*[46] the court found expenditure of $26.9 million in direct costs insufficient in the absence of construction. In *Avco Community Developers v. South Coast Regional Commission,*[47] which eventually led to the passage of California's development agreement statute, the developer had obtained all necessary permits but a building permit and had spent more than $2,000,000 in grading, infrastructure, and associated costs for a residential housing development. However, the California Supreme Court held that because it had not commenced vertical construction, Avco still needed a permit from the California Coastal Commission under later-applied coastal regulations. Similarly, in *Pete Drown Inc. v. Town of Ellenburg,*[48] a New York court held that $850,000 was insufficient under the circumstances to vest development rights.

Good Faith

Though technically not part of a vested rights theory and real property law, many courts require a landowner to have relied on, changed position, or otherwise acted "in good faith" in order for property rights to develop or

45. *See* Bregar v. Britton, 75 So. 2d 753 (Fla. 1954) ($28,000 for land preparation); Project Home, Inc. v. Town of Astatula, 373 So. 2d 710 (Fla. 1979) ($8,000 for water and sewer improvements); Town of Longboat Key v. Mezrah, 467 So. 2d 488 (Fla. 1985) ($40,000 for plans and permit procurement); Bd. of Comm'rs v. Lutz, 314 So. 2d 815 (Fla. 1975) ($100,000 for planning and other preparatory fees); Town of Largo v. Imperial Homes Corp., 309 So. 2d 571 (Fla. 1975) ($379,000 for land, architectural fees, interest, taxes, and sewer permits); City of N. Miami v. Margulies, 289 So. 2d 424 (Fla. 1974) ($600,000 for planning, architectural, engineering, and surveying fees). *See also* City of Miami Beach v. Clevelander Ocean, L.P., 338 So. 3d 16, 22 (Fla. 2022) (finding landowner's estimated expenses were sufficient to establish a vested rights claim).

46. 63 Cal. App. 3d 57 (Cal. Ct. App. 1976).

47. 553 P.2d 546 (Cal. 1976).

48. 646 N.Y.S.2d 205 (N.Y. App. Div. 1996).

continue developing a particular project to vest.[49] Rushing to complete or begin a project in order to knowingly avoid a possible change in zone classification has been held to constitute bad faith.[50]

The courts also require good faith and fair dealing on the part of elected and appointed officials. Thus, where a local government approved a request for rezoning with knowledge that a landowner's purchase of the subject property was contingent on that rezoning, and then attempted to downzone the land to prevent the development, the court held that the local government had acted in bad faith and permitted the landowner to develop notwithstanding the local government's downzoning of the land.[51] Bad faith has also been found where a unit of local government fails to provide an opportunity for conference or notice of a change in the plat review process, circumventing the traditional procedures to advocate for denial of necessary permits.[52] A more difficult case is presented by the issuance of an illegal building permit—or other clear error in official assurance of the legality of a proposed development—upon which a landowner relies in good faith. Allowing the development to proceed under such error may raise significant health and safety issues, as well as violate a "fundamental canon" of local government law that approvals wrongfully issued or given are void ab initio.[53] Therefore, most courts will not permit the illegal development to proceed.[54]

Although most jurisdictions do not permit the illegal development, some jurisdictions do estop local government from interfering with a land

---

49. Mandelker, *supra* note 1, § 6.18; Rhodes & Sellers, *supra* note 29, at 478–82; Siemon et al., *supra* note 29, at 29–32.

50. Smith v. City of Clearwater, 383 So. 2d 681 (Fla. 1980); Morris v. Postma, 196 A.2d 792 (N.J. 1964); Clackamas Cnty. v. Holmes, 508 P.2d 190 (Or. 1973); Boron Oil Co. v. Kimple, 284 A.2d 744 (Pa. 1971).

51. Town of Largo v. Imperial Homes Corp., 309 So. 2d 571 (Fla. 1975).

52. Honey Brook Ests., LLC v. Bd. of Supervisors of Honey Brook Twp., 132 A.3d 611, 621 (Pa. Commw. Ct. 2016).

53. Siemon et al., *supra* note 29, at 27; *see, e.g.*, Hunt v. Caldwell, 279 S.E.2d 138 (Va. 1981); Town of Blacksburg v. Price, 266 S.E.2d 899 (Va. 1980); State v. Missoula, 533 P.2d 1087 (Mont. 1975).

54. Mandelker, *supra* note 1, § 6.17. *Contra*, permitting the development to proceed anyway: Town of W. Hartford v. Rechel, 459 A.2d 1015 (Conn. 1983); Saah v. D.C. Bd. of Zoning Adjustment, 433 A.2d 1114 (D.C. 1981); City of Peru v. Querciagrossa, 392 N.E.2d 778 (Ill. 1979); City of Berea v. Wren, 818 S.W.2d 274 (Ky. 1991); Petrosky v. Zoning Hearing Bd., 402 A.2d 1385 (Pa. 1979); Abbeville Arms v. City of Abbeville, 257 S.E.2d 716 (S.C. 1979).

development project that is moving ahead based on invalid assurances and permits, so long as the landowner's reliance is substantial and in good faith, and the permission or approval is sufficiently definite and precise. In *Abbeville Arms v. City of Abbeville*,[55] the court directed the city to issue a building permit for a project on land erroneously zoned. There, the developer had both purchased the property and made substantial additional expenditures in reliance on both a defective zoning map and a letter of approval from the city's zoning administrator.[56]

A property owner or applicant also cannot rely on written statements made by a public official unless the official is authorized to make them.[57] In *Burchett v. City of Newport Beach*, the petitioner alleged a breach of a "written agreement with Defendant City of Newport Beach whereby said City agreed to allow Plaintiffs to improve said real property with a two story condominium structure and retain the existing driveway to said property."[58] The allegation was based on a letter from the Burchetts to the planning department asking for a permit to use an existing, nonconforming driveway, on which letter an assistant planner had marked a notation that the facts were "correct." The court first noted that the city's charter provided that it could not be bound by any contract "unless the same shall be in writing, approved by the city council and signed on behalf of the city by the mayor and the city clerk or by such officer or officers as shall be designated by the City Council."[59] Second, the assistant planner was neither the person to contact for an "encroachment permit" nor a member of the correct department. The court cited *Horsemen's Benevolent & Protective Ass'n v. Valley Racing Ass'n*[60] for the proposition that "[n]o government, whether state or local, is bound to any extent by an officer's acts in excess of his [or her] authority."[61] The court held:

> One who deals with the public officer stands presumptively charged with a full knowledge of that officer's powers, and is bound at his

55. 257 S.E.2d 716.

56. *See also Querciagrossa*, 392 N.E.2d 778 (setbacks); City of Coral Gables v. Puiggros, 376 So. 2d 281 (Fla. 1979).

57. Burchett v. City of Newport Beach, 33 Cal. App. 4th 1472 (Cal. Ct. App. 1995).

58. *Id.* at 1479.

59. *Id.*

60. 4 Cal. App. 4th 1538, 1563–64 (Cal. Ct. App. 1992).

61. *Burchett*, 33 Cal. App. 4th at 1479 (quoting *Horsemen's*, 4 Cal. App. 4th at 1563–64).

peril to ascertain the extent of his powers to bind the government for which he is an officer, and any act of an officer to be valid must find express authority in the law or be necessarily incidental to a power expressly granted.[62]

62. *Id.* (quoting *Horsemen's*, 4 Cal. App. 4th at 1564) (general law city was not bound by oral contract because it did not comply with California Government Code § 40602 and relevant city code provisions).

2

Development Agreements

The Development Agreement Solution

Developers and local governments face two difficult problems in the land development approval process. Local governments, on the one hand, are unable to exact dedications of land or fees of the "impact" or "in-lieu" variety without establishing a clear connection or nexus between the proposed development and the dedication or fee.[1] Developers, on the other hand, often are unable to "vest" or guarantee a right to proceed with development of a project until construction is commenced.[2] The development agreement offers a solution to both of these problems, as a well-crafted agreement can

1. *See* Judith Welch Wegner, *Moving toward the Bargaining Table: Contract Zoning, Development Agreements, and the Theoretical Foundations of Government Land Use Deals*, 65 N.C. L. Rev. 957, 1017–20 (1987) (describing the "rational nexus" test adopted by a majority of jurisdictions to assess the reasonableness of provisions requiring exactions of property in development agreements, and the expansion of the doctrine governing exactions to address the use of "impact fees"); Lyle S. Hosada, *Development Agreement Legislation in Hawaii: An Answer to the Vested Rights Uncertainty*, 7 U. Haw. L. Rev. 173 (1985); Takings: Land-Development Conditions and Regulatory Takings after Dolan and Lucas chs. 4, 9, 10, 11 (David L. Callies ed., 1996).

2. *See* John J. Delaney, *Vesting Verities and the Development Chronology: A Gaping Disconnect?*, 3 Wash. U. J. L. & Pol'y 603, 607–08 (2000) (noting that many states require, in addition to issuance of a building permit, action such as construction or expenditure of funds in reliance on the permit, to enjoy a vested right to continue with development notwithstanding changes in regulation).

provide a local government with public benefits that it otherwise could not achieve by regulation, while concurrently providing a developer with assurance that so long as its contractual obligations are met, the developer will be allowed to proceed with construction of its project. The development agreement also offers a mechanism to address a host of issues that commonly arise in the land development process between developers and local governments,[3] such as the timing of the provision of public facilities, the inclusion of certain types of housing, the annual number of building permits, and the like.

In considering whether a development agreement can be used successfully to address the challenges described above, the parties must first determine whether the local government may promise not to change certain land use regulations during the life of the agreement in order to achieve a broader public purpose, without illegally bargaining away its police power. The availability of specific statutory authority to enter into development agreements will be helpful, particularly in detailing required terms, specified scope, and/or procedural steps for the government to approve and enter into a development agreement. This legislative blessing can help ensure that the agreements effectuate a public purpose endorsed and recognized by the state. As is discussed later in this chapter, 16 states to date have adopted legislation enabling local governments to enter into development agreements with landowners and developers.[4]

---

3. *See generally* DEVELOPMENT AGREEMENTS: ANALYSIS, COLORADO CASE STUDIES, AND COMMENTARY (Erin J. Johnson & Edward H. Ziegler eds., 1993); DEVELOPMENT AGREEMENTS: PRACTICE, POLICY, AND PROSPECTS (Douglas R. Porter & Lindell L. Marsh eds., 1989); DAVID J. LARSEN, DEVELOPMENT AGREEMENTS MANUAL: COLLABORATION IN PURSUIT OF COMMUNITY INTERESTS (2002) (prepared for the Institute for Local Self Government, League of California Cities, Sacramento, California). For commentary on the British experience with development agreements, see David L. Callies & Malcolm Grant, *Paying for Growth and Planning Gain: An Anglo American Comparison of Development Conditions, Impact Fees, and Development Agreements*, 23 URB. LAW. 221 (1991). See Appendix 1 for a checklist on drafting agreements, and Appendices 2, 3, and 4 for sample development agreements.

4. *See* ARIZ. REV. STAT. ANN. § 9-500.05; CAL. GOV'T CODE § 65864; COLO. REV. STAT. §§ 24-68-101 to 24-68-106; FLA. STAT. ANN. § 163.3220; HAW. REV. STAT. ANN. § 46-123; LA. REV. STAT. ANN. § 33:4780.22; MD. CODE, LAND USE § 7-301; MINN. STAT. § 462.358, subdiv. C; NEV. REV. STAT. § 278.0201; N.J. STAT. ANN. § 40:55D-45.2; N.C. GEN. STAT. ANN. § 160D-1001; OR. REV. STAT. § 94.504; S.C. CODE ANN. § 6-31-10; UTAH CODE ANN. § 10-9a-102; VA. CODE ANN. § 15.2-2303.1 (applies only to New Kent County and developments there consisting of at least 1,000 acres); WASH. REV. CODE ANN. § 36.70B.170.

Does a Development Agreement Violate the Reserved Powers Doctrine or the Contract Clause of the U.S. Constitution?

The Reserved Powers Doctrine

Courts frequently have held that a local government may not contract away its authority to exercise the police power,[5] particularly in the context of zoning decisions.[6] Because land use and development regulations represent exercises of the police power, a development or annexation agreement binding a local government not to exercise these powers in the future arguably violates the reserved powers doctrine,[7] under which a government must reserve the exercise of certain regulatory or police powers for itself, and therefore is beyond the government's authority.[8]

---

5. *See* Carlino v. Whitpain Invs., 453 A.2d 1385, 1388 (Pa. 1982) (noting that "individuals cannot, by contract, abridge police powers which protect the general welfare and public interest").

6. *See* Azalea Lakes P'ship v. Par. of St. Tammany, 859 So. 2d 57 (La. Ct. App. 2003) (finding development agreement statute not unconstitutional because it does not attempt to delegate rezoning rights to developers); Pima Gro Sys. v. Bd. of Supervisors, 52 Va. Cir. 241, 244 (Va. Cir. Ct. 2000) ("Zoning must be governed by the public interest and not by benefit to a particular landowner"); Cederberg v. City of Rockford, 291 N.E.2d 249, 251–52 (Ill. App. Ct. 1972) (voiding restrictive covenant and rezoning ordinance because the law "condemns the practice of regulating zoning through agreements or contracts between the zoning authorities and property owners"); Houston Petroleum Co. v. Auto. Prods. Credit Ass'n, 9 N.J. 122, 129 (N.J. 1952) ("Contracts thus have no place in a zoning plan and a contract between a municipality and a property owner should not enter into the enactment or enforcement of zoning regulations."); V.F. Zahodiakin Eng'g Corp. v. Zoning Bd. of Adjustment, 86 A.2d 127, 131 (N.J. 1952) ("Zoning is an exercise of the police power to serve the common good and general welfare. It is elementary that the legislative function may not be surrendered or curtailed by bargain or its exercise controlled by the considerations which enter into the law of contracts.").

7. *See, e.g.*, Robert M. Kessler, *The Development Agreement and Its Use in Resolving Large Scale, Multi-Party Development Problems: A Look at the Tool and Suggestions for Its Application*, 1 J. Land Use & Env't L. 451, 464–69 (1985) (discussing the reserved powers doctrine and the inability of local governments to contract away police powers); Bruce M. Kramer, *Development Agreements: To What Extent Are They Enforceable?*, 10 Real Est. L.J. 29, 37–45 (1981) (discussing the history and current viability of the reserved powers doctrine in the context of development agreements); Shelby D. Green, *Development Agreements: Bargained-for Zoning That Is Neither Illegal Contract nor Conditional Zoning*, 33 Cap. U. L. Rev. 383, 405 (2004).

8. *See* Stone v. Mississippi, 101 U.S. 814, 817–18 (1879) (noting that "no legislature can curtail the power of its successors to make such laws as they may deem proper in matters of

On closer analysis, however, the cases demonstrate a greater concern with the duration or method of bargaining away that power, as opposed to an absolute prohibition on such bargaining.[9] The source of the doctrine, *Corporation of the Brick Presbyterian Church v. Mayor of New York*,[10] involved the municipal abrogation of a lease executed more than 50 years before. While some later cases do invalidate municipal actions only a few years old,[11] most invalidate behavior further back in time. The dominant view is that development and annexation agreements, drafted to reserve some governmental control over implementation of the agreement, in fact do not contract away the police power but rather constitute a valid present exercise of that power.[12]

A subsidiary question under the reserved powers doctrine is whether a city council, in exercising its power to contract, can make a contract that binds successor city councils. In *Carruth v. City of Madera*,[13] the city contended that obligations under an annexation agreement executed by a predecessor council were invalid because they deprived the successor city council of the power to determine city policy and act in the public interest. The court held that the city was bound, and that a contract, made by the council or other governing body of a municipality, that was fair, just, and reasonable at the time of its execution, is binding upon successor bodies. The court concluded that the contract was neither void nor voidable

---

police"); Corp. of the Brick Presbyterian Church v. Mayor of N.Y., 5 Cow. 538, 542 (N.Y. Sup. Ct. 1826) (noting that local governments have "no power to limit their legislative discretion by covenant"), *discussed in* Kramer, *supra* note 7, at 37–39.

9. *See* Green, *supra*, note 7, at 403; Ramsin G. Canon, *Participatory Democracy and the Entrepreneurial Government: Addressing Process Efficiencies in the Creation of Land Use Development Agreements*, 89 CHI.-KENT L. REV. 781, 796–97 (2014).

10. 5 Cow. 538.

11. *See, e.g.*, Hartnett v. Austin, 93 So. 2d 86, 89–90 (Fla. 1956) (affirming lower court's permanent injunction of a proposed revision of a zoning ordinance that had not yet taken effect); *V.F. Zahodiakin*, 86 A.2d at 131–32 (affirming lower court's invalidation of a decision made earlier by the local board of adjustment that purported to grant a "variance" from zoning requirements).

12. For good analogous authority of such premise, see, for example, *Morrison Homes Corp. v. City of Pleasanton*, 58 Cal. App. 3d 724, 734–35 (Cal. Ct. App. 1976) (holding that the effect of the general rule is to void only a contract that amounts to a city's "surrender" or "abnegation" of its *control* of a properly municipal function, and that the city's reservation of control over the land subject to an annexation agreement, as well as the "just, reasonable, fair and equitable" nature of the agreement, rendered the agreement valid and enforceable against the city).

13. 233 Cal. App. 2d 688 (Cal. Ct. App. 1965).

merely because some of its executory features may operate to bind a successor council.[14]

Similarly, in *Home Builders Ass'n of Central Arizona v. City of Maricopa*,[15] development agreements between a county and developers were found to be binding upon a city where the city became successor of the county upon its incorporation of the land subject to the agreements. The City of Maricopa sought by ordinance to impose development fees on newly incorporated land in violation of the preexisting development agreements, which provided that no fees would be assessed upon developers. These agreements were stipulated to be binding upon the respective successors of the county and the developer. Finding that the city was the successor in interest of the county, the appeals court concluded that the agreements were binding upon the city.

One of the strongest decisions supporting the use of development agreements consistent with a city's police power is the Nebraska Supreme Court opinion upholding development agreements in *Giger v. City of Omaha*.[16] The opponents claimed that development agreements were a form of contract zoning, thereby illegal on their face. The Nebraska Supreme Court rejected this claim, instead characterizing such agreements as a form of conditional zoning that actually increased the city's police power, rather than lessened it, by permitting more restrictive zoning (attaching conditions through agreement) than simply rezoning the property to a district in which a variety of uses would be permitted of right.[17]

---

14. *Id.* at 695–96; *see also* Denio v. City of Huntington Beach, 140 P.2d 392, 397 (Cal. 1943) (holding that a "fair, just, and reasonable" contract entered into by a governing body of a municipality "is neither void nor voidable merely because some of its executory features may extend beyond the terms of office of the members of [the governing] body"), *overruled by* Fracasse v. Brent, 494 P.2d 9 (Cal. 1972).

15. 158 P.3d 869 (Ariz. Ct. App. 2007).

16. 442 N.W.2d 182 (Neb. 1989).

17. *Id.* at 192. The court reasoned:

> In sum, we find that there is not clear and satisfactory evidence to support the appellants' contention that the city has bargained away its police power. The evidence clearly shows that the city's police powers are not abridged in any manner and that the agreement is expressly subject to the remedies available to the city under the Omaha Municipal Code. Further, we find that the agreement actually enhances the city's regulatory control over the development rather than limiting it.

Id.

The less supportive decision, *Morgran Co., Inc. v. Orange County,*[18] illustrates the limitations on agreements that threaten to bargain away municipalities' police powers. In *Morgran,* the development agreement obligated the county to "support and expeditiously" process Morgran's rezoning application.[19] The court declared the agreement void, finding the county's assurance of support for Morgran's rezoning request constituted an illegal contracting away of its police powers.[20]

California courts have repeatedly acknowledged the validity of development agreements that act to advance the public's interest in implementing land use regulations. In *Stephens v. City of Vista,* the Stephenses purchased property in 1973 to develop an apartment complex of approximately 140 to 150 units.[21] Subsequently, the City of Vista lowered the access street to the property, frustrating the Stephenses' contemplated use, and downzoned the property. The Stephenses sued. The city and the Stephenses eventually entered into a settlement agreement providing for a specific plan and zoning that permitted construction of a maximum of 140 units. After rezoning the property, the city denied a site development plan, in part because it again wanted the Stephenses to reduce the density. The Stephenses renewed their lawsuit. The city argued that the settlement agreement unlawfully contracted away its police power. The court disagreed. The court first noted that when the city entered into the settlement agreement, it understood it was obligated to approve 140 units. Further, relying on *Morrison Homes Corp. v. City of Pleasanton,*[22] the court held that while generally a local government cannot contract away its legislative and governmental functions, this rule applies only to void a contract that amounts to a "surrender" of the local government's control of a municipal function.[23] Therefore, the city could contract for a guaranteed density and exercise its discretion in the site development process without surrendering control of all of its land use authority. The court awarded $727,500 in damages for breaching the agreement based on the difference between the value of the property with an entitlement of 140 units and the value of the

18. 818 So. 2d 640 (Fla. Dist. Ct. App. 2002).
19. *Id.* at 642.
20. *Id.* at 643; *see also* Canon, *supra* note 9, at 795.
21. 994 F.2d 650 (9th Cir. 1993).
22. 58 Cal. App. 3d 724 (Cal. Ct. App. 1976).
23. *Stephens*, 994 F.2d at 655.

property with a developable density of 55 units (the current zoning).[24] In the same way, a development agreement that obligates a local government to permit a certain density and type of development should be enforceable by the developer.

Similarly, in *Santa Margarita Area Residents Together (SMART) v. San Luis Obispo County Board of Supervisors*, a California appellate court squarely upheld a development agreement that was challenged directly on "surrender of police power" grounds, holding that a "zoning freeze in the Agreement is not . . . a surrender or abnegation [of the police power]."[25] The court rejected an area residents' association contention that because San Luis Obispo County had entered into a development agreement freezing zoning for a property for five years, when the project was not yet ready for construction, the county improperly contracted away its zoning authority. In rejecting this reasoning, the court observed that land use regulation is an established function of local government, providing the authority for a local government to enter into contracts to carry out the function. The county's development agreement required that the project be developed in accordance with the county's general plan, did not permit construction until the county had approved detailed building plans, retained certain of the county's discretionary authority in the future, and allowed a zoning freeze of limited duration only. The court found that the zoning freeze in the county's development agreement was not a surrender of the police power but instead served to advance the public interest by preserving future options.

In *Neighbors in Support of Appropriate Land Use v. County of Tuolumne*,[26] the court voided a development agreement that would have allowed a property zoned for agricultural uses to be used commercially for weddings and similar events, contrary to what was otherwise permitted under the county's zoning code. The court found the agreement violated state law by failing to meet the uniformity requirement of California Government Code section 65852. Rather than focusing on a concern that the police power had been bargained away, the court stressed that zoning ordinances would be undermined if local governments made exceptions to them, favoring some property owners' interests over those of others

24. *Id.* at 657.
25. 84 Cal. App. 4th 221, 233 (Cal. Ct. App. 2000).
26. 157 Cal. App. 4th 997 (Cal. Ct. App. 2007).

through the use of development agreements. In this particular case, the development agreement would have permitted a use disallowed by the zoning ordinance without utilizing any of the county's procedures available to all landowners, including rezoning, issuing a conditional use permit in compliance with the existing zoning, or granting a variance.

In *Mammoth Lakes Land Acquisition LLC v. Town of Mammoth Lakes*,[27] the court upheld a $30 million damage award against the town in favor of the developer for the town's anticipatory breach of a 1997 development agreement in which the town had agreed, among other things, to act reasonably in moving the developer's proposed hotel/condominium project along. The court first reviewed the legislative history of development agreements in California and held that "a legislatively-approved development agreement gives both parties vested contractual rights."[28] The court then found the evidence of the town's repudiation of the agreement and failure to cooperate with the developer in advancing the project supported the developer's breach of contract claim and the jury's damage award. In so ruling, the court rejected the town's argument that the developer was required to first exhaust its administrative remedies, and instead focused on the contractual nature of a development agreement, which allowed the developer to pursue a breach of contract claim following the town's failure to cure its defaults. Courts have continued to treat development agreements that provide vested contractual rights for both parties as enforceable contractual obligations.[29]

In sum, notwithstanding some judicial use of the reserved powers clause to abrogate development agreements, many courts have attempted to find other grounds to uphold those contracts that are fair, just, reasonable, and advantageous to the local government and/or the public.[30] Finally, it is increasingly unlikely that courts will fall back on the reserved powers

---

27. 191 Cal. App. 4th 435 (Cal. Ct. App. 2010).

28. *Id.* at 444.

29. *See* N. Murrieta Cmty., LLC v. City of Murrieta, 50 Cal. App. 5th 31, 44–45 (Cal. Ct. App. 2020) (holding that terms of development agreement regarding imposition of future additional, generally applicable fees prevailed over protections under vesting tentative map statute in light of binding contractual nature of development agreement).

30. *See, e.g.*, Carruth v. City of Madera, 233 Cal. App. 2d 688, 695 (Cal. Ct. App. 1965) (holding contract entered into by city can be enforced, even if it extends beyond the legislative term, if the contract is fair, just, reasonable, and advantageous to the city); *see also* Kramer, *supra* note 7, at 41 (discussing *Carruth*).

clause to invalidate development agreements passed pursuant to state statute, especially if the agreements have a fixed termination date that is not many decades away.

The Contracts Clause of the U.S. Constitution

The Contracts Clause of the U.S. Constitution also provides a basis for upholding development and annexation agreements in the face of a complaint that the local government has illegally bargained away its police power. Article I of the U.S. Constitution provides: "No State shall . . . pass any . . . Law impairing the Obligation of Contracts. . . ."[31] Whether defined as a legislative or administrative act, a development agreement will be treated as a contract "when the language and circumstances evince a legislative intent to create private rights of a contractual nature enforceable against the State."[32]

However, the Contracts Clause is neither literal nor absolute.[33] The U.S. Supreme Court has held that the Contracts Clause limitation cannot operate to eclipse or eliminate "'essential attributes of sovereign power' . . . necessarily reserved by the States to safeguard the welfare of their citizens."[34] The test in *United States Trust Co. v. New Jersey*, as refined in *Allied Structural Steel Co. v. Spannaus*,[35] requires a balancing of the exercise of the police power against the impairment resulting from its exercise. The decisions suggest that any exercise of the police power that impairs any government obligations under a development agreement would be subject to strict scrutiny and must be justifiable as an act "reasonable and necessary

31. U.S. Const. art. I, § 10, cl. 1.

32. United States Trust Co. v. New Jersey, 431 U.S. 1, 17 n.14 (1977). For a full discussion, see Wegner, *supra* note 1, at 995–1003 (making the case that although writers have simply assumed that development agreements are contractual in nature, it would be more correct to characterize development agreements as possessing a hybrid contractual-regulatory nature); *see also N. Murrieta Cmty.*, 50 Cal. App. 5th at 44 ("development agreements are contracts, enforceable like normal contracts").

33. *See* Eric Sigg, *California's Development Agreement Statute*, 15 Sw. U. L. Rev. 695, 720–22 (1985) (discussing tension between the Contracts Clause and the reserved powers doctrine, and describing various tests to determine whether a particular contract surrenders an essential attribute of a state's sovereignty).

34. *United States Trust Co.*, 431 U.S. at 21 (quoting Home Bldg. & Loan Ass'n v. Blaisdell, 290 U.S. 398, 435 (1934)).

35. 438 U.S. 234 (1978).

to serve an important public purpose."[36] Just what constitutes an "important public purpose" sufficient to justify the impairment of contract obligations is a factual determination. In *United States Trust Co.*, bondholders' security interests outweighed the state's interest in pollution control, rapid transit, and resource conservation. Similarly, in *Allied Structural Steel*, the state's interest in protecting its citizens' pensions failed to prevail over a private company's rights in its own pension plan.[37]

Thus, a strict application of the Contracts Clause that would enforce the terms of a development agreement with the result of prohibiting the local government from imposing a new law or regulation necessary to address a genuine health, safety, or welfare crisis likely would not be judicially tolerated. A court would likely void the agreement or the offending provision as violating the reserved powers doctrine, notwithstanding the Contracts Clause.

---

36. *United States Trust Co.*, 431 U.S. at 25.

37. For a thorough discussion of the *United States Trust Co.–Allied Structural Steel Co.* test, see *Anthony v. Kualoa Ranch, Inc.*, 736 P.2d 55 (Haw. 1987), in which the Hawaii Supreme Court applied the Contracts Clause doctrine to strike down a state statute requiring landlords to pay for leasehold improvements, at the tenant's option, as an unconstitutional impairment of contractual rights. *See also* Quality Refrigerated Serv., Inc. v. City of Spencer, 908 F. Supp. 1471 (N.D. Iowa 1995) (granting city's motion to dismiss, in part because plaintiff failed to state a cause of action under the Contracts Clause of the U.S. Constitution where it failed to show that city zoning ordinance substantially impaired a contractual relationship or that legitimate government interests would not justify such an impairment if it existed); William G. Holliman, *Development Agreements and Vested Rights in California*, 13 URB. LAW. 44, 52–53 (1981) (concluding that "*United States Trust* and *Allied Structural Steel* suggest that any subsequent exercise of the police power which impairs the obligations under a development agreement would be subjected to a strict scrutiny test for reasonableness and necessity"); Kramer, *supra* note 7, at 35 (concluding that "[s]ubsequent legislative action seeking to amend, modify, or repeal [a] development agreement would undoubtedly impair the obligation of the contract and if less onerous alternatives were available to the legislature to achieve the same policy goals they would have to be taken"); Sigg, *supra* note 33, at 720–22 (concluding "it would appear that impairment by a city or country of its own development agreement would have to survive the heightened scrutiny of a 'reasonable and necessary to serve important state purposes' test"). For an exhaustive discussion of the reserved powers doctrine and its applicability to local government contracts (and its Contracts Clause limitations), see Janice C. Griffith, *Local Government Contracts: Escaping from the Governmental/Proprietary Maze*, 75 IOWA L. REV. 277 (1990).

Statutory Authority: Critical for Development Agreements

As discussed previously, courts that have rejected development and annexation agreements are most concerned with the abdication of police powers needed to protect the general welfare and the "bartering . . . [of] legislative discretion for emoluments that had no bearing on the merits of the requested amendment."[38] Such judicial inclination to protect a local government's future legislative power makes statutory authority to enter into such agreements an important, and often critical, component for parties contemplating use of a development agreement to establish future development rights. In crafting legislation to establish a local government's authority to bind itself in a development agreement, there are several key areas that a legislature should address for inclusion in any state statute authorizing such agreement.

Protection of General Welfare

The first issue—protection of general welfare—is best disposed of by strong public policy language in the statute. The control of land use and development within a community has consistently been determined to be a necessary police power to protect the general welfare of the community and its residents.

Permitted Scope of the Agreement

As to the bartering away of unrelated (to land use) emoluments, a well-drafted statute generally limits such agreements to specific land use matters, with a catch-all for related matters. Florida's development agreement statute contains this language.[39] What the statutes contemplate is the trade-off of zoning for development-generated public infrastructure needs

---

38. Hedrich v. Vill. of Niles, 250 N.E.2d 791, 796 (Ill. App. Ct. 1969).
39. Florida Statutes Annotated section 163.3227 provides:

> (1) A development agreement shall include the following:
>
> > (a) A legal description of the land subject to the agreement, and the names of its legal and equitable owners;
> >
> > (b) The duration of the agreement;
> >
> > (c) The development uses permitted on the land, including population densities, and building intensities and height;

(whether or not, it should be added, such public infrastructure needs are generated by the instant development). This is confirmed by cases upholding cooperative and annexation agreements;[40] low-rent housing for zoning;[41] annexation, zoning, and sewer connections for annexation and annexation fees;[42] and redevelopment agreements.[43]

(d) A description of public facilities that will service the development, including who shall provide such facilities; the date any new facilities, if needed, will be constructed; and a schedule to assure public facilities are available concurrent with the impacts of the development;

(e) A description of any reservation or dedication of land for public purposes;

(f) A description of all local development permits approved or needed to be approved for the development of the land;

(g) A finding that the development permitted or proposed is consistent with the local government's comprehensive plan and land development regulations;

(h) A description of any conditions, terms, restrictions, or other requirements determined to be necessary by the local government for the public health, safety, or welfare of its citizens; and

(i) A statement indicating that the failure of the agreement to address a particular permit, condition, term, or restriction shall not relieve the developer of the necessity of complying with the law governing said permitting requirements, conditions, term, or restriction.

(2) A development agreement may provide that the entire development or any phase thereof be commenced or completed within a specific period of time.

40. *See* Housing Redev. Auth. v. Jorgensen, 328 N.W.2d 740, 742–43 (Minn. 1983) (holding that cooperation agreement entered into between city and housing and redevelopment authority required city to issue conditional permits for development of low-income housing project).

41. *See* Housing Auth. v. City of Los Angeles, 243 P.2d 515, 524 (Cal. 1952) (holding that city was bound by cooperative agreement with housing authority that approved development and construction of low-rent housing project).

42. *See* Morrison Homes Corp. v. City of Pleasanton, 58 Cal. App. 3d 724, 733–34 (Cal. Ct. App. 1976) (holding that annexation agreements entered into between city and developer that required city to provide sewage service to planned development were binding and enforceable against the city); Meegan v. Vill. of Tinley Park, 288 N.E.2d 423, 426 (Ill. 1972) (dismissing developer's mandamus action for issuance of building permit to build a gasoline station pursuant to annexation agreement within a reasonable time after expiration of annexation agreement's statutory five-year period of validity).

43. *See* Mayor of Balt. v. Crane, 352 A.2d 786, 791–92 (Md. 1976) (holding that where a developer conveyed a strip of property to city for highway purposes under zoning ordinance

The California, Florida, Hawaii, and Nevada statutes contain minimum standards for describing the basic character of a proposed development subject to a development agreement. These include the size and shape of buildings. In a decision that clearly signals the extent of flexibility possible in California, a California court of appeal upheld a development agreement containing no such precise standards.[44] According to the court, it was sufficient that the zoning ordinance contained height and use limitations in the zone where the proposed project was to be constructed.[45]

This clearly indicates the importance of a well-drafted statute to support the legality of the development agreement, particularly in the face of a reserved powers/bargaining away of the police power challenge. Indeed, there is only one significant case upholding a development agreement against this and other challenges without the benefit of a statute.[46] It is worth noting what other basic provisions are contained in a typical development agreement statute. Sixteen states[47] presently have such statutes. The most detailed comes from Hawaii, and so the citations that follow are primarily to that statute. However, California remains the state in which the vast majority of development agreements appear to be negotiated and are in effect.

Enabling Ordinance

A preliminary issue is whether an enabling statute is sufficient to grant local government the authority to enter into development agreements. There is some authority for requiring a local government to pass an enabling ordinance setting out the details of development agreement/annexation agreement procedures and requirements, although this requirement has, so far, been limited to development agreements rather than annexation

---

that allowed developer's proposed development to contain the same density of dwelling units as if the land had not been conveyed, the developer acquired vested contractual rights that were enforceable against the city).

44. *See* SMART v. San Luis Obispo Cnty. Bd. of Supervisors, 84 Cal. App. 4th 221, 225–26 (Cal. Ct. App. 2000) (upholding development agreement that froze zoning on the proposed development property in exchange for developer's commitment to submit a specific construction plan in compliance with county land use requirements).

45. *Id.* at 231.

46. *See* Giger v. City of Omaha, 442 N.W.2d 182 (Neb. 1989).

47. *See supra* note 4.

agreements. Thus, the Hawaii[48] and Florida[49] statutes appear to require that local governments desiring to negotiate development agreements first pass a local resolution or ordinance to that effect. In Hawaii, the state legislature has delegated the authority to the county to enter into development agreements, provided, however, that the county first passes an enabling ordinance establishing the procedures that the county executive branch must follow.[50] While the language of the Hawaii statute does not clearly require counties to draft such an ordinance, all of Hawaii's four counties have passed them.

---

48. Hawaii Revised Statutes sections 46-123 to 46-124 provide:

> General authorization. Any county by ordinance may authorize the executive branch of the county to enter into a development agreement with any person having a legal or equitable interest in real property, for the development of such property in accordance with this part; provided that such an ordinance shall:
>
> > (1) Establish procedures and requirements for the consideration of development agreements upon application by or on behalf of persons having a legal or equitable interest in the property, in accordance with this part;
> >
> > (2) Designate a county executive agency to administer the agreements after such agreements become effective;
> >
> > (3) Include provisions to require the designated agency to conduct a review of compliance with the terms and conditions of the development agreement, on a periodic basis as established by the development agreement; and
> >
> > (4) Include provisions establishing reasonable time periods for the review and appeal of modifications of the development agreement.
>
> Negotiating development agreements. The mayor or the designated agency appointed to administer development agreements may make such arrangements as may be necessary or proper to enter into development agreements, including negotiating and drafting individual development agreements; provided that the county has adopted an ordinance pursuant to section 46-123.

The final draft of each individual development agreement shall be presented to the county legislative body for approval or modification prior to execution. To be binding on the county, a development agreement must be approved by the county legislative body and executed by the mayor on behalf of the county. County legislative approval shall be by resolution adopted by a majority of the membership of the county legislative body.

49. *See* Fla. Stat. Ann. § 163.3223 ("Any local government may, *by ordinance*, establish procedures and requirements, as provided in ss. 163.3220–163.3243, to consider and enter into a development agreement with any person having a legal or equitable interest in real property located within its jurisdiction.") (emphasis added).

50. Haw. Rev. Stat. § 46-123.

Requirements for Approval and Adoption

Although one governmental body may enter into the negotiation stage of the development agreement, another may be authorized to approve the final product. In Hawaii, for example, the mayor is the designated negotiator, with the final agreement presented to the county legislative body (city council) for approval. If approved, the city council must then adopt the development agreement by resolution.[51] In California, a development agreement must be approved by ordinance. In Washington, development agreements must be approved either by ordinance or by resolution after public hearing.[52]

A development agreement may also be entered into early in the planning process.[53] In *SMART*, an association composed of area residents contended that a development agreement entered into by San Luis Obispo County was invalid because the project in contention had not been approved for actual construction. In rejecting this contention and holding for the county, the court stated that the development agreement statute should be liberally construed to permit local government to make commitments to developers at the time the developer makes a substantial investment in the project.

The court found that the agreement entered into by the county conformed to the statute because, by focusing on the planning state of the project, the agreement met rather than evaded the purpose of the statute. The county's agreement maximized the public's role in final development,

---

51. Hawaii Revised Statutes section § 46-124 provides:

> Negotiating development agreements. The mayor or the designated agency appointed to administer development agreements may make such arrangements as may be necessary or proper to enter into development agreements, including negotiating and drafting individual development agreements; provided that the county has adopted an ordinance pursuant to section 46-123.
>
> The final draft of each individual development agreement shall be presented to the county legislative body for approval or modification prior to execution. To be binding on the county, a development agreement must be approved by the county legislative body and executed by the mayor on behalf of the county. County legislative approval shall be by resolution adopted by a majority of the membership of the county legislative body.

52. Wash. Rev. Code § 36.70B.200. *See also* Belleau Woods II, LLC v. City of Bellingham, 208 P.3d 5 (Wash. Ct. App. 2009).

53. SMART v. San Luis Obispo Cnty. Bd. of Supervisors, 84 Cal. App. 4th 221, 230 (Cal. Ct. App. 2000).

increased control over the inclusion of public facilities and benefits, and permitted the county to monitor the planning of the project to assure compliance with its existing land use regulations.

Conformance to Plans and Other Reviews

Development agreements must often comply with local government plans as a condition of enforceability, either by statute or because of the rubric that the zoning bargained for must accord with comprehensive plans. The Hawaii[54] and California[55] development agreement statutes both so require. In California, the development agreement must be consistent with the general plan and any applicable specific plans.[56] A fully negotiated development agreement is a "project" under the California Environmental Quality Act,[57] and as such is subject to environmental review. This is true even when the development agreement is not directly approved by the local government but is instead submitted to the voters for approval.[58]

If, prior to incorporation of a new city or annexation to an existing city, a county has entered into a development agreement with the developer, the development agreement remains valid for the duration of the agreement, or for eight years from the effective date of the incorporation or annexation, whichever is earlier, or for up to 15 years upon agreement between the developer and the city.[59] This statute applies to incorporations where the development agreement was applied for prior to circulation of the incorporation petition and entered into between the county and the developer prior to the date of the incorporation election. The statute also allows the

---

54. *See* HAW. REV. STAT. § 46-129 ("No development agreement shall be entered into unless the county legislative body finds that the provisions of the proposed development agreement are consistent with the county's general plan and any applicable development plan, effective as of the effective date of the development agreement.").

55. *See* CAL. GOV'T CODE § 65867.5(b) ("A development agreement shall not be approved unless the legislative body finds that the provisions of the agreement are consistent with the general plan and any applicable specific plan."); *but see* Rialto Citizens for Responsible Growth v. City of Rialto, 146 Cal. Rptr. 3d 12, 20 (Cal. Ct. App. 2012) (noting a court will not invalidate a development agreement for a failure to make the required consistency findings if there is no prejudicial error).

56. CAL. GOV'T CODE § 65867.5(b).

57. CAL. PUB. RES. CODE § 21000 *et seq.*

58. Citizens for Responsible Gov't v. City of Albany, 66 Cal. Rptr. 2d 102 (Cal. Ct. App. 1997).

59. CAL. GOV'T CODE § 65865.3.

incorporating or annexing city to modify or suspend the provisions of the development agreement if it finds an adverse impact on public health or safety in the jurisdiction. However, as to annexations, if the proposal for annexation is initiated by a petitioner other than a city, the development agreement is valid unless the city adopts written findings that implementation of the development agreement would create a condition injurious to the health, safety, or welfare of the city's residents.[60]

The importance of the plan is demonstrated by the Idaho Supreme Court in *Sprenger, Grubb & Associates, Inc. v. City of Hailey*.[61] There, the court upheld a rezoning over the objections of the developers of property subject to what the court called a development agreement (arguably an annexation agreement), on the ground that the applicable plan was sufficiently broad in that it supported the contested downzoning.[62] Largely to the same effect is a California court of appeal decision where the existence of, and need to conform to, applicable plans was critical in upholding a development agreement in the face of a broad and direct challenge to such agreements generally.[63]

Another issue arising frequently is whether a public hearing is required before a development agreement can be entered into and, if so, what proceedings are required. Both Hawaii[64] and California[65] explicitly require that a public hearing be held prior to adoption of the development agreement.

---

60. *Id.*

61. 903 P.2d 741 (Idaho 1995).

62. *Id.* at 750 ("The Council's conclusion that the 'downsizing' . . . is consistent with Hailey's comprehensive plan is not clearly erroneous, and is affirmed.").

63. *See* SMART v. San Luis Obispo Cnty. Bd. of Supervisors, 84 Cal. App. 4th 221 (Cal. Ct. App. 2000).

64. *See* Haw. Rev. Stat. § 46-128 (stating, "No development agreement shall be entered into unless a public hearing on the application therefore first shall have been held by the county legislative body.").

65. California Government Code section 65867 provides:

> A public hearing on an application for a development agreement shall be held by the planning agency and by the legislative body. Notice of intention to consider adoption of a development agreement shall be given as provided in Section 65090 and 65091 in addition to any other notice required by law for other actions to be considered concurrently with the development agreement.

Binding of State and Federal Agencies

Hawaii and California diverge on another key point: the binding inclusion of state or federal agencies. Hawaii seeks to bind them;[66] California does not. California initially appears to limit agreements to cities and counties, although it contemplates coastal commissions as parties under certain circumstances. Hawaii, on the other hand, appears determined to include state and federal agencies in development agreements.

Amendment or Cancellation of the Agreement

Generally, mutual consent of both parties is needed to amend or cancel the agreement.[67] In Hawaii, if the proposed amendment would substantially alter the original agreement, a public hearing must be held.[68] In California, a local government may terminate or modify a development agreement if it finds and determines, on the basis of substantial evidence, that the applicant or successor in interest thereto has not complied in good faith with its terms or conditions.[69]

---

66. Hawaii Revised Statutes section 46-126(d) provides:

> In addition to the county and principal, any federal, state, or local government agency or body may be included as a party to the development agreement. If more than one government body is made party to an agreement, the agreement shall specify which agency shall be responsible for the overall administration of the agreement.

67. *See* CAL. GOV'T CODE § 65868 ("A development agreement may be amended, or canceled in whole or in part, by mutual consent of the parties to the agreement or their successors in interest. . . ."); HAW. REV. STAT. § 46-130 ("A development agreement may be amended or canceled, in whole or in part, by mutual consent of the parties to the agreement, or their successors in interest.").

68. *See* HAW. REV. STAT. § 46-130 ("[I]f the county determines that a proposed amendment would substantially alter the original development agreement, a public hearing on the amendment shall be held by the county legislative body before it consents to the proposed amendment.").

69. CAL. GOV'T CODE § 65865.1.

Other Issues Affecting Development Agreements

Is the Approval a Legislative or Administrative Decision?

One of the thorniest problems in land use regulation is whether the amendment or changing of a regulation is legislative or quasi-judicial/administrative.[70] Legislative decisions like zoning amendments are subject to initiative and referendum in those states that authorize these ballot questions in development matters. However, quasi-judicial decisions like the granting of a special use permit are not. Legislative decisions like rezonings are, when appealed, usually heard de novo whereas quasi-judicial decisions, like the granting of a special use permit, are decided on the record made before the permitting agency, usually under a state's administrative procedure code.[71] What about the development agreement? On this issue, California and Hawaii again appear to differ—in the former, it is a legislative act,[72] whereas it is an administrative act in the latter.[73]

As with zoning, what follows from the statutory declarations—legislative in California, administrative/quasi-judicial in Hawaii—is more than a matter of form. Legislative decisions are subject to referendum.[74] Quasi-judicial ones are not.[75] Given the common use of the referendum in both California and Hawaii to address land use issues, development agreements

---

70. *See, e.g.*, Town v. Land Use Comm'n, 524 P.2d 84, 90–91 (Haw. 1974) (holding a reclassification of land by a state land use commission to be quasi-judicial); Fasano v. Bd. of Cnty. Comm'rs, 507 P.2d 23, 26 (Or. 1973) (holding a rezoning to be the same, despite the general rule that such "rezonings" are generally held to be legislative in character).

71. *See* Julian Conrad Juergensmeyer & Thomas E. Roberts, Land Use Planning Control Law §§ 531, 533, 538 (1998); *see also* David Callies et al., *Ballot Box Zoning: Initiative, Referendum, and the Law*, 39 Wash. U.J. Urb. & Contemp. L. 53 (1991). But as to federal due process, both administrative and legislative decisions appear to be referendable following the Court's decision in *City of Cuyahoga Falls v. Buckeye Community Hope Foundation*, 538 U.S. 188 (2003).

72. *See* SMART v. San Luis Obispo Cnty. Bd. of Supervisors, 84 Cal. App. 4th 221, 227 (Cal. Ct. App. 2000); Ctr. for Cmty. Action & Env't Just. v. City of Moreno Valley, 26 Cal. App. 5th 689, 712 (Cal. Ct. App. 2018).

73. *See* Haw. Rev. Stat. § 46-131 ("Each development agreement shall be deemed an administrative act of the government body made party to the agreement.").

74. *See* Cal. Gov't Code § 65867.5(a) ("A development agreement is a legislative act . . . and is subject to referendum.").

75. Juergensmeyer & Roberts, *supra* note 71, §§ 5.5, 5.9. *But see Buckeye Community Hope*, 538 U.S. 188.

in Hawaii, at least, are likely to be "referendum-proof," as well as protected against government change, during the life of a development agreement. However, California limits the opportunity to repeal a development agreement to 30 days from the date the local government approved the agreement.[76] Thereafter, both the agreement and the proposed land development are immune from subsequent changes by referendum.[77] In *Midway Orchards v. County of Butte*,[78] a California court held a development agreement was invalid because the general plan amendment relied on for consistency was timely referended.[79] The court stated:

> The development agreement was therefore unlawfully approved and executed. A contract entered into by a local government without legal authority is "wholly void," ultra vires and unenforceable. Such a contract can create no valid rights. Therefore, Midway can claim no right to develop its property based on a development agreement void from the beginning.[80]

In *Community Action & Environmental Justice v. City of Moreno Valley*,[81] the court held that the California development agreement statute does not permit adoption of a development agreement by initiative. The court cited (1) the statutory language, which specifies that adoption of a development agreement is a "legislative act . . . subject to referendum" but omits any reference to initiative;[82] (2) its determination that the statutory scheme was of statewide concern, which supported inferring a legislative intent to exclude initiatives;[83] and (3) the fact that the legislative history

---

76. *See* Midway Orchards v. Cnty. of Butte, 220 Cal. App. 3d 765, 778–82 (Cal. Ct. App. 1990) (holding that where development agreements are approved by legislative act of resolution that do not include referendum mechanism, constitutional right to referendum requires 30-day delay in effectiveness of the agreement to allow for referendum procedure).

77. *See* Cecily Talbert Barclay & Matthew S. Gray, California Land Use and Planning Law 317 (38th ed. 2022).

78. 220 Cal. App. 3d 765.

79. *Id.* at 778–82.

80. *Id.* at 783 (internal citations omitted). *See also* 216 Sutter Bay Assocs. v. Cnty. of Sutter, 58 Cal. App. 4th 860 (Cal. Ct. App. 1997) (holding that an interim urgency zoning ordinance and a parallel "ordinary" urgency ordinance, adopted by a newly elected board of supervisors within the 30-day "referendum period," successfully stopped a development agreement adopted by the preceding, lame-duck board).

81. 26 Cal. App. 5th 689 (Cal. Ct. App. 2018).

82. *Id.* at 699.

83. *Id.* at 706–07.

was consistent with an intent to prevent adoption of development agreements by initiative.[84]

Since a development agreement is a legislative act, a local government's decision not to enter into a development agreement need not be supported by findings.[85]

Under the California development agreement statute, mutuality of consideration is not required. As a practical matter, however, it is usually present as the developer obtains a "freeze" on applicable land use regulations while the public often obtains increased control over the development, certain assurances that the project will go forward, and perhaps other concessions from the developer that could not be obtained through the standard land use exaction process.

Finally, there is the question in California of whether the legislature can declare something to be a legislative act if it is not one anyway, even though this might take away a right reserved in the California Constitution to the people of a city to rezone by initiative.[86] Three California appellate courts have declared that a development agreement is a legislative act.[87] One of those courts, however, concluded that while development agreements approved by the legislative body are subject to referendum (as expressly provided in California's development agreement statute), they may not be approved by voter initiative.[88] This issue does not arise in Hawaii, both because the state constitution does not so provide, and because the Hawaii statute expresses a preference against such agreements being legislative acts. Other states have decided the question in the courts alone.[89]

---

84. *Id.* at 712.

85. Native Sun/Lyon Communities v. City of Escondido, 15 Cal. App. 4th 892 (Cal. Ct. App. 1993).

86. California Government Code section 65867.5 is the statute declaring a development agreement to be a legislative act.

87. SMART v. San Luis Obispo Cnty. Bd. of Supervisors, 84 Cal. App. 4th 221, 227 (Cal. Ct. App. 2000); Mammoth Lakes Land Acquisition LLC v. Town of Mammoth Lakes, 191 Cal. App. 4th 435, 442 (Cal. Ct. App. 2010); *Ctr. for Cmty. Action & Env't Just.*, 26 Cal. App. 5th at 712.

88. *Ctr. for Cmty. Action & Env't Just.*, 26 Cal. App. 5th at 712.

89. *See, e.g.*, Geralnes B.V. v. City of Greenwood Vill., 583 F. Supp. 830, 835 (D. Colo. 1984) (holding that city's zoning actions are quasi-judicial).

What Happens in the Event of a Breach?

There are essentially two kinds of breaches that commonly occur during the term of a development agreement: change in land use rules by the local government and failure to provide a bargained-for facility, dedication, or hook-up by either the developer or the local government.

When Local Government Changes the Land Development Rules

Recall that the overriding concern of the landowner in negotiating an annexation or development agreement is the vesting of development rights or the freezing of land development regulations during the term of the agreement. Whether these regulations are changed just prior to the execution of the agreement, and whether the landowner may need further permits that are not subject to a particular agreement, raise different, but related, questions. Here, we deal only with the effect on the landowner and the agreement should the local government change development regulations during the term of the agreement. Development agreement statutes usually contemplate such a freeze of development regulations.[90] In general, development agreements can freeze existing regulation but cannot grant or promise future approvals or changes.[91]

The California Supreme Court, in *City of West Hollywood v. Beverly Towers*,[92] made it abundantly clear in a footnote that landowner protec-

---

90. For example, the California code provides:

> Unless otherwise provided by the development agreement, rules, regulations, and official policies governing permitted uses of the land, governing density, and governing design, improvement, and construction standards and specifications, applicable to development of the property subject to a development agreement, shall be those rules, regulations, and official policies in force at the time of execution of the agreement. A development agreement shall not prevent a city, county, or city and county, in subsequent actions applicable to the property, from applying new rules, regulations, and policies which do not conflict with those rules, regulations, and policies applicable to the property as set forth herein, nor shall a development agreement prevent a city, county, or city and county from denying or conditionally approving any subsequent development project application on the basis of such existing or new rules, regulations, and policies.

CAL. GOV'T CODE § 65866.

91. Kenneth R. Kupchak et al., *Arrow of Time: Vested Rights, Zoning Estoppel, and Development Agreements in Hawaii*, 27 U. HAW. L. REV. 17, 61 (2004/2005).

92. 805 P.2d 329 (Cal. 1991).

tion from development regulation changes is a major factor in executing development agreements:

> Development agreements . . . between a developer and a government limit the power of that government to apply newly enacted ordinances to ongoing developments. Unless otherwise provided in the agreement, the rules, regulations, and official policies governing permitted uses, density, design, improvement, and construction are those in effect when the agreement is executed.[93]

The purpose of a development agreement, said the court, was "to allow a developer who needs additional discretionary approvals to complete a long-term development project as approved, regardless of any intervening changes in local regulations."[94]

The few courts that have dealt with local government changes in land use regulations have no difficulty in finding them inapplicable to the property subject to the agreement, provided the agreement itself is binding. Thus, in *Meegan v. Village of Tinley Park*,[95] the Illinois Supreme Court held that the original zoning of the subject property was valid during the term of the annexation agreement and any change by the village was void during that time. Indeed, since the village's attempted zoning change was void, said the court, there was no breach by the village.[96]

On the other hand, careful drafting is necessary to avoid the later application of land development regulations of a different sort than those contemplated in the agreement. Thus, in the California case *Pardee Construction Co. v. City of Camarillo*,[97] the court held applicable to the subject

---

93. *Id.* at 334 n.6. *See also* Daniel J. Curtin, Jr., *Protecting Developers' Permits to Build: Development Agreement in Practice in California and Other States*, 18 Zoning & Plan. L. Rep. 85, 85–92 (1995) (discussing various tests for determining when a developer's rights have vested and local government is estopped "from enacting or applying subsequent zoning changes to prevent the completion of the project or substantially reduce the return upon the developer's investment").

94. *Beverly Towers*, 805 P.2d at 334–35; *see also* Mammoth Lakes Land Acquisition LLC v. Town of Mammoth Lakes, 191 Cal. App. 4th 435, 442 (Cal. Ct. App. 2010).

95. 288 N.E.2d 423 (Ill. 1972).

96. *Id.* at 426; *cf.* Cummings v. City of Waterloo, 683 N.E.2d 1222, 1230 (Ill. App. Ct. 1997) (holding the city's amendment to its zoning ordinance that was contrary to the provisions of an annexation agreement was unenforceable against property subject to the annexation agreement).

97. 690 P.2d 701 (Cal. 1984).

property a transportation impact fee on the ground that it was different from the land development regulations listed in the agreement as frozen. While this seems to require a certain amount of prescience from the landowner at first blush, a local government can hardly be estopped from exercising its police power in enforcing a new breed of land development regulations that were not contemplated years before by either party, under the exercise of its police power.

Country Meadows West Partnership v. Village of Germantown[98] represents an entirely different perspective. There the court struck down the village's imposition of a new impact fee against a subdivider, holding that because of a subdivision agreement between the village and the subdivider, the subdivider was not obligated to pay the impact fee. However, an increase in fees or regulation can occur if permitted by a term of the development agreement, as in *Building Industry Ass'n of Central California v. City of Patterson*.[99] The development agreement in this case bound the developer to a revision of the affordable housing in-lieu fee, provided the increase was "reasonably justified." The fee was subsequently increased from $734 per unit to $20,946 per unit. Finding that the city failed to show that the fee increase was "limited to the cost of that portion of a public program attributable to the development," the appeals court reversed the trial court's determination that the increase was "reasonably justified" as required by the agreement.[100]

While most development agreement statutes either contain a limitation on the duration of such agreements[101] or provide that the agreement must recite one,[102] many states appear to permit annexation agreements (and, in some states like Nebraska and California, development agreements) without the benefit of such a statutory mandate. It is, therefore, theoretically possible for an annexation agreement to be relatively open-ended with respect to matters such as the zoning of the subject property. The results

98. 614 N.W.2d 498 (Wis. Ct. App. 2000).

99. 171 Cal. App. 4th 886 (Cal. Ct. App. 2009).

100. *Id.* at 889.

101. *See, e.g.*, FLA. STAT. ANN. § 163.3229 ("The duration of a development agreement shall not exceed 20 years. It may be extended by mutual consent of the governing body and the developer, subject to a public hearing. . . .").

102. *See, e.g.*, CAL. GOV'T CODE § 65865.2 ("A development agreement shall specify the duration of the agreement. . . ."); HAW. REV. STAT. ANN. § 46-126(a) ("A development agreement shall . . . (4) Provide a termination date . . . .").

can be unfortunate for the landowner since it is, of course, black-letter law that a landowner has no vested right in a zoning classification absent activity that vests such rights.[103] Thus, where the agreement is silent on the time period, at least one court has held that a landowner is without remedy if, a few years after annexation pursuant to an annexation agreement, the annexing local government changes the zoning to a classification that makes the originally contemplated land development impossible.[104]

Nonperformance of a Bargained-for Act: Dedications, Contributions, and Utility Connections

Equally common is the failure of a landowner or local government to live up to the terms of the agreement, generally by failing to provide a public facility or money therefor, or by refusing to provide utility services to the subject property.[105] Under such circumstances, the courts have been strict in forcing the parties to live up to their bargains, even when unusual difficulties would appear to render such performance nearly impossible. Thus, in the California case *Morrison Homes Corp.*, the court of appeal directed the local government to provide sewer connections to the landowner's property, as agreed in an annexation agreement, even though a superior governmental entity, a state regional water quality control board, ordered the local government not to do so.[106] After deciding that the agreement did not amount to the city's illegally contracting away its police power, the court stated: "The onset of materially changed conditions is not a ground

103. *See* David L. Callies, *Land Use: Herein of Vested Rights, Plans, and the Relationship of Planning and Controls*, 2 U. Haw. L. Rev. 167, 168 (1979) ("While it is fair to say that most jurisdictions are satisfied with an expenditure of funds in reliance upon a preexisting zone classification to support a claim for these so-called vested rights, some jurisdictions have disregarded all together fairly large amounts so expended.") (footnote omitted).

104. *See* Carty v. City of Ojai, 77 Cal. App. 3d 329, 341 (Cal. Ct. App. 1978) ("The reliance of the Cartys on the conduct of the city in the case before us has most tenuous predicates. No representations were made by any public official from the city as to the length of the time that the zone 'C-1' would continue.").

105. For other items bargained for and litigated, see *Van Cleave v. Village of Seneca*, 519 N.E.2d 63, 64 (Ill. App. Ct. 1988) (exemptions from real estate taxes), and *O'Malley v. Village of Ford Heights*, 633 N.E.2d 848, 849 (Ill. App. Ct. 1994) (exemption from environmental ordinances, which did not survive legal challenge).

106. 58 Cal. App. 3d 724, 724 (Cal. Ct. App. 1976); *but cf.* Keystone Bituminous Coal Ass'n v. DeBenedictis, 480 U.S. 470, 492 (1987) (upholding governmental refusal to perform development agreement when health and safety issue is involved); Goldblatt v. Town of Hempstead, 369 U.S. 590, 593–94 (1962) (same).

for voiding a municipal contract which was valid when made, nor is the contracting city's failure to have foreseen them."[107] In the California case *Mammoth Lakes*, the court of appeal upheld a $30 million jury award for the town's anticipatory breach of a development agreement.[108]

Are There Limits on What Conditions, Exactions, and Dedications May Be Imposed by a Local Government Pursuant to a Development Agreement?

While every governmental action must be invested with a public purpose, there are few conditions, exactions, or dedications that a local government may not legitimately bargain for in negotiating such agreements. Certainly, local governments may require landowners and developers to make reasonable contributions toward whatever services and other resources the government will need to provide as a result of a proposed development.[109] But this is so under existing law on development conditions and exactions entirely apart from such agreements.[110] The question is whether the local government may go further since the development agreement is indeed a voluntary agreement that neither government nor landowner is compelled to either negotiate or execute. So long as the agreement is indeed voluntary, the answer is almost certainly yes.[111]

---

107. *Morrison Homes Corp.*, 58 Cal. App. 3d at 735.

108. Mammoth Lakes Land Acquisition LLC v. Town of Mammoth Lakes, 191 Cal. App. 4th 435, 476 (Cal. Ct. App. 2010).

109. *See* Award Homes, Inc. v. Cnty. of San Benito, 287 Cal. Rptr. 3d 254, 263 (Cal. Ct. App. 2021) (requiring developer to pay the amount owed by the city to the county for each single-family dwelling unit because development agreement required developer to "fully pay for all costs of the City associated with or anticipated to result from such development").

110. *See* David L. Callies, *Exactions, Impact Fees, and Other Land Development Conditions, in* Zoning and Land Use Controls ch. 9 (Eric Damian Kelly ed., 2001); *see also* Dolan v. City of Tigard, 512 U.S. 374, 391 (1994) (holding that the Takings Clause of the Fifth Amendment requires that "the city must make some sort of individualized determination that the required dedication is related both in nature and extent to the impact of the proposed development"); Nollan v. Cal. Coastal Comm'n, 483 U.S. 825, 834–35 (1987) ("We have long recognized that land-use regulation does not effect a taking if it substantially advances legitimate state interests and does not deny an owner economically viable use of his land. . . . [A] broad range of governmental purposes and regulations satisfies these requirements.") (internal quotations omitted).

111. *See* City of Annapolis v. Waterman, 745 A.2d 1000, 1025 (Md. 2000) (conditions agreed to by the subdivider as part of an earlier subdivision agreement were not an unconstitutional taking of the subdivider's property). For a contrary view that would impose the same

Whether or not development agreements successfully avoid or survive nexus and proportionality challenges may depend, however, upon how willing the courts are to accept the underlying "voluntary" rationale. Nevertheless, some argue that exactions agreed to under a voluntary development agreement must bear a rational nexus to the needs created by the development.[112] The argument states that the "rational nexus" and "substantial advancement" standards of *Nollan* are not limited to just those instances where the municipality requires an exaction from an uncooperative landowner, but also apply to voluntary permit conditions. Under this view, the type and extent of exactions permissible under development agreements would not differ from the type and extent available under other traditional exaction mechanisms such as impact fees.

The rationale supporting such a view is that requiring the *Nollan* standard to be satisfied serves to prevent governmental abuse of the mechanism, as it is "difficult to tell whether a landowner's acceptance of a condition is truly voluntary or is instead a submission to government coercion."[113] Thus:

> A municipality could use . . . regulations to exact land or fees from a subdivider far out of proportion to the needs created by his subdivision in order to avoid imposing the burden of paying for additional services on all citizens via taxation. To tolerate this situation would be to allow an otherwise acceptable exercise of police power to become grand theft.[114]

---

strict nexus and proportionality requirements upon such agreements as upon "freestanding" local government development dedications, exactions, and other conditions, see generally Sam D. Starritt & John H. McClanahan, *Land-use Planning and Takings: The Viability of Conditional Exactions to Conserve Open Space in the Rocky Mountain West after* Dolan v. City of Tigard, *114 S. Ct. 2309 (1994)*, 30 Land & Water L. Rev. 415 (1995).

112. *See* Michael H. Crew, *Development Agreements after* Nollan v. California Coastal Commission, *483 U.S. 826 (1987)*, 22 Urb. Law. 23, 27 (1990) ("In applying this standard, courts considered . . . the cost of existing public facilities and their manner of financing, the extent to which existing development has already contributed to the cost of these facilities, and the extent to which the proposed project will contribute to the cost of the existing facilities in the future.").

113. *Id.* at 46.

114. Collis v. City of Bloomington, 246 N.W.2d 19, 26 (Minn. 1976) (upholding statute authorizing municipalities to require dedication of land or payment of fees as condition of subdivision approval as constitutional since enabling legislation and implementing ordinance limited the amount of land to be dedicated to a "reasonable" percentage of the property).

The Hawaii development agreement statute provides that "[p]ublic benefits derived from development agreements may include, but are not limited to, affordable housing, design standards, and on- and off-site infrastructure and other improvements. Such benefits may be negotiated for in return for the vesting of development rights for a specific period."[115] According to one commentator:

> [T]he government can require the developer to provide public benefits unrelated to the proposed project in exchange for the municipality granting her the right to develop. . . . [T]he statute leads municipalities to believe that the granting of development rights confers a governmental benefit on the developer. This is not the case. *Nollan* clearly holds that "the right to build on one's own property—even though its exercise can be subjected to legitimate permitting requirements—cannot remotely be described as a 'governmental benefit.'"[116]

However, while it is true that the right to develop on one's own land is not a governmental benefit, the right to develop is not the bargaining chip being tendered by the government in a development agreement. The authorities cited in support of the above-quoted argument concern exactions imposed as required conditions to development. In the case of a development agreement, the municipality is not granting the landowner the right to develop or imposing conditions on such development, but instead is promising to protect the developer's investment by not enforcing any subsequent land use regulation that may burden the project. Because the developer does not require any such guarantee to exercise a right or privilege to build, and may certainly choose to avail itself of such a guarantee and to negotiate for it, one could argue that the development agreement does indeed convey a "governmental benefit" upon the developer, since "[i]t is well established that there is no federal Constitutional right to be free from changes in land use laws."[117] The municipality should therefore be free to negotiate its best terms in exchange for the benefit conferred, regardless of nexus. Because development agreements are adopted as a result of nego-

---

115. Haw. Rev. Stat. § 46-121.

116. Crew, *supra* note 112, at 49 (quoting Nollan v. Cal. Coastal Comm'n, 483 U.S. 826, 833 n.10 (1987)).

117. Lakeview Dev. Corp. v. City of S. Lake Tahoe, 915 F.2d 1290, 1295 (9th Cir. 1990).

tiations between a local government and a developer, they are not subject to the *Dolan* or *Nollan* decisions.[118]

In *Hermosa Beach Stop Oil Coalition v. City of Hermosa Beach*,[119] the court held that the developer, who had failed to establish an entitlement to vested rights to develop an oil business on property leased from the city, could have protected itself from subsequent regulatory changes by asking that the city enter into a development agreement. The court noted that it was likely that the city would have demanded additional consideration for either a risk-adjustment provision in the existing lease or a separate development agreement, and that having at least implicitly decided to forgo such protection against future regulatory changes, the developer must accept the consequences of its judgment to do so.[120]

A trial court held that developers' rights vested at the time of signing a development agreement, and thus a city could not use wording within the agreement to allow it to raise sewer connection fees.[121] Developers and the city entered into a 15-year written agreement allowing for the development of a residential subdivision, allowing that the city may charge any "new taxes, assessments, or development impact fees on the implementation of the Project" only if those same charges are levied on all other similar developments within the city.[122] Six years after the parties signed the contract, the city raised the monthly wastewater connection fees and initial capital surcharge for each residential unit during the period covered by the contract, and the developers sued for breach of contract because their development rights had vested at the time of the initial agreement. A trial court agreed, but said that plaintiffs could not challenge the increased costs for potential future homeowners.[123]

---

118. *See* Leroy Land Dev. Corp. v. Tahoe Reg'l Plan. Agency, 939 F.2d 696 (9th Cir. 1991) (holding settlement agreement not subject to *Nollan*); *see also* David L. Callies & Julie A. Tappendorf, *Unconstitutional Land Development Conditions and the Development Agreement Solution: Bargaining for Public Facilities after* Nollan *and* Dolan, 51 Case W. Rsrv. L. Rev. 663 (2001).

119. 86 Cal. App. 4th 534 (Cal. Ct. App. 2001).

120. *Id.* at 558.

121. Referred to in the subsequent appeal, *Operating Engineers Funds, Inc. v. City of Thousand Oaks*, No. B137879, 2002 WL 44253 (Cal. Ct. App. Jan. 14, 2002) (unpublished decision) (holding that because the plaintiffs did not succeed in each of its claims, they could not qualify for attorney fees).

122. *Id.* at *1.

123. *Id.* at *2.

In *City of North Las Vegas v. Pardee Construction Co. of Nevada*,[124] a developer lost the appeal to define a cost-based fee as an impact fee in order to invalidate it through the parties' development agreement, which prohibited only impact fees. The municipality in this case regulated water issues on a regional level, and to respond to Nevada's growth spurt, the region passed a capital improvements plan to supplement the existing, overstrained water supply system.[125] The city had to join the regional water authority because its own water supply could not accommodate any more growth. Upon joining, the city had to pay for the connection to the new system through citywide assessments and water delivery, connection, and commodity fees.[126] To meet these payments, the city passed the costs on to the consumers at a direct rate, not making any profit.[127] Plaintiffs contended that these new charges were really impact fees and violated the terms of their development agreement.[128] Because the city did not make a profit, but based the charges on those charges it must pay to the regional authority, with no money going toward capital improvements, the court found that the charge was simply cost-based and within the parameters of the development agreement.[129]

While courts regularly label sewer, water, and stormwater systems as typical government functions, development agreements often provide that the subdivision developer install the water, sewer, and stormwater lines needed within the subdivision and connect them to existing lines. Sometimes a development agreement also requires payments for upgrades to the city's facilities to manage the greater flow requirements of the new development. In return for the improvements, the city agrees to maintain the pipe infrastructure within and connected to the subdivision.

---

124. 21 P.3d 8 (Nev. 2001).
125. *Id.* at 9.
126. *Id.*
127. *Id.* at 10.
128. *Id.*
129. *Id.* at 11.

3

Annexation Agreements

Introduction

An annexation agreement is really just another form of a development agreement. Many of the legal and procedural issues discussed in Chapter 2 apply equally to both types of agreements, and both the theory and the principal reasons for entering into these agreements are the same. In both types of agreements, the developer desires to protect its ability to develop its property once it has obtained all land use approvals. The municipality wants as many concessions and conditions as possible beyond what it could reasonably require through its normal exercise of its police power.

The difference between the two agreements is that an annexation agreement applies to unincorporated property proposed to be annexed to a municipality rather than to property already within municipal boundaries. In exchange for the municipality's agreement to annex the property, the developer will obtain a variety of services and protections but is also subject to the municipality's land use regulations and payment of property and other taxes. The municipality will obtain additional tax revenues and a larger tax base but must provide police, fire, and often utility services to the newly annexed territory.

In drafting and negotiating an annexation agreement, certain legal and procedural issues should be considered. The legal issues relate to the municipality's police power and its authority to enter into an annexation agreement. The procedural issues include public hearings if necessary, approval and adoption of the agreement, conformance with plans, amendment or cancellation of the agreement, and restrictions on conditions. The existence of a state statute to govern these procedural issues may determine whether and how these issues must be addressed in the negotiation or drafting of the annexation agreement.

Legal Issues

Authority

While statutory authority might be important in the context of development agreements, annexation agreement statutes seem less critical. In fact, while every state has a statute dealing with annexation, only a minority of states have adopted legislation enabling municipalities to enter into annexation agreements, including Arizona, California, Colorado, Illinois, Minnesota, North Carolina, Ohio, and Washington.[1] Because most states have statutes governing annexation itself, those statutory annexation provisions, together with a recognition that local governments have the powers they need to exercise their authorized powers (such as annexation), have likely convinced most courts considering the matter to uphold the annexation agreement in the absence of enabling statutes. For example, California courts of appeal have held that the statutory sources of a city's authority to discharge its annexation, sewage, and nuisance abatement functions, while not expressly vesting it with the authority to contract for either purpose by means of an annexation agreement, have that effect by necessary implication: "a city has authority to enter into contracts which enable it to carry out its necessary functions, and this applies to powers expressly conferred upon a municipality and to powers implied by necessity."[2]

Illinois Compiled Statutes authorize a municipality to enter into an annexation agreement with owners of land that is contiguous or becomes contiguous:[3]

---

1. Arizona: ARIZ. REV. STAT. § 9-500.05; California: CAL. GOV'T CODE §§ 65864 to 65869.5; Colorado: COLO. REV. STAT. § 31-12-121; Illinois: 65 ILL. COMP. STAT. 5/11-15.1-1 to 11-15.1-5; Minnesota: MINN. STAT. § 414.0325; North Carolina: N.C. GEN. STAT. §§ 160A-58.21 to 160A-58.28; Ohio: OHIO REV. CODE § 709.192; Washington: WASH. REV. CODE § 36.70B.170.

2. City of Ventura v. City of Moorpark, 24 Cal. App. 5th 377, 388–89 (Cal. Ct. App. 2018) (citing Morrison Homes Corp. v. City of Pleasanton, 58 Cal. App. 3d 724, 734 (Cal. Ct. App. 1976)).

3. *See* 65 ILL. COMP. STAT. 5/11-15.1-1.

> § 11-15.1-1. The corporate authorities of any municipality may enter into an annexation agreement with one or more of the owners of record of land in unincorporated territory. That land may be annexed to the municipality in the manner provided in Article 7 at the time the land is or becomes contiguous to the municipality. The agreement shall be valid and binding for a period of not to exceed 20 years from the date of its execution.

Similarly, North Carolina authorizes municipalities to enter into agreements concerning future annexation to "enhance orderly planning by such cities as well as residents and property owners in areas adjacent to such cities."[4] North Carolina General Statutes provide: "§ 160A-58.21. *Purpose.* It is the purpose of this Part to authorize cities to enter into binding agreements concerning future annexation in order to enhance orderly planning by such cities as well as residents and property owners in areas adjacent to such cities."

Arizona, California, and Washington authorize municipalities and owners to enter into "development agreements" relating to property located *outside* of the municipality's boundaries.[5] Arizona's statute provides as follows:

> § 9-500.05. Development Agreements; public safety; definitions
> A. A municipality, by resolution or ordinance, may enter into development agreements relating to property in the municipality and to property located outside the incorporated area of the municipality. If the development agreement relates to property located outside the incorporated area of the municipality, the development agreement does not become operative unless annexation proceedings to annex the property to the municipality are completed within the period of time specified by the development agreement or any extension of such time.

California provides as follows:

> § 65865. Authorization, procedures and requirements; recovery of costs; compliance with § 66006

4. *See* N.C. Gen. Stat. § 160A-58.21.

5. *See* Ariz. Rev. Stat. § 9-500.05; Cal. Gov't Code §§ 65864 to 65869.5; Wash. Rev. Code § 36.70B.170.

(a) Any city, county, or city and county, may enter into a development agreement with any person having a legal or equitable interest in real property for the development of the property as provided in this article.

(b) Any city may enter into a development agreement with any person having a legal or equitable interest in real property in unincorporated territory within that city's sphere of influence for the development of the property as provided in this article. However, the agreement shall not become operative unless annexation proceedings annexing the property to the city are completed within the period of time specified by the agreement. If the annexation is not completed within the time specified in the agreement or any extension of the agreement, the agreement is null and void.

Washington's statute states, in part, as follows:

§ 36.70B.170. Development agreements—Authorized

(1) A local government may enter into a development agreement with a person having ownership or control of real property within its jurisdiction. A city may enter into a development agreement for real property outside its boundaries as part of a proposed annexation or a service agreement. A development agreement must set forth the development standards and other provisions that shall apply to and govern and vest the development, use, and mitigation of the development of the real property for the duration specified in the agreement. A development agreement shall be consistent with applicable development regulations adopted by a local government planning under chapter 36.70A RCW.

Colorado authorizes a municipality to enter into annexation agreements with property owners as a condition to the provision of municipal services:

§ 31-12-121. Provision of municipal services to outside consumers—agreement to annex

Any municipality, as a condition precedent to the supplying of municipal services pursuant to contract, may require a contemporary agreement by such consumers, who are owners in fee of real

> property so supplied, to apply for or consent to the annexation of the area to be supplied with such municipal services to the supplying municipality at such future date as the area supplied, or any portion thereof, becomes eligible for annexation pursuant to the provisions of this part 1. The agreement to annex shall be enforceable by an action for specific performance filed in the district court of the judicial district containing all or part of the supplying municipality. A memorandum of such agreement, setting forth the names of the owners in fee of real property supplied and the legal description of such area, shall be recorded in the office of the county clerk and recorder of the county in which such area is located and shall constitute constructive notice of such agreement to all persons not parties thereto. In no event shall the board of directors of any quasi-municipal corporation organized under part 5 or 6 of article 25 of this title, article 8 of title 29, part 2 of article 20 of title 30, or title 32 (except article 8), C.R.S., or any other law of this state be permitted to obligate or require property owners within any such district to sign any such agreement in order to obtain water service from a municipality.[6]

Even without specific statutory authority, courts have generally upheld annexation agreements, recognizing that municipalities have the authority they need to exercise their authorized powers (such as annexation).[7] For example, in *Morrison Homes v. City of Pleasanton*,[8] the court upheld an annexation agreement without the benefit of a statute. In doing so, the court recognized:

> The cited sources of a city's authority to discharge the annexation or sewage functions do not expressly vest it with the authority to contract for either purpose, but they have this effect by *necessary implication*: "A city has authority to enter into contracts which

---

6. Colo. Rev. Stat. § 31-12-121.

7. *See, e.g.*, Bradley v. City of Trussville, 527 So. 2d 1303, 1306 (Ala. Civ. App. 1988); Town of La Plata v. Faison-Rosewick LLC, 434 Md. 496, 515–16 (Md. 2013) (citing Rockville v. Brookville Tpk. Constr. Co., 246 Md. 117, 134–35 (Md. 1967)).

8. 130 Cal. Rptr. 196 (Cal. Ct. App. 1976).

enable it to carry out its necessary functions, and this applies . . . to powers implied by necessity."[9]

In drafting an annexation agreement, reference should be made to the municipality's authority to enter into the agreement. Typically, this can be noted in the recitals of the agreement or an approving ordinance or resolution that includes a simple statement that the municipality has the authority to enter into the annexation agreement pursuant to an express state statute or, in the absence of a statute, other municipal authority such as the statutory authority to annex property or the general police powers.

Jurisdiction

Another legal issue distinct to annexation agreements is the question of jurisdiction over the unincorporated land subject to an annexation agreement prior to the formal annexation of the land to the annexing municipality. In Illinois, zoning and building jurisdiction is established by state statute, which provides as follows:

> § 11-15.1-2.1. Annexation agreement; municipal jurisdiction.
>
> (a) Except as provided in subsections (b) and (c), property that is the subject of an annexation agreement adopted under this Division is subject to the ordinances, control, and jurisdiction of the annexing municipality in all respects the same as property that lies within the annexing municipality's corporate limits.
>
> (b) This Section shall not apply in (i) a county with a population of more than 3,000,000, (ii) a county that borders a county with a population of more than 3,000,000 or (iii) a county with a population of more than 246,000 according to the 1990 federal census and bordered by the Mississippi River, unless the parties to the annexation agreement have, at the time the agreement is signed, ownership or control of all property that would make the property that is the subject of the agreement contiguous to the annexing municipality, in which case the property that is the subject of the annexation agreement is subject to the ordinances, control, and jurisdiction of

9. *Id.* at 202 (emphasis added) (citing Carruth v. City of Madera, 233 Cal. App. 2d 688, 695 (Cal. Ct. App. 1965); McBean v. City of Fresno, 112 Cal. 159, 161–63, 170 (Cal. 1896)).

the municipality in all respects the same as property owned by the municipality that lies within its corporate limits.

(b-5) The limitations of item (iii) of subsection (b) do not apply to property that is the subject of an annexation agreement adopted under this Division within one year after the effective date of this amendatory Act of the 95th General Assembly with a coterminous home rule municipality, as of June 1, 2009, that borders the Mississippi River, in a county with a population in excess of 258,000, according to the 2000 federal census, if all such agreements entered into by the municipality pertain to parcels that comprise a contiguous area of not more than 120 acres in the aggregate.

(c) Except for property located in a county referenced in subsection (b) of this Section, if property that is the subject of an annexation agreement is located more than 1.5 miles from the corporate boundaries of the annexing municipality, that property is subject to the ordinances, control, and jurisdiction of the annexing municipality unless the county board retains jurisdiction by the affirmative vote of two-thirds of its members.

(d) If the county board retains jurisdiction under subsection (c) of this Section, the annexing municipality may file a request for jurisdiction with the county board on a case by case basis. If the county board agrees by the affirmative vote of a majority of its members, then the property covered by the annexation agreement shall be subject to the ordinances, control, and jurisdiction of the annexing municipality.

The statute makes an interesting distinction between various counties in Illinois with respect to zoning and building code jurisdiction over unincorporated land subject to an annexation agreement. For those counties surrounding the City of Chicago (commonly referred to as the "collar counties"), the statute does not grant a municipality in one of those counties zoning or building code authority over unincorporated land subject to an annexation agreement. However, for all other counties in Illinois, a municipality has zoning and building code jurisdiction over land subject to an annexation agreement. That statutory distinction was the subject of a "special legislation" challenge in *Village of Chatham v. County of Sangamon.*[10]

10. 837 N.E.2d 29 (Ill. 2005).

The Village of Chatham had entered into an annexation agreement governing unincorporated land in Sangamon County. The village exercised its zoning and building code authority over the property in processing various permit applications, and the county challenged the village's jurisdiction in court. The court determined that based on the above-cited statute, the village had both zoning and building code jurisdiction over the unincorporated land that was subject to the annexation agreement. The court upheld the statute's differential treatment between "collar counties" and downstate counties and found that it was neither special legislation nor an invalid exercise of the police power. The court rejected the county's argument that a landowner could bargain with unlimited municipalities across the state for the best zoning deals even though an annexation might never occur because of the statutory contiguity requirement.[11]

Another jurisdictional issue arises when there are competing interests in a particular territory by neighboring governmental entities. For example, in *Sugarcreek Township v. City of Centerville*,[12] the township sued the city to challenge certain provisions contained in a preannexation agreement between the city and the owner of two parcels of land located in both the township and city. The court ultimately held that the township had standing to challenge the preannexation agreement even though it was not a party because it would be affected by the provisions relating to the establishment of a tax increment financing (TIF) plan within the annexed territory.

Issues of priority and timeliness also arise with conflicting annexation claims between two local government authorities. In *In re Petition to Annex Certain Territory to the Village of Lemont*,[13] a village engaged in a domino-like annexation project: after property owners for the parcels filed voluntary annexation petitions, the village annexed neighboring property that would create the necessary contiguity to properly annex the petitioned-for parcels. However, in the interim between the petitions and the annexation of the connecting property, residents of a neighboring village filed a forcible annexation petition to annex some of the identified property to their

---

11. *See also* Vill. of Orland Hills v. Citizens Utils. Co. of Ill., 807 N.E.2d 590 (Ill. App. Ct. 2004) (finding that where property is subject to competing claims of jurisdiction, the annexing municipality's subdivision and zoning jurisdiction overrides another municipality's statutory grant of planning jurisdiction over the unincorporated planning area).

12. 921 N.E.2d 655 (Ohio Ct. App. 2009), *rev'd on other grounds*, 133 Ohio St. 3d 467 (Ohio 2012).

13. 97 N.E.2d 43 (Ill. App. Ct. 2017).

community. The court found that the voluntary proceedings had priority over the forcible proceedings because there was no evidence that the voluntary annexation petitions were abandoned while the village was working to incorporate the connecting territory.

Limits on Conditions and Zoning Provisions

Under existing law on development conditions and exactions, municipalities have traditionally had broad authority to require developers to make reasonable contributions toward whatever services and other resources the government will need to provide as a result of an annexation. The question is, can a municipality go further than what is permitted under exactions law based on an argument that the annexation agreement is a voluntary agreement? Provided the agreement is truly voluntary, the answer is almost certainly yes, particularly where the conditions are imposed through an annexation agreement.[14] One commentator suggests that annexation agreements are simply beyond the scope of the *Nollan-Dolan* cases (discussed in Chapter 1):

> Although at first glance, *Nollan* and *Dolan* may have made these negotiated deals between local government and landowner subject to new and substantial constitutional hurdles, some particularly popular discretionary agreements may actually fall beyond the heightened scrutiny and more stringent substantive standards articulated in those cases. Specifically, annexation agreements and planned development agreements, where municipal governments exercise absolute discretion to accept or reject landowner proposals, appear to provide a context in which the *Nollan-Dolan* standards are simply inapplicable.[15]

14. *See* David L. Callies & Glenn H. Sonoda, *Providing Infrastructure for Smart Growth: Land Development Conditions*, 43 Idaho L. Rev. 351 (2007); *see also* Daniel J. Curtin, Jr. et al., *Exactions Update: When* Nollan/Dolan *Heightened Scrutiny Does Not Apply*, 37 Urb. Law. 539, 540 (2005) ("Development and annexation agreements are adopted as a result of negotiations between a city or county and a developer; therefore, they are not subject to the *Nollan/Dolan* heightened scrutiny standard the courts apply to determine whether an exaction is a valid condition on development or an unconstitutional taking.").

15. Laurie Reynolds & Carlos A. Ball, *Exactions and the Privatization of the Public Sphere*, 21 J. L. & Pol. 451, 472 (2005).

Although this commentator suggests that municipal involvement in these type of negotiated agreements is a sign that cities are ignoring the mandate of *Nollan-Dolan* by bargaining "outside the constitutionally required parameters," it is perhaps more accurate to suggest that these agreements are simply beyond the scope of the rules articulated in those cases. In the case of both an annexation agreement and a planned development, for example, local governments have absolute discretion to accept or reject proposals, and landowners will always have alternative development potential guaranteed as a matter of right. *Nollan-Dolan*'s standards of essential nexus and rough proportionality (which impose a limitation on the extent to which government can condition the landowner's right to development approval) simply do not appear to apply to an agreement in which the parties have reached a mutually agreeable set of terms.[16] This analysis seems consistent with the U.S. Supreme Court's decision in *Koontz v. St. John's River Water Management District*,[17] where the Court relied on the unconstitutional conditions doctrine to hold that a local government could not coerce a developer to give up its constitutionally protected rights in exchange for the benefit of developing on designated wetlands.[18] *Koontz*, *Nolan*, and *Dolan* do not go so far as to suggest that voluntary entry into an agreement with local government would trigger constitutional issues—rather, local governments must be careful in raising exactions so as to avoid the appearance or effect of coercion vis-à-vis landowners, and continue to exercise their police powers consistently with their authority and discretion.[19]

As the Colorado Supreme Court stated in *City of Colorado Springs v. Kitty Hawk Development Co.*:[20]

> A municipality is under no legal obligation in the first instance to annex contiguous territory, and may reject a petition for annexation for no reason at all. It follows then that if the municipality

16. *Id.* at 472–73; *see also* Curtin et al., *supra* note 14.
17. 570 U.S. 595 (2013).
18. *Id.* at 619.
19. *See* Old Cutters, Inc. v. City of Hailey, 488 B.R. 130, 152 (Bankr. D. Idaho 2012) (finding annexation fee and community housing provisions of annexation to be unenforceable where it was "unquestionably in excess" of fees required to compensate city for actual costs resulting from annexation).
20. 392 P.2d 467 (Colo. 1964).

> elects to accept such territory solely as a matter of discretion, it may impose such conditions by way of agreement as it sees fit. If the party seeking annexation does not wish to annex under the conditions imposed, he is free to withdraw his petition to annex and remain without the city.[21]

Almost 50 years after deciding the *Kitty Hawk* case, the Colorado Supreme Court upheld Colorado Springs's imposition of $9 million in drainage fees through an annexation agreement.[22]

The Washington legislature, on the other hand, has limited the authority of municipalities to impose what would otherwise be unauthorized impact fees or dedications as part of an annexation agreement by providing that nothing in the annexation agreement statute authorizes municipalities to impose impact fees or dedications, or any other condition, unless these fees or dedications are expressly authorized by another state statute: "Nothing in [the development/annexation agreement statute] is intended to authorize local government to impose impact fees, inspection fees, or dedications or to require any other financial contributions or mitigation measures except as expressly authorized by other applicable provisions of state law."[23]

In the case of annexation agreements, it is the developer's *choice* to annex to a municipality and to decide to protect itself and its proposed development by attempting to freeze zoning or land use regulations through the agreement. To the extent that the developer chooses to annex its property to the municipality and to negotiate for any regulatory freezes or other development rights or protections, arguably the annexation agreement does convey a "governmental benefit" on the developer. The municipality should, therefore, be free to negotiate its best terms in exchange for the benefit conferred.[24]

---

21. *Id.* at 472.

22. Wolf Ranch, LLC v. City of Colo. Springs, 220 P.3d 559 (Colo. 2009).

23. Wash. Rev. Code § 36.70B.210.

24. *See* I-57 & Curtis, LLC v. Urbana & Champaign Sanitary Dist., 164 N.E.3d 99 (4th Dist. 2020) ("The statute [governing annexation agreements] does not condition that authority on the agreement's being unmotivated by economic incentives or annexation leverage."); *see also* Shelby D. Green, *Development Agreements: Bargained-for Zoning That Is Neither Illegal Contract nor Conditional Zoning*, 33 Cap. U.L. Rev. 383, 394, 407 (2004) ("[A] municipality is able to set definite conditions that govern the process of development, thus limiting the potential negative impacts from the development on neighboring land and the community.").

Parties must be careful to follow applicable statutory procedures for approving the zoning of the property and the proposed project plans that are the subject of the annexation agreement. Simply including zoning provisions in an annexation agreement without following necessary notice, hearing, and other zoning procedures will likely result in the invalidation of the zoning.[25] For example, in *Crumbaker v. Hunt Midwest Mining, Inc.*,[26] neighboring property owners challenged the validity of various land use provisions in an annexation agreement between the City of De Soto and a mining company that would allow the expansion of an existing rock quarry operation. Although the annexation agreement itself contained provisions authorizing the quarry use, the city had not scheduled the zoning matter for a hearing before the planning commission nor adopted a separate zoning ordinance. Because the city failed to follow the zoning procedures in state law and city ordinances to authorize the continuation and expansion of the quarry operations, the court invalidated those provisions of the annexation agreement that dealt with land use. The Kansas Supreme Court has since cited the *Crumbaker* opinion with approval, reinforcing its holding that "the purpose of the annexation statutes is to protect the rights of the landowners against unilateral action by a city annexing *their* land."[27] Thus, the policy justifications underlying proper annexation procedures are familiar and largely impenetrable on the same grounds as due process rights in land use processes generally.

At least one court has held, however, that a municipality need not amend the underlying annexation agreement in approving amendments to zoning approvals for a property subject to an annexation agreement. In *Lane Ranch Partnership v. City of Sun Valley*,[28] an annexation agreement was approved in 1986. The agreement contained various zoning provisions that authorized fewer residential units than would otherwise be allowed under the zoning ordinance. In 2001, a subsequent owner applied for zoning approvals that would increase the number of residential units allowed on the property in excess of that allowed by the annexation agree-

25. *See* Wallingford v. Moab City, 2020 UT App 12, ¶¶ 24–25 (holding that adoption of "Zoning Status Agreement," made in the context of annexation, without a public hearing was unlawful contract zoning).

26. 69 P.3d 601 (Kan. 2003).

27. Stueckemann v. City of Basehor, 348 P.3d 526, 535 (Kan. 2015) (citing *Crumbaker*, 69 P.3d at 610; City of Lenexa v. City of Olathe, 660 P.3d 1368, 1373 (Kan. 1983)).

28. 166 P.3d 374 (Idaho 2007).

ment. After the city denied the applications, stating that the annexation agreement would have to be amended to authorize the revised development plans, the owner sued. Ultimately, the Idaho Supreme Court held that the annexation agreement did not need to be amended to authorize the rezoning because the agreement was silent as to any prohibition on rezoning of the property. The court emphasized that the annexation agreement did not result in a waiver or forfeiture of the owner's right to apply for or obtain approval of a rezoning of the property.

Courts will generally grant municipalities broad authority to enforce conditions and zoning provisions of an annexation agreement. Moreover, in interpreting provisions of an annexation agreement, courts will typically defer to the municipality's interpretation. For example, in *Pen & Ink, LLC v. Alpine City*,[29] the owners of property subject to an annexation agreement challenged the city's denial of a proposed development plan that was based on the city's interpretation of certain plans approved as part of the annexation agreement. The court first determined that the plans were incorporated into the annexation agreement. The court then acknowledged that the language of the annexation agreement concerning maximum lot size was somewhat ambiguous and subject to two interpretations. However, based on the presumption of validity accorded to zoning ordinances in Utah, the court held that the plaintiffs failed to establish that the city's denial of its application was arbitrary or capricious.

Obviously, it is important to review any applicable state statutes and cases to determine the extent to which a municipality can impose these fees, dedications, or other conditions.

Binding on Successors

Like development agreements, the obligations contained within the annexation agreement are generally binding on successor owners. That has not prevented successor owners from challenging annexation agreements or attempting to disconnect from the municipality in order to avoid obligations in the annexation agreement. Most courts have held these successor owners to the benefit of their (or their predecessor's) bargain.[30] For

29. 238 P.3d 63 (Utah Ct. App. 2010).

30. *See, e.g.*, Town of Florence v. Florence Copper Inc., 493 P.3d 891 (Ariz. Ct. App. 2021); United City of Yorkville v. Fid. & Deposit Co. of Md., 2019 IL App (2d) 180230; BMC Promise Way, LLC v. Cnty. of San Benito, 287 Cal. Rptr. 3d 269 (Cal. Ct. App. 2021).

example, in *Jewell v. City of Beardstown*,[31] subsequent owners challenged an annexation agreement entered into by the original developer of their subdivision. The court upheld the annexation agreement, finding:

> [O]nce a land owner has given consent to annexation in return for valuable consideration from the annexing city and the consideration significantly improves his or her land by the provision of city water and sewer services, the landowner is then estopped from gaining the benefit of his or her bargain without also exercising its obligations.[32]

Similarly, in *Humphrey Property Group, LLC v. Village of Frankfort*,[33] the court held that a municipality could invoke equitable estoppel against a successor owner's challenge to the validity of a zoning amendment. The village had argued that because the successor owner "stands in the shoes of its predecessor in interest," the owner is estopped from contesting the validity of an amendment to the agreement and zoning of the property.

However, the determination of whether a party may properly be considered a successor is not always straightforward. In *Doyle v. Village of Tinley Park & Malone*,[34] for example, the court found that individual purchasers of lots in a subdivision could not properly argue they were successors to bind the developer to its promise to construct a functional drain system. Rather, only a successor owner who might take title to the entire property could be bound by the agreement's terms.[35] Other courts have taken the position, however, that equitable principles may permit a party to an annexation agreement to apply "proportionate responsibility" to partial successor owners (purchasers for less than the entire lot contemplated in the agreement) in order to obtain security for the construction of public improvements for the proposed residential development.[36]

---

31. 260 S.W.3d 348 (Ky. Ct. App. 2008).

32. *Id.*

33. 925 N.E.2d 219 (Ill. App. Ct. 2009); *see also United City of Yorkville*, 2019 IL App (2d) 180230.

34. 115 N.E.3d 1069 (Ill. App. Ct. 2018).

35. *Id.* ¶¶ 30–32 (determining the "subject property" could only properly be interpreted as the entire subdivision, avoiding the absurd result that individual homeowners could legally take on the obligations of the developer).

36. *See* Vill. of Kirkland v. Kirkland Props. Holdings Co., 2022 IL App (2d) 200780.

In *In re Southcreek Development, LLC*,[37] the village and Southcreek Development entered into an annexation agreement in 1996, amended in 1997, to govern the annexation and development of 314 acres in unincorporated Kankakee County. The property was subsequently annexed and zoned. In 2009, the village sued Southcreek to enforce its obligation under the agreement to improve the Frontage Road because construction had not yet commenced. Shortly thereafter, Southcreek filed for bankruptcy and listed the village as a creditor for the estimated costs of improving Frontage Road. The village filed a motion to protect its interest in the property, and argued that the property could not be sold without satisfaction of the road improvement requirement of the annexation agreement. The bankruptcy trustee filed a motion to dismiss, challenging the validity of the annexation agreement. The court denied the trustee's motion to dismiss, holding that the bankruptcy trustee's challenge to the annexation agreement was barred by the one-year statute of limitations for challenges to annexation agreements.

At least one state annexation agreement statute (Illinois) specifically provides that annexation agreements are "binding upon the successor owners of record of the land which is the subject of the agreement and upon successor municipal authorities of the municipality and successor municipalities."[38] The Arizona statute implicitly provides the same:

> § 9-500.05 Development Agreements; public safety; definitions
>
> C. A development agreement may be amended, or cancelled in whole or in part, by mutual consent of the parties to the development agreement or by their successors in interest or assigns.[39]

Disconnection

One legal issue distinct to annexation agreements is the benefit/burden of the annexation of unincorporated land to the annexing municipality. Does the promise (or obligation) of annexing the unincorporated land to the municipality "estop" a property owner from disconnecting the property in the future? Some courts have said yes, even where the annexation

37. No. 10-C-2136, 2010 WL 4683607 (C.D. Ill. Oct. 25, 2010).
38. 65 Ill. Comp. Stat. 5/11-15.1-4.
39. Ariz. Rev. Stat. § 9-500.05(C).

agreement is silent on the issue of disconnection and even in cases where the annexation agreement has expired.

In *Gaylor v. Village of Ringwood*,[40] a property owner voluntarily entered into an annexation agreement with the village for a term of 20 years. However, seven years into the agreement, the owner filed a petition for disconnection. The village argued that, although the petitioner's proposed disconnection satisfied the statutory conditions required for disconnection, the property was not entitled to disconnection because the terms of the binding annexation agreement had not yet expired. The appellate court determined that the disconnection statute requires two findings: (1) that the petition allegations are true, and (2) that the land is "entitled to disconnection." In this case, although the statutory requirements in the disconnection petition were met, the appellate court determined that the language of the second requirement implies that the existence of a valid, unexpired annexation agreement is an affirmative defense to a disconnection action and that the village could raise equitable estoppel against disconnection.

The Illinois Appellate Court took it one step further in *Falcon Funding LLC v. City of Elgin*.[41] Similar to the facts in the *Gaylor* case, the property in question was subject to an annexation agreement. However, in this case, the annexation agreement had expired when the owner filed a petition for disconnection. The city claimed that the owner was equitably estopped from disconnecting the subject property because the owner induced the city to provide more than $9 million in sewer and water connections to the subject property in reliance on the annexation agreement, and the petitioner never developed the property. The owner claimed that the city was not entitled to use the doctrine of equitable estoppel as an affirmative defense in a disconnection case because the agreement expired. The appellate court determined that, pursuant to the holding in *Gaylor v. Village of Ringwood*, the doctrine of equitable estoppel was available as an affirmative defense in disconnection cases even where the annexation agreement had expired. However, because the city failed to sufficiently plead the elements for an equitable estoppel, the property was subject to disconnection.[42]

40. 842 N.E.2d 1241 (Ill. App. Ct. 2006).

41. 924 N.E.2d 1216 (Ill. App. Ct. 2010).

42. The *Falcon Funding* court laid out six discrete elements for a municipality to successfully raise an equitable estoppel claim: (1) the petitioner misrepresented or concealed material facts; (2) the petitioner knew the representations were untrue when they were made; (3) the municipality did not know the representations were untrue when they were made and

When a Municipality Changes the Land Development Rules

The overriding concern of the developer in negotiating an annexation agreement (besides the annexation itself) is the vesting of development rights or the freezing of land development regulations during the term of the agreement.

The Illinois annexation agreement statute sets forth the proper scope of these agreements that would allow the agreement to continue in effect any subdivision, zoning, plan, building, or housing regulation. In addition, the statute allows the agreement to limit any increases in permit fees during the life of the agreement. The Illinois statute further provides that any action taken by the municipality during the period the agreement is in effect, if applied to the property subject of the agreement, would be a breach of such agreement, and would not apply to that property without an amendment to the agreement.[43] Similarly, Washington statutes provide that any development standards incorporated into an annexation agreement will govern during the term of the agreement and are not subject to any zoning or other development change adopted after the effective date of the agreement.[44] California provides that the rules, regulations, and official policies governing permitted uses, density, design, improvement, and construction standards in effect at the time of execution of the agreement will be applicable to the development of the land subject to the agreement, unless otherwise provided by the agreement.[45]

The courts that have dealt with municipality changes in land use regulations have had no difficulty finding them inapplicable to the property subject to the agreement, provided the agreement itself is binding. For example, in two Illinois decisions, *Meegan v. Tinley Park*[46] and *Cummings v. City of Waterloo*,[47] courts held that no zoning change would be valid during the term of the annexation agreement. However, if the municipality fails to comply with required state and local notice-and-hearing requirements

---

acted upon; (4) the petitioner reasonably expected or intended for the municipality to act upon the representations; (5) the municipality reasonably relied upon the representations in good faith and to its detriment; and (6) the municipality would be prejudiced by its reliance on the representations if the petitioner were permitted to deny their truth. *Id.* at 1229.

43. 65 Ill. Comp. Stat. 5/11-15.1-2.

44. Wash. Rev. Code § 36.70B.180.

45. Cal. Gov't Code § 65866.

46. 288 N.E.2d 423 (Ill. 1972).

47. 683 N.E.2d 1222 (Ill. App. Ct. 1997).

in approving the zoning for property subject to an annexation agreement, courts may invalidate the zoning and find no vested right to continue or expand a use that was not properly authorized.[48]

One interesting question is whether the zoning and other development standards survive upon termination of the agreement. In *Bank of Waukegan v. Village of Vernon Hills*,[49] the Illinois Appellate Court held that the zoning provisions in the agreement expired upon expiration of the agreement, an obvious problem. Following that decision, in 1995, the Illinois legislature amended the annexation agreement statute to state that zoning provisions in the agreement remain in effect beyond termination of the agreement.[50]

Bargaining Away of the Police Power

The issue of whether a municipality bargains away its police power by entering into an agreement under which it promises not to change its land use regulations during the life of the agreement is the same for annexation agreements as it is for development agreements. Local governments may not "contract away the police power,"[51] particularly in the context of zoning decisions.[52] In other words, government cannot bind itself to not exercise its police powers.

Because the zoning power is an aspect of the police power, a municipality may not enter into a private contract for rezoning subject to restrictions. It is considered to be against public policy to permit the bargaining of zoning and subdivision regulations for agreements and stipulations on the part of developers to do or refrain from doing certain things. Courts often look to the law on conditional or contract zoning in analyzing the

48. Crumbaker v. Hunt Midwest Mining, Inc., 69 P.3d 601 (Kan. 2003); *but see* Stueckemann v. City of Basehor, 348 P.3d 526, 534–35 (Kan. 2015) (holding that the Kansas annexation statute was not violated where a city gave proper notice and an opportunity to be heard).

49. 626 N.E.2d 245 (Ill. App. Ct. 1993).

50. 1995 Ill. Pub. Act. 432 (Lexis 2022).

51. Carlino v. Whitpain Invs., 453 A.2d 1385 (Pa. 1982). *See also* Monumental Task Comm., Inc. v. Foxx, 240 F. Supp. 3d 487 (E.D. La. 2017) ("[I]f a public corporation enters into a contract that barters away or otherwise restricts the exercise of its legislative or police powers, then the contract is ultra vires and void ab initio.").

52. Cederberg v. City of Rockford, 291 N.E.2d 249 (Ill. App. Ct. 1972). *See also* Houston Petroleum Co. v. Auto. Prods. Credit Ass'n, 9 N.J. 122, 129 (N.J. 1952) ("Contracts thus have no place in a zoning plan and a contract between a municipality and a property owner should not enter into the enactment or enforcement of zoning regulations."); *see also* Zahodiakin Eng'g Corp. v. Zoning Bd. of Adjustment, 86 A.2d 127 (N.J. 1952).

validity of annexation agreements that contain zoning provisions and conditions.[53] Notwithstanding these legal limitations, some courts recognize that it is "disingenuous to condemn a method of zoning because it benefits private interests in some way."[54] If an annexation agreement is drafted to reserve some governmental control over the agreement, it does not contract away the police power, but instead constitutes a valid present exercise of that power.[55]

The prohibition against bargaining away the police power finds its source in the "reserved powers" doctrine.[56] Under this doctrine, bargaining away the police power is the equivalent of a current legislature attempting to exercise legislative power reserved to later legislatures.[57] In *Carruth v. City of Madera*,[58] the city argued that its obligations under an annexation agreement approved by a previous council were invalid because they deprived the later city council of the power to determine city policy and act in the public interest. The court, however, found the agreement to be fair, just, and reasonable at the time of its approval and, therefore, the city

53. *See* Cnty. of Volusia v. City of Deltona, 925 So. 2d 340 (Fla. Dist. Ct. App. 2006) (remanding case for determination as to whether annexation agreement was an improper delegation of legislative authority based on substantial obligations on the city); *see also* Rockville v. Rylyns Enters., Inc., 814 A.2d 469 (Md. 2002) (finding conditional or contract zoning invalid even through annexation agreement); *but see* City of Bowie v. MIE Props., Inc., 922 A.2d 509 (Md. 2007) (upholding annexation agreement against an illegal contract zoning challenge).

54. Lamar Advert. of S.D., LLC v. City of Rapid City, 944 N.W.2d 793, 802 (S.D. 2020) (citing Dacy v. Vill. of Ruidoso, 845 P.2d 793, 798 (N.M. 1992)).

55. *See, e.g.*, Morrison Homes Corp. v. City of Pleasanton, 130 Cal. Rptr. 196 (Cal. Ct. App. 1976) (holding that the effect of the general rule is to void only a contract that amounts to a city's "surrender" or "abnegation" of its control of a properly municipal function, and that the city's reservations of control over the land subject to an annexation agreement, as well as the "just, reasonable, fair and equitable" nature of the agreement, rendered the agreement valid and enforceable against the city).

56. *See* Bruce M. Kramer, *Development Agreements: To What Extent Are They Enforceable?*, 10 REAL EST. L.J. 29 (1981); *see also* Robert M. Kessler, *The Development Agreement and Its Use in Resolving Large Scale, Multi-Party Development Problems: A Look at the Tool and Suggestions for Its Application*, 1 J. LAND USE & ENV'T L. 451 (1985).

57. *See* Stone v. Mississippi, 101 U.S. 814 (1879); *see also* Corp. of the Brick Presbyterian Church v. Mayor of N.Y., 5 Cow. 538 (N.Y. Sup. Ct. 1826), *discussed in* Kramer, *supra* note 56, at 37–39.

58. 43 Cal. Rptr. 855 (Cal. Ct. App. 1965).

was bound to its terms. The contract was neither void nor voidable merely because some of its provisions could bind a successor council.[59]

Similarly, in *Village of Orland Park v. Federal Savings & Loan Ass'n of Chicago*,[60] a bank attempted to avoid obligations contained in an annexation agreement approved pursuant to the Illinois annexation agreement statute. Noting that the bank's cited authority involved agreements that proceeded without statutory authority, the Illinois Appellate Court observed:

> The authorization of preannexation agreements by statute, such as 11-15.1-1, serves to further important governmental purposes, such as the encouragement of expanding urban areas and to do so uniformly, economically, efficiently and fairly, with optimum provisions made for the establishment of land use controls and necessary municipal improvements including streets, water, sewer systems, schools, parks, and similar installations. This approach also discourages fragmentation and proliferation of special districts. Additional positive effects of such agreements include controls over health, sanitation, fire prevention and police protection, which are vital to governing communities.[61]

Also, where an owner tried to disconnect its territory from the City of Greenwood Village, Colorado, in part on the ground that the annexation agreement under which the property was first annexed inhibited the city's future zoning power, the federal district court held that preannexation agreements that impose zoning conditions "have been upheld as valid and enforceable" in Colorado.[62] The court found that the city's zoning in this case fell into that category. Similarly, several state court decisions uphold annexation agreements that restrict a local government's power to later change zoning that was granted and guaranteed during the life of the agreement.[63]

---

59. *Id.*; *see also* Denio v. Huntington Beach, 140 P.2d 392 (Cal. 1943).

60. 481 N.E.2d 946 (Ill. App. Ct. 1985).

61. *Id.* at 950. Illinois courts have since recognized a general "public policy in favor of ensuring the fulfillment of an annexation agreement." *See* United City of Yorkville v. Fid. & Deposit Co. of Md., 2019 IL App (2d) 180230.

62. Geralnes B.V. v. City of Greenwood Vill., Colo., 583 F. Supp. 830 (D. Colo. 1984).

63. Rockville v. Brookeville Tpk. Constr. Co., 228 A.2d 263 (Md. 1967); Union Nat'l Bank v. Glenwood, 348 N.E.2d 226 (Ill. App. Ct. 1976); French v. Lincolnshire, 335 N.E.2d 29 (Ill. App. Ct. 1975); Beshore v. Town of Bel Air, 206 A.2d 678 (Md. 1965).

Where a developer sued to recover payment to Colorado Springs for the acquisition of public parks made under an annexation agreement, the majority held that since the developer had obtained water and sewer services for its development under the agreement, as well as annexation to the city, it could not now seek to set aside the agreement.[64] In *City of Colorado Springs v. Kitty Hawk Development Co.*, the court stated that the parties "each got what it bargained for"—the city wanted the property annexed and the property owners wanted water and sewer services.[65] The court emphasized that a "municipality is under no legal obligation in the first instance to annex contiguous territory, and may reject a petition for annexation for no reason at all." Thus, the court held that a municipality may impose through an annexation agreement "such conditions by way of agreement as it sees fit."[66] Opining that "the majority opinion amounts to the longest and most dangerous step yet taken by this court in the general direction of emasculation of property rights,"[67] the dissent suggests that annexation agreements cannot require of a landowner that which the city could not constitutionally exact under the police power if the subject territory were already within the city's jurisdiction, even if that exaction is a trade-off for that which the developer seeks, such as the discretionary annexation of its land. Recent cases follow the majority position in the *Kitty Hawk* case and uphold municipal policies that require property owners to enter into annexation agreements or consent to annexation as a condition to the provision of utility services.[68]

Today, courts have no difficulty supporting annexation agreements against any reserved powers or bargaining away the police power argument, particularly if supported by state legislation,[69] and if the agreements

---

64. City of Colo. Springs v. Kitty Hawk Dev't Co., 392 P.2d 467 (Colo. 1964).

65. *Id.* at 472.

66. *Id.*

67. *Id.* at 473.

68. Clark v. Greene Cnty. Combined Health Dist., 108 Ohio St. 3d 427 (Ohio 2006); Bakies v. City of Perrysburg, 108 Ohio St. 3d 361 (Ohio 2006); *see also* City of Springfield v. Ameren Ill. Co., 127 N.E.3d 703, 710 (Ill. App. Ct. 2018) (citing Gaylor v. Vill. of Ringwood, 842 N.E.2d 1241 (Ill. App. Ct. 2006)).

69. *See* David L. Callies et al., Bargaining for Development: A Handbook on Development Agreements, Annexation Agreements, Land Development Conditions, Vested Rights, and the Provision of Public Facilities 118–19 n.705 (2003).

have a fixed termination date—and that date is not decades away.[70] It is rare today for a court to apply the reserved powers clause to abrogate government-private contracts, and courts have attempted to find other grounds to uphold those contracts that are fair, just, reasonable, and advantageous to the municipality.[71]

Procedural Issues

Approval and Adoption of the Agreement

In addition to the legal issues discussed earlier, there are several procedural issues that should be considered in negotiating and drafting annexation agreements. Typically, an annexation agreement is approved through some formal action of the corporate authorities. For example, in Illinois, an annexation agreement must be approved by either resolution or ordinance and must be passed by a vote of two-thirds of the corporate authorities then holding office.[72] Both Arizona[73] and Washington[74] also require that annexation agreements be approved by resolution or ordinance and that they be recorded in the county in which the property is located.

It is important to review the statute authorizing annexation agreements to ensure that the negotiation and adoption of an annexation agreement complies with the applicable procedural requirements. If no enabling statute exists, any procedures required by local ordinance or the annexation agreement itself must be followed.[75]

Public Hearing

States that have adopted statutes authorizing annexation agreements typically require that the municipality hold a public hearing. For example, the

70. 65 Ill. Comp. Stat. 5/11-15.1-1 *et seq.* See Appendix 3 for a sample annexation agreement.

71. Carruth v. City of Madera, 43 Cal. Rptr. 855 (Cal. Ct. App. 1965). *But cf.* Cnty. of Volusia v. City of Deltona, 925 So. 2d 340 (Fla. Dist. Ct. App. 2006).

72. 65 Ill. Comp. Stat. 5/11-15.1-3.

73. Ariz. Rev. Stat. § 9-500.05.

74. Wash. Rev. Code § 36.70B.190.

75. Weiss v. City of Gainesville, No. 05-C-158, 2010 WL 1192303 (N.D. Fla. Mar. 23, 2010), *aff'd,* Weiss v. City of Gainesville, 462 F. App'x 898 (11th Cir. 2012) (holding annexation agreement unenforceable where agreement required approval by referendum and referendum failed).

Illinois, North Carolina, and Washington annexation agreement statutes all require a public hearing prior to the approval of an annexation agreement. An annexation agreement should contain appropriate language confirming that the public hearing has been held and any required notices have been provided.

Conformance to Plans

Depending on the jurisdiction, annexation agreements must often comply with municipal plans as a condition of enforceability because the zoning that is bargained for in the agreement must be consistent with comprehensive plans. For example, Arizona's annexation agreement statute explicitly requires that an agreement be consistent with the municipality's general plan.[76] The Idaho Supreme Court in *Sprenger, Grubb & Associates, Inc. v. City of Hailey*[77] upheld a rezoning over the objections of the developers of property subject to an annexation agreement on the ground that the applicable plan was sufficiently broad in support of the contested downzoning. The Illinois Appellate Court denied a motion to dismiss and allowed a lawsuit to proceed that challenged an annexation agreement and annexation ordinances where the plaintiffs alleged that the annexation was not in harmony with the village's comprehensive plan in *Whipple v. Village of North Utica*.[78] In those states that require that the annexation agreement comply with the comprehensive plan and other planning documents, language should be incorporated into the agreement setting forth findings by the municipality that the agreement is consistent with the plan.

Amendment or Cancellation

Generally, both parties must mutually consent to amend or cancel the agreement. In Illinois and North Carolina, an amendment to an annexation agreement must follow the same procedures as required for the original approval, including the holding of a public hearing and approval by a resolution or ordinance.

---

76. Ariz. Rev. Stat. § 9-500.05(B).

77. 903 P.2d 741 (Idaho 1995).

78. 79 N.E.3d 667, 675–76 (Ill. App. Ct. 2017) (finding silica and salt mines inconsistent with comprehensive plan showing annexed property zoned for agricultural use).

Because property often changes hands after development, the annexation agreement might include language requiring that the owner provide notice to the municipality of any transfer of the property so that the municipality knows the proper owner in the event of any potential amendment or if there is a dispute or question about the agreement. In addition, a provision setting forth the procedures for amendment should be incorporated into the agreement so that there is no question later about how the agreement should be amended.

Contents of an Annexation Agreement

An annexation agreement typically will describe the terms and conditions of the development of the property that have been negotiated between the parties, including annexation of the property to the municipality, zoning of the property, approval of subdivision and development plans, restrictions on the development of the property, construction of the required improvements, including utility facilities, and dedication of property or payment of fees in lieu of dedication. In addition to these property-specific provisions, certain provisions are fairly standard in an annexation agreement, including performance security requirements for the development and provisions for the issuance of building and other permits.

Illinois's annexation agreement statute includes a broad series of subjects authorized in an annexation agreement:

> The continuation in effect, or amendment, or continuation in effect as amended, of any ordinance relating to subdivision controls, zoning, official plan, and building, housing and related restrictions; provided, however, that any public hearing required by law to be held before the adoption of any ordinance amendment provided in such agreement shall be held prior to the execution of the agreement, and all ordinance amendments provided in such agreement shall be enacted according to law.
>
> A limitation upon increases in permit fees required by the municipality.
>
> Contributions of either land or monies, or both, to any municipality and to other units of local government having jurisdiction over all or part of land that is the subject matter of any annexation agreement entered into under the provisions of this Section shall

be deemed valid when made and shall survive the expiration date of any such annexation agreement with respect to all or any part of the land that was the subject matter of the annexation agreement.

The granting of utility franchises for such land.

The abatement of property taxes.

Any other matter not inconsistent with the provisions of [the annexation statute], nor forbidden by law.[79]

Very few provisions in annexation agreements have been found to be invalid, and both municipalities and developers have had a difficult time freeing themselves from the terms and conditions of annexation agreements, which may later be deemed obsolete or undesirable. For example, if a developer agrees that a certain portion of the property will be commercially developed, he cannot force a change in that provision of the annexation agreement even if commercial users of the property have not been found for ten years, and the construction of additional single-family or multi-family residences would be immediately and highly successful. In that case, a developer can ask for an amendment to the annexation agreement to change the zoning, but the municipality is under no obligation to approve that request.

By the same token, a municipality cannot enter into annexation agreements only to later deny rights properly conferred to a developer under that agreement. In *Town of Florence v. Florence Copper Inc.*,[80] for example, a town's attempt—through various tools and eventual litigation—to deny the mining rights of a successor owner to annexed property was rejected by the court. Because the party that preceded the owner had never abandoned its right to mine the property, and subsequent attempts to rezone the property or amend the planned unit development plan did not impact that right, the successor owner adopted the vested right of its predecessor to use the land for mining. In so deciding, the court was steadfast: "The Town points to no authority that local governments may enter and then flout their statutorily authorized contracts—all without judicial review."[81]

79. 65 Ill. Comp. Stat. 5/11-15.1-2.

80. 493 P.3d 891 (Ariz. Ct. App. 2021).

81. *Id.* ¶ 23.

Some of the most common provisions in an annexation agreement include the following:

Zoning

No real estate developer will exercise its option over vacant property or annex land to a municipality, if already purchased, without having some assurance that the necessary zoning and other land use approvals will be granted to the property, along with any necessary variances and special uses, including planned unit developments. If zoning cannot be agreed to, then the land will not be and should not be annexed. Most annexation agreements contain much more information about zoning than simply the zoning districts involved. Depending on the size of the proposed project and the demands of the municipality, annexation agreements can contain significant detail about the type and nature of the development. For example, an annexation agreement for the development of a residential development will often pin a developer down regarding the number and type of single-family residential units and will contain an appropriate level of standards regarding the quality of the homes to be built. The agreement might also contain a specific number of permitted units or, instead, allow some flexibility in unit number depending on final engineering considerations. A similar level of detail should be shown with regard to any townhouses and multi-family units.

A greater flexibility is generally needed for commercial or industrial development, because the developer generally does not know the particular size or configuration of the structures that will be built. In any case where the structures are not definitively shown on a site plan, the municipality needs to retain a substantial degree of site plan approval. What is usually relatively established at the time of the annexation agreement is the proposed road network and the general location of land that will be devoted to public use, such as school and park sites, public safety buildings, and municipal buildings or sites, where appropriate.

Utilities

One of the major costs whenever a municipality expands its jurisdiction through is the availability and capacity of municipal utility systems and facilities and the method in which those systems and facilities will serve the property that will be annexed. Since utility lines generally run within the right-of-way of municipal or other public streets, the general location for the utilities is often determined at this stage of development. In some special circumstances, major trunk utility lines may be located outside municipal rights-of-way and in land devoted to park use, detention facilities, or bike or pedestrian paths. The subdivision ordinance of the municipality will usually detail the minimum size of utility lines that will need to be constructed by the developer to serve the proposed development.

In many cases, one of the largest costs associated with utilities is the expansion or replacement of an existing municipal water or sanitary sewer system. In most cases, the developer will be asked to pay for the expansion or replacement of these systems in advance, with the hope of recapturing some or all of the funds expended by the developer to create any excess capacity from benefited properties. In a smaller community, several planned, large-scale developments generally produce enough residential units to pay for substantial utility improvements or new plants and mains, the replacement of which may be long overdue in the existing system. In addition, utility systems are generally built to certain established sizes so that the improvements may serve the existing population and the expanded population from the new developments with, perhaps, some additional capacity. That capacity should be available to allow for the quick expansion of commercial facilities, the need for which is brought on by the increased population.

There is a limit to the amount of extra capacity that any development can be asked to bear. In the negotiations relating to the developer's obligations, the parties should total up the costs of land donation, impact fees to governmental bodies, utility charges, utility oversizing, and any special conditions unique to the community that might drive up certain costs. Each developer has a sense of the level of public improvements and charges that a successful development can bear. Annexation negotiations are directed at making certain that the municipality is not shortchanged, but that the developer has a product that will sell and provide a reasonable profit and return on investment. Developers are willing to make these payments because they may be unable or unwilling to develop without entering into annexation agreements, and they have learned over a period of years that developments fail where there are inadequate utilities, parks, schools, and at least the promise of significant growth. In return for these payments and the risk involved in generally borrowing the money to advance the cost of the utilities, the developer will rightly ask for a reservation of capacity so that the system the developer helped to pay for will not be made freely available to some other developer who arrives on the scene later.

In some situations, when a municipality requests oversizing that may be beyond the capacity of the developer to provide, it will agree to allow the developer to recapture a portion of the oversizing costs from future system users. A developer may also ask for the benefit of tax-exempt borrowing by utilizing special service area bonds to build a sewage treatment plant expansion or for the construction of new wells or water systems. These costs are known as "off-site costs" because these facilities may generally be built off the land at some location where services can be easily provided for a community or large areawide system. These special service area bonds are guaranteed not by the credit of the municipality, or the rates of its utility users, but rather constitute a lien on the developer's land. The bonds are usually paid back through a tax, either imposed when the property is sold or levied on each lot and paid out over years by the new property owners. Some municipalities have also agreed to issue special service area bonds for certain "on-site improvements" such as streets, sidewalks, water mains, sanitary sewers, storm sewers, and even the cost of land on which the detention or retention basins will be located. On-site special service area bonds are often treated as liens on the property, which can be assumed by the first homeowners. Although those bonds can generally be paid off early without penalty, the new homeowners could pay the debt over the term of the bonds and, in certain cases, may benefit from the continued tax-exempt interest rate. The community should ensure that the developer informs the homebuyers of this new debt at the time of closing. Since most of these special service areas require recordation of the ordinance or authorizing documents, homebuyers should also be on notice of their obligations during due diligence.

Impact Fees for Public Improvements and Services

Municipalities are often limited in the type and nature of impact fees that can legitimately be sought from developers whose land has already been annexed and that is outside the annexation or development agreement context. If the land to be developed is outside of the borders of the community, however, developers can be required to pay impact fees to various governmental bodies that can be negotiated in the annexation agreement. Impact fees are generally intended to cover the increased cost for services such as libraries, schools, fire departments, and parks that governments will be required to spend on the new residents who will be generated by the development.

Municipalities must be mindful, however, of any limits placed on the assessment of impact fees by statute or case authority. In Washington State, for example, there is a statute that limits the use of impact fees to those that a local government "can demonstrate are reasonably necessary as a direct result of the proposed development or plat to which the dedication of land or easement is to apply."[82] This limitation is consistent with the constitutional constraints on exactions discussed previously, and has been cited by at least one court to strike down a formulaic fee imposed by a city that did not exhibit a "site-specific relationship" to the value of the land to be dedicated. Even in the context of a voluntary agreement, the court found that the city was bound to the terms of the statute, which had no exception for discretionary annexation authority.[83]

Impact fees are generally paid either by the conveyance of land, the contribution of cash, or both. If, for example, a municipality (or a park district where the parks program is operated by a separate government body) maintains a large existing park system, it might choose to accept cash donations from the developer in an amount that might be the equivalent of the additional park land that would be necessary to be added to the system except for, in this case, the availability of existing land. The same rule would apply to schools or libraries (or a school or library district where these programs are operated by a separate government body). Although these governmental bodies will bear the costs of additional residents and students, where the government body is separate from the municipality, they are often given no role in the establishment and collection of impact fees. Municipalities that make the decision on annexation and development have the ability, but not the obligation, to collect impact fees and, where appropriate, to turn them over to the respective governmental entities. It is not unusual to have a municipality collecting only modest impact fees for itself with the great bulk of these collected fees being distributed to other governmental bodies.

---

82. Wash. Rev. Code § 82.02.020.

83. *See* Vintage Constr. Co. v. Bothell, 922 P.2d 828 (Wash. Ct. App. 1996), *aff'd*, 959 P.2d 1090 (Wash. 1998).

In some cases, other governmental bodies urge the municipality to impose unacceptably large impact fees. A municipality must resist this temptation, especially if it has many needs itself as a growing community with few revenue sources other than real estate taxes. Also, for that reason, municipalities should not turn over impact fees to other governmental bodies unless those governments enter into an intergovernmental agreement to hold harmless and defend the municipality if disputes should arise regarding the impact fees. This is especially important since, as pointed out earlier, the municipality itself will often serve only as a conduit for the payment of these fees.

Freezing of Regulations or Fees

An annexation agreement will often contain a provision that either freezes fees at their existing level or places limitations on future fee increases. During periods of low inflation, these agreements may make sense, but a municipality with little experience in administering large-scale developments certainly cannot safely freeze its fee structure. This issue is generally a subject of substantial negotiations in annexation agreements.

Annexation agreements will also often provide the developer with a guarantee that any changes to a municipality's zoning ordinance will not affect the development during the annexation agreement. That is a sensible provision because otherwise a municipality could zone a parcel to the R-4 district (which may allow three-story buildings) only to change the ordinance the next year to allow only single-story buildings in that district. Municipalities also generally agree to freeze their subdivision ordinances, except to the extent the community is required to make changes by a superior governmental body such as the state legislature or a state or federal agency with jurisdiction over the property or its development.

Developers are often concerned that the municipality will pass some type of regulatory ordinance that may, effectively, apply only to their project. As a result, changes in municipal ordinances that would apply to land covered under an annexation agreement must usually be general in nature and apply to other similar projects. Another developers' concern, other than the lack of stability, is that the municipality will pass an ordinance that will make it impossible for a home to be built for the price already agreed to with a buyer. For that reason, many annexation agreements provide that ordinances relating to building codes will only take effect, for example, six months after their passage. This will generally give the developer an adequate period of time to reprice products made more expensive by code changes. Agreements also frequently provide that the building code changes cannot make the construction of previously approved homes impossible or impractical.

Health and safety codes unrelated to construction raise another issue. A municipality should generally be able to enact ordinances relating to health, safety, or welfare and make them apply generally throughout the community. That is especially the case if there is a tragedy of some sort that might have been prevented if a municipal ordinance required some safety device, such as a smoke detector or, in a case of some recent interest, sprinklers. Negotiations often take place as to how ordinances of this nature will take effect.

4

Other Agreements

Affordable Housing Agreement

For decades, communities across the country have seen serious and ever-increasing demand for affordable housing, particularly in urbanized coastal areas where stringent land use regulations and historically high demand for new housing have depleted the availability of housing that is affordable to individuals and families with lower incomes. Many local governments have adopted and continue to implement a variety of programs in an effort to meet this ever-growing need for affordable housing.[1] Many of these regulatory programs include a requirement that rental or for-sale units be made available to families of very low, low, or moderate incomes at prices and rents affordable to lower-income families. Local governments, in turn, frequently require the developers of market-rate housing to enter into an "affordable housing agreement" that documents the terms and conditions upon which these inclusionary affordable housing requirements will be implemented.

The terms and conditions of many affordable housing agreements are influenced significantly by the agency's inclusionary housing program.

---

1. For a discussion of the content and legal controversies associated with various affordable housing programs adopted throughout the United States, including in California, Florida, Hawaii, Massachusetts, and New Jersey, see David L. Callies et al., *Local Government Inclusionary Programs and the Courts*, 63 Plan. & Env't L. 3 (2011).

Otherwise, the terms are a result of ad hoc negotiations between the agency and the market-rate developer. This section explores a host of factors that should be considered by the parties to the agreement as they begin their negotiations.

Mandatory or Voluntary Agreement

While numerous local governments have adopted mandatory inclusionary housing programs, others have made the programs voluntary, offering the developer of an otherwise market-rate unit project certain benefits, such as increased density, vested development rights, or reduced fees, in exchange for providing affordable housing. If the program is mandatory, the agreement will need to include the terms required by the program, serving to document compliance with the agency's program. If the program is voluntary, perhaps resulting from incentives to encourage developers to provide the affordable units, the agreement should document clearly that the agreement is entered into voluntarily and identify what benefits the developer is receiving in exchange for providing the inclusionary housing. It is possible, of course, that the agreement results from a hybrid voluntary-mandatory inclusionary housing approach such as that which has emerged in a number of fast-growing cities that have adopted growth management ordinances. In these communities, a growth restriction is imposed by an ordinance that limits the number of dwelling units that can be constructed in any given year. To determine which development applications will be approved, the city holds a "beauty contest" whereby project sponsors compete to present the most desirable project. By awarding points for the inclusion of affordable units in the proposed development, the agency is able to leverage its growth cap by encouraging developers to "volunteer" to include affordable units so as to enhance their chances of project approval.[2] Any such award of units under a growth management program in exchange for affordable units should be at least referenced in the agreement.

Class and Size of the Project

In the case of a large master-planned community, where different developers will be providing potentially different levels of affordable housing,

2. *See* Bill Higgins, Inclusionary Zoning and Affordable Housing after Homebuilders Ass'n of Northern California v. City of Napa 3 (2003).

the affordable housing agreement also should identify the classes of development (i.e., for-sale and rental residential, mixed-use, commercial, or industrial) that will be subject to inclusionary housing or a fee to subsidize construction of affordable housing, as well as the size of the project at which those requirements will apply. Typically, programs with mandatory inclusionary housing requirements have thresholds with a minimum of five to 20 units, with smaller projects being allowed to pay fees in lieu of construction. However, some agencies have adopted programs that set a relatively low threshold, while others are applying inclusionary policies to all projects, regardless of size.[3] The agreement should specify what the minimum requirements are, if any, and the specific requirements that are being provided by the developer that is a party to the agreement.

Amount and Type of Housing and Levels of Affordability

There is considerable variation among inclusionary housing programs with respect to the percentage of affordable units included in a project, and the levels of affordability required. Typically, more affluent cities and counties require more units at deeper levels of affordability, as those jurisdictions have the greatest challenges in meeting housing needs for lower-income families. Affordability levels generally range from 5 to 25 percent, depending upon whether local subsidies are available, with most agencies looking for requirements from 10 to 15 percent.[4] It is important that the agreement set out the percentage of the units that will be affordable, whether they will be rental or for-sale units, and the levels of affordability that will be provided.

Given the increased costs associated with constructing units affordable to households with low and very low incomes, affordable housing agreements may decrease the financial burden on the developer by providing income-targeting incentives in the agreement. For example, if an agency is seeking an increased number of lower-income units (which are in greater need because of the amount of government-subsidized financing available for very low-income units), the agreement could provide a credit against

3. *See* Expanding Housing Opportunity in Washington, D.C.: The Case for Inclusionary Housing 31 (2003).

4. *See* California Affordable Housing Law Project & Western Center on Law and Poverty, Inclusionary Zoning: Policy Considerations and Best Practices 5 (2002).

the moderate-income obligation in return for producing more low-income units. Thus, if an agency requires 20 percent affordability (with a mix of 10 percent moderate-, 5 percent low-, and 5 percent very low-income units) and a developer exceeds the 5 percent low-income requirement, the 10 percent obligation for moderate-income units could be reduced by an even greater amount.[5]

Timing of Construction of Affordable Units

The affordable housing agreement should specify the time by which inclusionary units are to be completed within the context of the overall development. For a variety of reasons, construction of affordable units may be delayed unless certain timing requirements are imposed within the context of the overall development. Absent concrete requirements agreed to up front, future financing may impair a developer's ability to produce affordable units early in construction. In addition, there is a risk of public opposition to the construction of affordable units within the project from new residents who might not have understood that affordable units were part of the project when they bought their homes. To avoid these problems and help ensure that inclusionary units are built, most jurisdictions will require that the inclusionary units be constructed up front or be phased in a way that is proportional to the rest of the development.

Location and Development and Design Standards

Along with timing issues, the affordable housing agreement should identify where the affordable units will be located and what design and development standards will be applied to the units. The agreement should specify the extent to which these units must be built to the same development standards and design guidelines as the market-rate units, as well as the extent to which units may be clustered or must be dispersed throughout the project. Requiring certain construction and design standards similar to market-rate requirements can assure the agency that the affordable units will consist of quality construction and will not be stigmatized within the project or the community. On the other hand, imposing such requirements in all aspects of design—particularly size and interior finishes and

5. *Id.* at 6.

amenities—can increase the cost of these units tremendously, potentially making their development infeasible.

In order to balance these competing concerns, many agreements require stricter controls for the exterior of the affordable units, but allow for the use of less expensive materials for interior features and the provision of fewer interior amenities. Another means of addressing this issue is for the agreement to provide the developer with financial incentives to construct affordable and market-rate units in a uniform manner. For instance, in return for providing affordable homes that mirror the more expensive housing in the project, developers could be permitted to charge an additional amount (perhaps 5 or 10 percent) for the affordable homes; however, in jurisdictions where lower affordability levels need to be obtained to meet local and regional housing needs, such an arrangement may not be practical.[6]

Length of Time That Inclusionary Units Must Remain Affordable

Typically, affordable housing agreements require units to remain affordable for a period of 30 to 50+ years, although the length of time can range from as little as five years to perpetuity depending upon the jurisdiction. Various policy considerations come into play when negotiating what this time period should be. On the one hand, if affordability is required for only a short period of time, this imposes a significant burden on the community to produce additional affordable units within a relatively short time frame in order to maintain the affordable housing stock. On the other hand, a requirement that units remain affordable in perpetuity may unreasonably penalize developers and disserve individual owners of inclusionary units by reducing their ability to benefit from the financial opportunities afforded by homeownership or their ability to remodel or refurbish units.[7] Additionally, many financing programs, such as federal and state income tax

6. *See* Karen Destorel Brown, Brookings Institution Center on Urban and Metropolitan Policy, Expanding Affordable Housing through Inclusionary Zoning: Lessons from the Washington Metropolitan Area 26 (2001).

7. To balance the goals of preserving affordability and promoting wealth-building opportunities of homeownership, many inclusionary programs establish shared appreciation formulas to allow the program and the inclusionary homeowner to share resale profits. *See* Expanding Housing Opportunity in Washington, D.C.: The Case for Exclusionary Housing, *supra* note 3, at 33.

credits, require a period of affordability that may exceed what the agreement provides.

Qualifications of Individuals and Families

The affordable housing agreement should establish the criteria by which the applicants for the affordable units will be evaluated to ensure their income qualifies them for such units; clear guidelines should assist the jurisdiction and the developer in administering the program and ensuring fairness. Among the issues to consider is how the inclusionary program will define very low-, low-, and moderate-income households. Most inclusionary programs use the definitions provided by the U.S. Department of Housing and Urban Development, though others may follow state definitions. Another item to consider is how the income limits will be adjusted for family size and the method by which income limits will be revised. Particularly difficult is what happens in the event the tenants of a "very-low" income unit have increased income, due perhaps to career advancement or a family member's new employment. Should there be annual tenant income reporting requirements, and if a formerly low-income unit is now occupied by a moderate- or higher-income family, should that unit's rent be increased to a higher rate and another unit provided? One obvious problem with including such a provision in an affordable housing agreement is that the program could encourage lower-income tenants to keep lower incomes rather than become more financially independent.

Preserving Affordability

In order to ensure that inclusionary units remain affordable for a significant period of time, most affordable housing agreements contain some affordability controls that are often recorded against the property that is subject to the program. Without such long-term controls, inclusionary units may become lost in the system and resold or rented at market rates, thereby creating a windfall to the owner at the expense of lost public and private investment. Such recorded controls may include (1) sales price restrictions; (2) a program for determining eligibility of applicants; (3) the setting of a specific period of time during which the inclusionary units must remain affordable; and (4) enforcement and monitoring mechanisms to ensure these requirements are met.

To effectively implement such affordability controls and related monitoring and enforcement mechanisms, a considerable amount of staff supervision is required. Accordingly, agencies need to consider these administrative issues when crafting their inclusionary programs and negotiating their affordable housing agreements. Agencies adopt various approaches to administering their programs and agreements. While some cities, towns, and counties administer inclusionary housing and affordable housing agreements with existing staff, others contract with outside sources—possibly paid for by the developer or other assessments—to administer this staff-intensive activity.[8]

Enforcement and Monitoring Mechanisms

With respect to ownership units, affordability controls generally are implemented, enforced, and monitored through resale and rental restrictions. For resale housing, such restrictions can include (1) "soft" second mortgages for the difference between the appraised value and the delivered price; (2) terms for repayment of such mortgages upon sale and/or forgiveness over ten to 20 years; (3) ownership of the underlying land by a land trust; and (4) other related devices such as the city's right of first refusal and regulatory agreements to lock in specific commitments of owners, tenants, and inclusionary homeowners over time.[9]

In order to evaluate the effectiveness of their inclusionary programs, some agencies have initiated reviews or refinements once they have been in place for a number of years. One way to accomplish this objective is to require annual reporting in all affordable housing agreements, providing the agency with the information to review milestones to ensure that its inclusionary program is effective in meeting affordable housing goals and is maximizing inclusionary opportunities with its affordable housing agreements.

8. *Id.*

9. *See* Dieckmeyer v. Redev. Agency of City of Huntington Beach, 127 Cal. 4th 248 (Cal. Ct. App. 2005) (upholding the redevelopment agency's authority to require the purchaser of a subsidized low-income unit to pay an "equity share" of the profit earned upon subsequent resale to a market-rate buyer).

Community Benefits Agreement

A community benefits agreement (CBA) is a private contract negotiated between a prospective developer and community representatives (e.g., neighborhood groups, unions, environmental organizations, religious communities). These agreements seek to win support for a proposed development and address the concerns of all parties involved. Unlike a development agreement between a developer and a municipality, a CBA is an agreement among private parties. This means that CBAs can address matters far beyond the land use and environmental issues generally considered in development agreements.[10] The issues addressed in CBAs often go far beyond those that would survive scrutiny under the U.S. Supreme Court's "nexus" requirement (which states that there must be a connection between an exaction imposed on a developer and the development being constructed).[11] Other issues include the use of unionized labor, hiring of local residents, purchasing materials from local suppliers, and traditional land use issues like building low-income housing and creating streets, sewers, and water pipes for the community.

Development of the Community Benefits Agreement Model

CBAs have a relatively short history. One of the first CBAs negotiated in 2001 was the $2.5 billion Staples Center development in Los Angeles.[12] This CBA contains a number of benefits for the community, including $1 million for parks, funding for a residential parking program, a living-wage commitment, job training and local hiring programs, and affordable housing provisions.[13] The Staples Center CBA was initially proposed as a means to redevelop a disadvantaged community, home to many low-income and minority residents.[14] These residents, fearing gentrification and

10. *See* Patricia E. Salkin, *Community Benefits Agreements: Opportunities and Traps for Developers, Municipalities, and Community Organizations*, 59 PLAN. & ENV'T L. 3, 3 (2007), for a discussion about the difference between exactions and CBAs.

11. *See Nollan v. California Coastal Commission*, 483 U.S. 825 (1987), for a discussion of the nexus requirement for exactions imposed on developers by municipal governments.

12. William Ho, *Community Benefits Agreements: An Evolution in Public Benefits Negotiation Processes*, 17 J. AFFORDABLE HOUS. & CMTY. DEV. L. 7, 27 (2007/2008).

13. Patricia E. Salkin & Amy Lavine, *Understanding Community Benefits Agreements: Equitable Development, Social Justice, and Other Considerations for Developers, Municipalities, and Community Organizations*, 26 UCLA J. ENV'T L. & POL'Y 291, 302 (2008).

14. *Id.* at 303.

congestion, used the CBA model to obtain a seat at the negotiating table.[15] Using the possibility of litigation as leverage during the negotiations, the coalition was able to win many of the benefits its members sought.[16]

Encouraged by the success of the Staples Center CBA, the Los Angeles City Council decided to utilize the CBA model in its Los Angeles International Airport (LAX) expansion. In December 2004, the Council approved an $11 billion agreement on airport expansion reached between Los Angeles World Airports (LAWA), the public administrator of LAX airport, and 22 community groups.[17] These community groups represented local school districts, religious organizations, environmental groups, and labor unions. The CBA's provisions included job training, living-wage requirements, and the soundproofing of local schools, city buildings, and homes. Environmental groups were particularly pleased to obtain a promise from LAWA to conduct a $2 million study on air pollution, the most comprehensive study of its kind ever undertaken in the United States. Despite a lawsuit from a group not involved in the CBA negotiating process, the project has proceeded and is widely regarded as a success.

Another significant CBA was the $3.5 billion Atlantic Yards arena in Brooklyn.[18] Based on the Staples Center CBA, this project, which sought to construct a new stadium for the National Basketball Association's New Jersey Nets, was negotiated by eight community groups.[19] This CBA also included affordable housing and living-wage provisions, and offered free basketball tickets for neighborhood residents.[20] However, unlike the generally positive response from the community to the Staples Center CBA, the Atlantic Yards CBA has met much criticism.[21] First, the Atlantic Yards CBA is not incorporated into a development agreement with the city, making enforcement difficult.[22] Second, many community organizers have charged that the eight community groups with whom the developer negotiated were not representative of the community, and were too close to the developer.

15. *Id.*

16. *Id.*

17. Salkin & Lavine, *supra* note 13, at 304–05.

18. *Id.* at 308.

19. Nathan Markey, *Atlantic Yards Community Benefit Agreement: A Case Study of Organizing Community Support for Development*, 27 Pace Env't L. Rev. 377, 384 (2010).

20. Salkin & Lavine, *supra* note 13, at 309.

21. Markey, *supra* note 19, at 385.

22. Salkin, *supra* note 10.

Later revelations that one of the eight community groups received $5 million in funds from the developer after the signing of the CBA only fueled this speculation.[23]

Another major New York City CBA is the Columbia University expansion. In this $6 billion project, Columbia will construct 16 to 18 new buildings over the span of 20 years.[24] The expansion is projected to transform the neighborhood surrounding the university and create a considerable number of jobs.[25] The CBA process differed markedly from that of Atlantic Yards. The city and Mayor Bloomberg strongly supported the project, and authorized County Board 9 to create a local development corporation to negotiate with the university over the CBA. County Board 9 appointed the community leaders on this board who represented a wide range of constituents and interests. The deal was completed in December 2007 and committed the university to paying $150 million in benefits to the community, including a university-run public school.[26]

Advantages to Community Benefits Agreements

CBAs can be advantageous for the developer because they can garner support from local organizations that may otherwise challenge the development through judicial proceedings. CBAs eliminate the costs, risks, and delays associated with these challenges, while gaining public support for the development.[27]

CBAs are also advantageous for the community, as they provide a mechanism to ensure that community concerns are heard and addressed. This counters the argument of many low-income residents that municipal economic development programs seek to force them from their neighborhoods by encouraging gentrification and rising property values. A CBA can also ensure that a developer's promises regarding community benefits are legally enforceable.[28] By creating an enforcement mechanism or expanding

---

23. Salkin & Lavine, *supra* note 13, at 310.

24. *Id.* at 314.

25. *Id.*

26. *Id.* at 316.

27. *See Community Benefits Agreements Seen as Vital for Growing Cities*, 34 No. CD-14 HDR Current Devs. 9, for a discussion on the important role that CBAs have played in the past decade in many cities in the South and West.

28. *See* Julian Gross, *Community Benefits Agreements: Definitions, Values, and Legal Enforceability*, 17 J. Affordable Hous. & Cmty. Dev. L. 35, 35 (2007/2008), for an examination of promises made by developers to communities and their legal enforceability.

the class of parties who can enforce the CBA, developers can be legally bound to follow through on their promises.

Problems Raised by Community Benefits Agreements

CBAs also raise certain problems. First, it is unclear how an organization secures a seat at the negotiating table.[29] Since not all groups may be represented, challenges from parties left out of the negotiations may impede the development. Furthermore, the developer may contract only with groups sympathetic to its goals, as seen in the Atlantic Yards CBA.

Second, CBAs may not always be effectively enforced. It may prove difficult to monitor compliance with the agreement, while the remedies for the breach of a particular point of the contract may be difficult to determine.

Third, CBAs often contain ambiguous language, like provisions stating that the developer "seeks to" do something, or "intends to" do another thing.[30] It often is unclear whether these are enforceable promises.

Fourth, problems arise when CBAs are incorporated into an agreement between a developer and a local government. Under judicial scrutiny, these agreements may be considered government exactions subject to constitutional limitations.

Finally, because the community organizations that enter into CBAs are sometimes loosely organized, have rotating leadership, and may not have permanent funding sources, developers can find themselves without necessary negotiating partners when it becomes necessary to modify or amend certain provisions of a long-term CBA.

Many legal scholars worry that CBAs will not survive judicial scrutiny because community groups do not provide any real consideration in these contracts.[31] The developers provide extensive benefits to the community, in return for the promise of community organizations not to oppose the development, a potentially questionable form of consideration. Furthermore, even if a court does hold that these promises constitute valid consideration, questions arise as to who can enforce the CBA's provisions.

---

29. The Atlantic Yards CBA serves as a poignant example. Many community members charged that the community groups party to the CBA did not represent their interests, but rather those of the developer. This diminished the credibility of the CBA and threatened to spur opposition from community members to the development.

30. Vicki Been, *Community Benefits Agreements: A New Local Government Tool or Another Variation on the Exactions Theme?*, 77 U. Chi. L. Rev. 5, 29 (2010).

31. *See* Been, *supra* note 30; Salkin & Lavine, *supra* note 13.

Contract law generally permits only contract signatories to enforce the provisions of a contract, meaning that community groups who have not signed a CBA have no means of enforcing its provisions.

Conservation Agreement

A conservation agreement is a written agreement between a landowner and a qualified conservation organization or public agency in which the landowner (grantor) promises to keep the land in its original condition, and the conservation organization or public agency (grantee) is granted the right to enforce the covenants of the agreement to maintain the property in this original condition.[32] A conservation agreement stipulates ways in which the land can be used in the future, as well as restrictions upon its use. When creating a conservation agreement, a landowner does not relinquish ownership of the property.[33] Instead, he or she merely gives up the development rights specified in the conservation agreement.[34]

A conservation agreement may be known by various names, including a conservation easement, a grant of development rights, a historic preservation agreement, a facade easement, an agricultural easement, a farmland agreement, and a working forest easement.

Purpose of a Conservation Agreement

A conservation agreement is intended to preserve property in its natural, undeveloped condition. This serves as a public benefit, as it conserves lands, forests, streams, and other ecosystems.[35] Due to this public benefit, significant federal, state, and local tax incentives exist for landowners who create conservation agreements.[36] In fact, some programs exist that make grants available for the purchase of conservation agreements from

32. For a recent and comprehensive overview of the use of conservation easements, see Shea B. Airey, *Conservation Easements in Private Practice*, 44 Real Prop. Tr. & Est. L.J. 745 (2010); William R. Sylvester et al., *The Current Status, at the Beginning of 2010, of Land Conservation Issues*, *in* The ACREL Papers (ALI-ABA, Spring 2010).

33. 26 U.S.C. § 2031(c)(8)(A).

34. *Id.*

35. *Id.* § 170(h)(4)(A)(iii) (2006).

36. *See id.* § 170(h).

landowners on certain eligible lands.[37] Conservation agreements often work best for landowners motivated by a desire to preserve their land while obtaining income tax deductions, tax credits, and a reduction in the value of their potential estate. Ideally, land conveyed through a conservation agreement will not require intensive management.

In order to obtain federal income tax deductions, the land must be conveyed or restricted in perpetuity.[38] Conveyance must be made to a qualified grantee (generally a nonprofit organization or a public agency), and it must meet one of the following conservation purposes:

1. The preservation of land areas for outdoor recreation by, or the education of, the general public
2. The protection of a relatively natural habitat of fish, wildlife, or plants, or similar ecosystem
3. The preservation of open space (including farmland and forest land) where the preservation is for the scenic enjoyment of the general public and will yield a significant public benefit
4. The preservation of a historically important land area or a certified historic structure[39]

A landowner should prepare a natural resource inventory including maps, photographs of existing buildings and roads, a description of natural habitats, and a survey of wildlife.[40] This inventory allows the landowner to decide which conservation purpose is met and will distinguish ecologically sensitive areas from other areas that might be appropriate for other uses. Expenses associated with a conservation agreement typically include a land survey, an appraisal, accounting fees, legal fees for tax planning, recording

---

37. North Carolina has a program by which state government funds are available for the purchase of conservation easements on agricultural land. *See* U.S. Department of Agriculture Natural Resources Conservation Service, *Agricultural Land Easements—North Carolina*, https://www.nrcs.usda.gov/programs-initiatives/acep-agricultural-conservation-easement-program/north-carolina/agriculturall#:~:text=NRCS%20provides%20financial%20assistance%20to,conservation%20values%20of%20eligible%20land (last visited Dec. 18, 2023). https://www.ncagr.gov/SWC/easementprograms/landowner.html

38. 26 U.S.C. § 170(h)(2)(c) (2006).

39. *Id.* § 170(h)(4)(A).

40. Conservation and Historic Preservation Agreements Act, N.C. Gen. Stat. Ann. § 121-34-42 (West 2006).

fees, and sometimes a stewardship endowment to the grantee to help fund the maintenance of the land.[41]

Structure of a Conservation Agreement

A conservation agreement's restrictions are typically drafted to balance the interests of the landowner and grantee and their conservation goals. Most conservation agreements seek to preserve land in its pristine state.[42] However, conservation agreements may impose less comprehensive restrictions, such as limiting heavy commercial development, setting a limit upon maximum number of buildings that can be constructed on the property, or limiting the amount of resources, like timber, that can be removed from the property.[43] Other agreements might permit certain activities like hunting and fishing, agricultural use, the subdivision of the land into parcels, and even the construction of a limited number of new homes.[44] Public access is not a requirement, but most agreements grant access to the grantee at least once a year for the maintenance of the property and the enforcement of covenants.[45]

An entire tract does not need to be subject to a conservation agreement.[46] Certain parts of a tract may be subject to different types of conservation agreements. For example, a landowner may use an agricultural agreement on farmlands, while using a more restrictive conservation agreement in ecologically sensitive areas.

The grantor of a conservation agreement usually retains ownership of the land, along with the right and duty to manage the property.[47] However, in circumstances where the conservation organization has specialized experience managing a particular habitat, the grantee will often be given

41. Nancy A. McLaughlin, *Increasing the Tax Incentives for Conservation Easement Donations—A Responsible Approach*, 31 Ecology L.Q. 1, 26 (2004).

42. Julia D. Mahoney, *Perpetual Restrictions on Land and the Problem of the Future*, 88 Va. L. Rev. 739, 749 (2002).

43. *See* Md. Code Ann., Real Prop. § 2-118 (West 2006).

44. *Id.*

45. D.C. Code § 42-201-8; Okla. Stat. Ann. tit. 60, § 49.1-8. These statutes are based on the Uniform Conservation Easement Act, which has been adopted in a number of states.

46. Nicholas M. Agopian, *Conservation Easements—Preserving Privately Owned Natural Habitats: Guidance for Interpreting 26 U.S.C. § 170(h)(4)(a)(II),* Glass v. Commissioner of Internal Revenue, *124 T.C. 258 (2005)*, 6 Wyo. L. Rev. 447, 476 (2006).

47. 26 U.S.C. § 2031(c)(8)(A).

the right to undertake the management of the land and the enforcement of the restrictive covenants of the conservation agreement.[48]

Tax Advantages Resulting from a Conservation Agreement

The grantor of a qualifying conservation agreement may claim the value of the conservation agreement as a deduction for income and estate tax purposes.[49] Tax reductions are not available for the sale of conservation agreements.

Federal Estate Tax

Conservation agreements are an ideal way to prevent the levy of heavy estate taxes, as they provide protection against the appreciation of property values over time. Section 2031(c) of the Internal Revenue Code provides that 40 percent of the value of the land subject to a conservation agreement (not to exceed $500,000) may be excluded from a landowner's estate, provided the agreement reduces the value of the land by at least 30 percent.[50] If the conservation agreement has been executed during the grantor's lifetime, only the restricted value of the property under a conservation agreement will be included in the owner's estate, resulting in a lower estate tax.[51] This can provide protection against the breakup of family farms or estates that would otherwise occur due to heavy estate tax liability.

Federal Income Tax

If the conservation agreement is executed during the grantor's lifetime and the land provides a long-term capital gain, the grantor may claim a federal income tax deduction for the full fair market value of the interest subject to the conservation agreement.[52] However, to prevent a grantor from using the deduction to avoid paying taxes, the Internal Revenue Service places a cap on the deduction that can be claimed in the year the conservation agreement is executed to 50 percent of the taxpayer's contribution base.[53]

---

48. Timothy Lindstrom, *The Tax Benefits of Conservation Easements*, 79 Mich. Bar J. 690, 691 (2000).

49. 26 U.S.C.A. § 170.

50. *Id.* § 2031.

51. 9B Nichols Cyclopedia of Legal Forms § 228:234 (2022).

52. 26 U.S.C.A. § 170.

53. *Id.* § 170(b)(1)(E)(i).

Any unused portion of the donation may be carried over for each of the next 15 years.[54]

State Income Tax and Local Property Taxes

Many states grant special income tax credits for the donation of land through a conservation agreement. Colorado and Virginia have made these tax credits transferable, which has created a market for the buying and selling of the tax credits.[55] Local property taxes can also be reduced due to the lower appraisal of the property resulting from the conservation agreement.

Value of the Agreement

For tax purposes, the value of the property subject to the agreement is assessed by an appraiser using a before-and-after test. This measures the value of the property before the agreement compared to what it is after, making the conservation agreement the difference between the two.[56] However, if the conservation agreement increases the property value of an adjoining property owned by the grantor, the value of the conservation agreement will be reduced by the amount of the benefit to the adjoining property.[57] A professional appraiser should be used in assessing the value of the agreement, as substantial penalties will be imposed on the grantor and appraiser for any overvaluation.[58]

Conveyance of Land Subject to a Conservation Agreement

Land subject to a conservation agreement can be sold, mortgaged, or conveyed, but it will always remain subject to the agreement.[59] The value of the land as a security will be its value as restricted by the agreement, not its potential value for all unrestricted purposes and uses.[60] The land may also be subdivided, subject to any specific prohibition or limitation in the agreement against subdivision.[61] If there is a preexisting deed of trust on

---

54. *Id.* § 170(b)(1)(E)(ii).
55. Lindstrom, *supra* note 48, at 695.
56. 26 U.S.C.A. § 170(e)(1).
57. Lindstrom, *supra* note 48, at 692.
58. *See* Whitehouse Hotel Ltd. P'ship v. Comm'r, 131 T.C. 112, 117–18 (2008).
59. 26 U.S.C.A. § 170.
60. *Id.*
61. Lindstrom, *supra* note 48, at 693.

the land, it must be subordinated to the conservation agreement before the agreement is granted.[62]

For a grantor to convey land subject to a conservation agreement that qualifies for a federal tax deduction, a conservation agreement document must be prepared, along with an inventory of the property, an appraisal, title work, a survey and legal description, and a Form 8283 (an attachment to the federal tax return of all individuals claiming non-cash charitable contributions).[63]

Amendment or Revocation

Amendment or revocation of conservation agreements is difficult.[64] Revocation is usually accomplished only through a court proceeding and depends upon demonstrating that due to a change in circumstances, such as surrounding land use, the original conservation purposes of the agreement can no longer be achieved.[65] If the agreement is extinguished, the interest in the land is allocated to the grantee and the grantor in proportion to the value of the agreement and the value of the land.[66]

In rare circumstances an easement may be amended, but only with the agreement of both parties.[67] This is usually done to clarify an ambiguity in the easement and will not be allowed if the amendment diminishes the conservation values protected by the easement or enriches the landowner without properly compensating the grantee.[68] In *Vo-land v. Village of Bartlett*,[69] the plaintiff sued to invalidate a restrictive covenant requiring it to keep 96 acres of its property as open land. The plaintiff claimed that since it was seeking to disconnect this land from the village, it was no longer bound by the conservation agreement. The court rejected this argument, noting that the village zoning board refused to release the plaintiffs from the restrictive covenant.

---

62. *Id.*

63. 26 U.S.C.A. § 2031 (West 2006).

64. Nancy A. McLaughlin, *Amending Perpetual Conservation Easements: A Case Study of the Myrtle Grove Controversy*, 40 U. RICH. L. REV. 1031, 1072 (2006).

65. *Id.* at 1076.

66. *Id.*

67. *Id.*

68. *Id.* at 1079.

69. 919 N.E.2d 1 (Ill. App. Ct. 2009).

However, courts have proven reluctant to allow amendments to conservation easements. In *Bjork v. Draper*,[70] the court invalidated amendments to a conservation easement that a land trust approved at the request of new owners of the land subject to the easement. The land trust argued that since the state enabling statute provided that a conservation easement can be released by its holder, the trust had the right to release or amend the easement at will. While the court noted that the easement's language could be changed, it concluded that no amendment would be permissible if it conflicted with the easement's goal of perpetual conservation of the land. The court emphasized that tax-deductible conservation easements may not be substantially amended or released by their holders.

Courts will allow the amendment of a conservation easement when the original purpose of the easement can no longer be attained. In *In re Preservation Alliance for Greater Philadelphia*,[71] the court allowed the termination of a facade easement. The court determined that the building had deteriorated to the point that it could not be restored to any proper use, making the original purpose of the easement impossible to attain.

Disposition and Development Agreement

A disposition and development agreement (DDA) was a common contract between a developer and the redevelopment agency previously authorized under California's Community Redevelopment Law. DDAs involved the sale of agency-owned land and typically obligated the developer to proceed with development of the land consistent with the terms of the DDA and an approved redevelopment plan within a certain time.

A DDA is not the same as a "development agreement" adopted pursuant to the California Planning and Zoning Law (see Chapter 2). DDAs were approved, and entered into, by redevelopment agencies rather than cities and counties. Moreover, they do not convey the same type of vested rights to develop that are the hallmark of a development agreement. However, DDAs often include restrictions on the scope of the redevelopment agency's future amendments to its adopted redevelopment plans; thus, they may protect against certain future changes that would affect a property's development potential.

70. 886 N.E.2d 563 (Ill. App. Ct. 2008).

71. O.C. No. 759 (Ct. Com. Pl. Phila. Cnty. June 28, 1999).

Though California dismantled its redevelopment agencies in 2011, the DDA form of agreement—without the constraints previously imposed by the Community Redevelopment Law—continues to serve as a model for other public agencies to follow in selling or leasing land to developers for redevelopment.

Exclusive Negotiating Agreement

In the land use context, an exclusive negotiating agreement (ENA) is a contract between a public agency (typically a city, county, or redevelopment agency) and a developer that vests in the developer the exclusive right to negotiate with the agency regarding acquisition and development of particular property in which the agency, or some other public agency, has a legal or equitable interest. The parties agree that, during the specified negotiation period, the agency will negotiate exclusively with the developer regarding the proposed project and the land use approvals and agreements that are the subject of agency review and negotiation. During the negotiation period, the agency commits not to solicit or entertain offers or proposals from other parties concerning acquisition and development of the property.

Bases for Exclusive Negotiating Agreements

ENAs most typically arise in a context in which the agency is seeking proposals to redevelop property consistent with the agency's redevelopment goals and objectives and integrated with the existing development in the vicinity. The objective of the ENA is typically to reach terms on a comprehensive development or purchase agreement. Such longer-term agreement is intended to then provide the legal framework for transfer of the property to the developer and to obligate the developer to complete the project according to approved plans within a specified time frame.

ENAs allow agencies to impose structure and predictability on the initial negotiating phases of development or redevelopment of specific properties. The agency typically selects the developer pursuant to a qualifications-based procedure in which the agency details, in a request for proposals, the desired financial attributes and expertise. Such criteria generally include experience with development of the type of property involved (which often requires environmental remediation or poses other development challenges), financial capability to undertake the project, and organizational and staff capacity to manage the project. The agency also may require confirmation that the developer is able and willing to develop the project in conformance with the communities' goals, objectives, and vision for the project area.

Once the developer is selected, there is generally a period specified—usually 30 to 90 days, depending on the complexity of the project—during which the agency and developer will negotiate the terms of the ENA. In many cases, the agency will have a form of ENA based on prior agreements that it will use as the starting point for negotiations. If no agreement is reached in that time, the agency may select another developer candidate and undertake the same negotiation.

ENAs are attractive to developers for reasons similar to option agreements because they provide a set period—with possible extensions—during which the developer can perform due diligence and expend resources on planning and environmental work with the assurance that it will have the exclusive opportunity to negotiate and enter into an agreement for acquisition and development of the property. An additional benefit is an improved likelihood of obtaining necessary land use approvals for the project, since the legislative body approving the ENA and ultimate agreement(s) is often similar to the one vested with authority to grant the entitlements.

Structure and Content of Exclusive Negotiating Agreements

Core provisions of most ENAs include the negotiating term, grounds for extensions, descriptions of the agreements and other actions (such as environmental and land use approvals) required for the project, responsibility for costs of negotiation and entitlement processing, and grounds for and effect of termination.

All ENAs specify the term of the exclusive negotiating period and the objective of the negotiations. Most will also describe the circumstances under which the term may be extended, either automatically or at the discretion of the agency, if agreement has not been reached within the specified term. Provisions regarding extensions are often lengthy and generally call for automatic extension only if specified milestones have been reached (such as preparation and submittal of reports, studies, and development plans, or successful negotiation of essential terms of the ultimate agreements). Discretionary extensions are often predicated on a finding by the agency that significant progress on the negotiations has been achieved. The agreement generally provides for automatic termination unless the objectives of the exclusive negotiation (including one or more agreements concerning the development) have been achieved by the end of the term together with any extensions. Agreements sometimes will provide that either party may terminate the agreement before expiration of the term if certain milestones have not been reached and the party concludes, in good faith, that successful consummation of the negotiations is not reasonably possible.

Under the ENA, the developer is generally required to fund most or all of the costs incurred by the agency and its attorneys and consultants in negotiating the ENA as well as the ultimate agreements and in reviewing and processing development entitlements.

Facilities Improvement Agreement

A facilities improvement agreement (FIA) is a contract between a developer and a municipality to finance the construction of infrastructure such as roads, water pipes, sewers, flood control, and park improvements, among others.[72] These agreements involve detailed provisions of the development, from the performance bonds that will fund the project to the construction materials and workmanship that will be used.[73] These contracts ensure that each party receives that for which it bargained.

Financing Facilities Improvement Agreements

FIAs are often financed through the formation of community facility districts (CFDs). CFDs are entities through which a local government is empowered to levy special taxes and tax-exempt bonds for the purpose of financing public facilities and services.[74] In California, CFDs are authorized by the Mello-Roos Community Facilities Act of 1982[75] and have been used in dozens of projects over the past several decades. The bonds issued

---

72. Pinehurst, L.P. v. City of Chino Hills, No. RCV063815, 2004 WL 5911066, No. RCV063815, (San Bernardino County Superior Court, September 28, 2014).

73. *See* Facilities Improvement Agreement between Commonwealth of Kentucky, Department of Military Affairs, and Western Kentucky Gas Co. (Mar. 17, 1997), https://psc.ky.gov/tariffs/Natural%20Gas/Local%20Distribution%20Companies/Atmos%20Energy%20Corporation/Contracts/Lapsed/Western%20Kentucky%20Gas%20Contracts/Department%20of%20Military%20Affairs/1997-03-17_Facilities%20Improvement%20Agreement.pdf.

74. Camarillo v. Ventura, 26 Cal. App. 4th 1351, 1356 (Cal. Ct. App. 1994).

75. Cal. Gov't Code § 53311.

by CFDs are paid off through special taxes levied on the property being developed.

California also authorizes enhanced infrastructure facilities districts (EIFDs), which provide some of the financing powers of since-dissolved redevelopment agencies by allowing for the collection of tax increment generated from growth in property taxes collected within a designated district boundary.[76] EIFD proceeds can be used to finance a broad range of infrastructure work, including roads, parking facilities, transit facilities, flood control, parks and libraries, and child care facilities. They can also be used to finance environmental mitigation, affordable housing, and transit-oriented development projects, among other things. EIFDs have been used in connection with redevelopment of the former military base at Treasure Island/Yerba Buena Island in San Francisco, development of the San Francisco 49ers stadium in Santa Clara, California, and revitalization of the Los Angeles River.

Notable Facilities Improvement Agreements

A notable case involving a dispute over an FIA is *Richland Pinehurst, L.P. v. City of Chino Hills*.[77] There, a developer, Richland Pinehurst, entered into an FIA with the City of Chino Hills to construct public infrastructure improvements, including sewers, water pipes, and roads.[78] The developer and the city entered into a complex financing arrangement, in which a new CFD was created to issue bonds for the development. The bonds were secured by the developer's yet-undeveloped real property located in the city.[79] In exchange for allowing its property to be encumbered as a security for the repayment of the bonds, the developer received various credits that entitled it to receive funds from the city when they became available. However, when the funds did become available, the city refused to convey them to the developer. The developer sued, citing breach of contract as its cause of action.

The trial court noted that the word "reimbursement" was not defined in the FIA. Using *Black's Law Dictionary* to define the proper meaning of reimbursement, the court refused to consider any parol evidence. The trial

76. *Id.* § 53398.50 *et seq.*
77. No. E037242, 2006 WL 3602917 (Cal. Ct. App. Dec. 12, 2006).
78. *Id.*
79. *Id.*

court found in favor of the city, concluding that the developer's right to reimbursement was limited to actually expended construction costs, and not any promised credits. On appeal, the appellate court rejected the trial court's reasoning, finding that this complex financing agreement required a determination of the parties' intent. The court determined that the parties intended for the developer to be reimbursed for the tax credits and reversed the trial court's holding, finding in favor of plaintiffs.

Habitat Mitigation Agreement

Whether expanding roadways or building new commercial centers, developers are often forced to encroach on wetlands, habitats, and other environmentally sensitive areas. To preserve these natural areas and their ecological functions (i.e., flood control, habitat, and climate control), federal, state, and local governments impose environmental mitigation obligations on developers.[80]

Mitigation is the process of restoring degraded or destroyed natural resources to offset damage to other natural resources caused by development.[81] For every acre of degraded wetland or habitat, a developer may be required to "mitigate" the impact by restoring an equal or greater amount of degraded wetland or habitat on-site or off-site.[82]

For wetland impacts, the U.S. Army Corps of Engineers, with authority from the Clean Water Act, has set mitigation ratios that a developer must satisfy to obtain wetland permits.[83] For sensitive species habitats, federal

80. *See* Virginia C. Veltman, *Banking on the Future of Wetlands Using Federal Law*, 89 Nw. U. L. Rev. 654, 657 (1995).

81. Compensatory Mitigation for Losses of Aquatic Resources, 73 Fed. Reg. 19594-01, 19594 (U.S. Environmental Protection Agency et al. Apr. 10, 2008) ("Compensatory mitigation involves actions taken to offset unavoidable adverse impacts to wetlands, streams and other aquatic resources authorized by Clean Water Act section 404 permits and other Department of the Army (DA) permits. As such, compensatory mitigation is a critical tool in helping the federal government to meet the longstanding national goal of 'no net loss' of wetland acreage and function.").

82. *Id.*

83. *Id.* at 19602 ("[I]n a case where a project proponent is proposing to fill a degraded three acre wetland that provides one unit of wetland function per acre (as determined by a rigorous functional assessment method), the loss of that wetland may in some cases be offset by a compensatory mitigation project that provides fewer acres of high-functioning wetlands (as determined by the same functional assessment method). Conversely, where the impact is to a high-value resource, more than one-to-one replacement on an acreage basis may be

and state permitting agencies set similar mitigation ratios that require developers to restore habitat in other areas.[84]

Mitigation agreements (i.e., habitat mitigation agreements) structure and memorialize this offset arrangement. Mitigation agreements may focus on a single project and outline the developer's obligation to fund restoration work, standards, and provisions for preserving the restored natural resources and the amount of impacted land that is offset.

Given the wide range of project-specific options, mitigation agreements come in many sizes and shapes. Mitigation agreements may be entered into by a developer and regulatory agency to outline the developer's mitigation efforts in exchange for a permit. Alternatively, developers may use a mitigation agreement to outline the scope of services with an off-site conservation land trust or landowner for mitigation work that will be funded by the developer.

In some cases, a group of engineers, investors, and conservation groups will restore sensitive areas independent of any specific development and sell the credit to offset future impacts—a process known as banking. Habitat and wetland mitigation banks aggregate the patchwork of individual project impacts, offer readily available mitigation credits for developers, and maximize the ecological benefit of the off-site work (such as larger restoration projects and better habitat). For these larger banking projects, mitigation agreements provide the structure for creating and selling credits.

Regardless of the specific transaction, all mitigation agreements share a few fundamental elements in common. First, mitigation agreements identify the scope and terms of the mitigation project. Agreements will identify in detail the location of the off-site work, the size of the mitigation area, and the projected environmental benefits of the mitigation project or credit.[85]

---

necessary just to achieve functional equivalence between the impact and mitigation sites. Note that replacement ratios may also be greater than one-to-one for other reasons, such as to address uncertainty of success or temporal losses.").

84. *See* Robert D. Thornton, *Searching for Consensus and Predictability: Habitat Conservation Planning under the Endangered Species Act of 1973*, 21 Env't L. 605, 623 (1991) (discussing Endangered Species Act Habitat Conservation Plan agreements "that assure the private sector landowners and developers that, except as specifically set forth in the [mitigation] agreement, no further mitigation or compensation will be required in the interest of wildlife or their habitat on the mountain").

85. Michigan Department of Environmental Quality, Model Wetland Mitigation Banking Agreement, https://www.michigan.gov/-/media/Project/Websites/egle

Second, mitigation agreements incorporate, directly or by reference, a conservation easement over the restored land. To effectively offset wetland and habitat degradation, developers must not only restore habitat, but also protect that habitat once restored. The legal mechanism for protecting property from future development or adverse use is a conservation easement, often with a conservation land trust as beneficiary.[86]

Third, mitigation agreements create a right to the ecosystem services created by the restored habitat and then convey that right to the developer. These provisions assure the developer—and the regulating entity (i.e., the federal, state, and local governments)—that the restored area will not be "recycled" as an offset for other future development impacts.[87]

Finally, if federal or state permitting requirements are involved, mitigation agreements may incorporate agency review and oversight to assure quality and compliance. Mitigation agreements involving wetland or habitat banks often have additional language that addresses the process of creating, issuing, and recording restoration "credits."[88] Instead of funding a future project, developers purchase a wetland and habitat restoration "credit." To assure the developer and regulating entity that the "credit" represents a specific environmental benefit, mitigation agreements outline the process for creating the credit and transferring ownership of that credit to the developer. Federal and state agencies require strict documentation of mitigation credits to assure that each credit accurately represents a direct offset of the proposed impacts for purposes of Clean Water Act or Endangered Species Act compliance.

Memorandum of Agreement/Memorandum of Understanding

A memorandum of agreement (MOA) is a non-statutory agreement typically entered into by a local government and a prospective developer to lay out the process and terms by which the parties will process the developer's

---

/Documents/Programs/WRD/Wetlands/wetlands-bank-agreement-example.pdf?rev=216dd4ab919040a0adf3568c36ac8426.

86. *Id.*

87. *Id.*

88. Oregon Department of State Lands, Removal-Fill Guide: Applying for Permits to Work in Wetlands, Rivers, Streams, Lakes, and Other Oregon Waters ch. 8 (2023), https://www.oregon.gov/dsl/WW/Documents/Removal_Fill_Guide.pdf.

applications for land use approvals and/or negotiate the developer's potential purchase of land for development from the jurisdiction. MOAs are used to express the parties' shared intent to proceed with negotiations and consideration of a project, as well as to commit to certain fixed and binding provisions that structure the parties' future interactions. Such provisions are likely to set parameters for the timing of upcoming negotiations and events and may help minimize the risk of misunderstandings on the part of the community and the parties alike with regard to the process and content of the potential project and future transactions. MOAs serve to offer some assurances of mutual commitment to the parties before they invest further time, money, and effort.

A memorandum of understanding (MOU) is typically more conceptual than an MOA and simply provides a statement of understanding between the parties rather than any particular agreements or commitments by the parties. MOUs are intended to express the parties' intent to proceed with a project and to give general direction to staff, the local community, and perhaps other parties about how they might proceed with processing an anticipated project. While MOUs can prove helpful to ensuring that the parties share the same basic objectives and are discussing the relevant issues, they typically contain only nonbinding terms, ordinarily making it impossible for the signatories to breach or default.[89]

Structure of a Memorandum of Agreement

MOAs need not adhere to any particular structure, but frequently will address the following issues.

Process for Submission of Proposed Project Applications and Plans

MOAs often describe the process by which the prospective developer will submit, and the local government will review, development plans and applications. MOAs establish the mechanism and timing for public review and may commit the jurisdiction to following a predetermined timetable. That said, in jurisdictions such as California that require thorough

89. Although these non-statutory agreements are typically entered into by an agency and prospective developer, multiple public agencies, striving to achieve shared goals, also might enter into an MOA, or more likely an MOU, to help define their respective rights and obligations on pending development applications or other shared concerns.

environmental review, MOAs cannot bind a public agency to consider or approve a project before the environmental review process has been completed.

Identification of Ancillary Agreements

MOAs can identify ancillary agreements that will help implement the terms of the MOA and advance consideration of the project. MOAs also can require the parties to negotiate and jointly prepare future agreements, such as a purchase and sale agreement, in the event one of the parties is purchasing land from the other, but usually will not commit the parties in advance to including particular provisions in the latter agreements. MOAs frequently contain lists of provisions that the parties "anticipate" incorporating into ancillary documents. Compiling this list can become the focus of protracted negotiations even before agreement on an MOA is reached.

Financial Terms

MOAs often have a financial component, oftentimes requiring the prospective developer to make an initial deposit and/or further payments that may be refundable only under certain circumstances. The private party also may be responsible for reimbursing the costs incurred by the public agency in processing entitlements and responding to planning requests. Understandably, defining the amount, timing, and refundability of any deposits and additional payments can prove critical to both parties' willingness to proceed with the agreement. By requiring a private party to take certain steps or risk losing its deposit, MOAs can increase the pressure to comply.

Termination and Extension Provisions

As part of the overall timetable of development, MOAs can include provisions for their own extension and termination based on whether certain actions are, or are not, taken. These provisions guide the parties' expectations as to how long the development process will take unless and until the MOA is terminated or a further agreement that supersedes the MOA is reached.

Structure of a Memorandum of Understanding

In keeping with their nonbinding nature, MOUs tend to have a less formal structure than MOAs. MOUs typically contain a list of statements to which the parties agree; the list is intended to provide terms to guide future discussion and action. These provisions may include a shared understanding of the history to date and perceived need for an MOU at this stage. Other provisions may establish a general process and schedule for moving forward, though without binding the parties to a specific timetable as an MOA might. MOUs also can require one or all parties to take certain actions to advance the shared direction expressed by the agreement. However, such provisions typically are written in a sufficiently vague manner so as to be unenforceable under general contract law principles. Additionally, unlike an MOA, an MOU does not include any specific enforcement mechanisms, like a reimbursement provision, that could adversely affect the parties financially if they fail to adhere to the MOU's provisions.

Parkland Dedication and Improvement Agreement

Parkland dedication and improvement agreements are used by developers/landowners and municipalities to shift "community" or public elements of a development project (e.g., roads, sidewalks, or parks) to municipal ownership and control. Often parkland dedications are used to preserve open space and offset impacts of new development. In exchange for the dedicated property, the municipal entity provides long-term maintenance for the parkland and improvements that benefit the adjacent landowners.

Like any agreement, parkland dedication and improvement agreements begin with an offer and acceptance. Dedication of property to the public in a plat is not, alone, sufficient to convey that property or create any maintenance obligation on behalf of the municipality.[90] Statutory dedication occurs when the property owner files or records a plat that marks or notes on the plat portions of the premises as donated or granted to the public, and the public entity accepts the dedication, thus completing the transfer of ownership and maintenance obligations.[91] Acceptance by a municipality of an offer of dedication of land for road purposes may be proved by evidence of direct municipal action (i.e., filing of suit to establish dedication), municipal possession or maintenance of property, or public use of the road for substantial time.[92]

90. Bigelow v. City of Rolling Meadows, 865 N.E.2d 221 (Ill. App. Ct. 2007); Vill. of Elwood v. Newell, 197 N.E.2d 467 (Ill. App. Ct. 1964).

91. *Bigelow*, 865 N.E.2d 221.

92. First Ill. Bank of Wilmette v. Valentine, 619 N.E.2d 834 (Ill App. Ct. 1993).

Agreements allow the parties to establish clear standards for acceptance and to avoid subsequent disputes. Parkland dedication and improvement agreements formally recognize the developer's offer and the conditions upon which the municipality will accept the public dedication. The agreements identify the owner's intention to dedicate the property, the municipality's acceptance of the dedication on behalf of the public, and the compliance by the owner with all statutory requirements for subdividing land and recording plats prior to dedication.[93] Parkland dedication and improvement agreements should clearly identify the construction standards that must be met by the dedicator prior to the public's acceptance, as well as the maintenance obligations of both parties prior to acceptance and after acceptance.

Reimbursement and Processing Agreement

Reimbursement and processing agreements (RPAs) are typically negotiated between a project applicant and the local agency that will review and act upon applications. They are most frequently used where a proponent has applied for approval of a large, complex development project that will require considerable agency time and expense to process, including costs associated with outside consultants engaged by the agency.

RPAs frequently address such topics as:

- The process and timing for retention of consultants by the agency
- The applicant's approval rights over work scopes and budgets of project consultants
- Allocation of responsibility among agency consultants and applicant consultants for production of certain technical and environmental reports
- The process and sequence for any peer review by the local agency of technical reports submitted by the applicant's consultant team
- Schedule and time lines for reimbursement of agency out-of-pocket costs, including those for consultants
- Provisions for the advance deposit of funds to cover anticipated consultant costs and the continual replenishment of such deposited funds to ensure no local agency liability for out-of-pocket costs (sometimes referred to as an "evergreen" deposit)

93. Am. Nat'l Bank & Tr. Co. v. Harcros Chems., Inc., 997 F. Supp. 994 (N.D. Ill. 1998).

Why Would Parties Want a Reimbursement and Processing Agreement?

RPAs provide proponents of particularly large projects with a mechanism for ensuring that appropriate local agency resources are devoted to the review, processing, and consideration of their project applications. At the same time, such agreements provide local agencies with an opportunity to ensure prompt repayment of the city's out-of-pocket costs associated with processing a complex and costly development proposal. While MOAs or MOUs may provide policy directives or objectives and/or terms for negotiating the sale of public lands, RPAs are focused simply on assuring a method of reimbursement and processing project applications.

Considerations in Drafting a Reimbursement and Processing Agreement

While they can be very useful tools for the effective and efficient processing of complex applications, RPAs must be carefully drafted to protect the interests of both the local agency and the project applicant. The most important considerations for the local agency and the applicant include the following:

- In complex projects, the agency and the applicant may each have its own consultants addressing certain topics. The parties must clearly establish which—the agency or the applicant—has the contractual rights to direct the work of which consultants.
- The agency must be careful to expressly provide in any RPA that it is not committing to reach any particular determination on the applications being processed; indeed, except as may otherwise be required by law, the agency is not committing to take any decision-making action whatsoever on the applications by virtue of the RPA.
- The RPA should provide a mechanism for the applicant to review invoices of city consultants for which applicant reimbursement is required. Invoices containing privileged information (e.g., bills of special outside counsel hired by the agency and reimbursed by the applicant) should be exempted from such a process.
- The RPA should include a process for airing and resolving disagreements between the agency and applicant over the scope or amount of billed fees that are subject to reimbursement.

- The agency will want an unequivocal right to stop processing any applications where the applicant has failed to timely reimburse for agency-incurred costs or has failed to maintain an "evergreen" deposit consistent with the terms of the agreement.

School Mitigation Agreement

A school mitigation agreement is a contract between a developer and a school district (and in some cases a city or county) that provides for mitigation of the impacts of proposed development on the district's educational facilities. Although school mitigation agreements are referenced in some state statutes, there is no established legislative framework for such agreements (in contrast, for example, to development agreements). They are individually negotiated agreements, enforceable under general contract law, containing provisions addressing the particular issues at hand. Also, although in rare instances involving significant commercial or industrial development, the developer and school district may enter into a school mitigation agreement, most of these agreements involve single-family and multifamily developments since these have the most direct impact on the district's school facilities.

School mitigation agreements generally arise in contexts in which the district lacks the facilities necessary to house the project's students, state or local financing is insufficient to pay for the needed facilities, and any legally mandated mitigation payable by the developer is inadequate.[94] The school

94. The portion of the cost of new school facilities funded by the state as opposed to the school district or other local agencies or developers varies widely across the nation. Between 2005 and 2008, the average state share of funds for capital school facility projects was 30 percent. This ranged from 11 states contributing no funds for school facility projects to three states and the District of Columbia paying 100 percent of the cost of school facility projects. Mary Filardo et al., 21st Century School Fund & National Clearinghouse for Educational Facilities, State Capital Spending on PK–12 School Facilities (2010), https://files.eric.ed.gov/fulltext/ED516065.pdf. For a 2021 assessment of the prior decade's lagging investment in school maintenance and infrastructure nationally, see Victoria Jackson & Nicholas Johnson, Center on Budget and Policy Priorities, America's School Infrastructure Needs a Major Investment of Federal Funds to Advance an Equitable Recovery (2021), https://www.cbpp.org/sites/default/files/5-17-21sfp.pdf. For a 2022 assessment of California's system of school facility finance over the years, see Julien Lafortune et al., Public Policy Institute of California, Equitable State Funding for School Facilities (2022),

mitigation agreement specifies the mitigation—in the form of school fees, public or private financing, construction, or other requirements—that, alone or together with other funding sources, will ensure provision of new or rehabilitated facilities to accommodate the students from the development. Where new developing areas involve several developers or landowners with different development schedules, the agreement may involve multiple parties and provide for the dedication of land and construction or financing of facilities by the first to develop, as well as the recapture of fees, assessments, or taxes from subsequent developments. Additionally, in jurisdictions where cities or counties and school districts have overlapping responsibilities for school facilities, the city or county is commonly a party to the school mitigation agreement.

Bases for School Mitigation Agreements

There is a wide spectrum of motivations underlying school mitigation agreements. Housing and schools are closely intertwined, and the quality of schooling is frequently cited as the most important issue in the selection of a home.[95] Indeed, ensuring adequate educational facilities can be one of the most significant issues to be addressed in the planning of new communities. Together with school districts and cities, developers are important stakeholders in the quality of school facilities as the schools play such a large role in the marketability of new homes. At the same time, as traditional sources of financing for educational facilities (property taxes, bonded indebtedness, and income taxes) have declined, a larger share of the cost of school facilities has been transferred to developers in the form of impact fees and other exactions.[96] Both developers and public agencies thus share a strong interest in ensuring availability of timely, high-quality facilities in tandem with new development and a desire to clearly identify each party's relative responsibility for funding or constructing those facilities.

Despite these shared interests, developers and districts often differ over the appropriate contribution by the developer toward school facility needs. Even when school mitigation is provided by state or local laws (typically

https://www.ppic.org/?show-pdf=true&docraptor=true&url=https%3A%2F%2Fwww.ppic.org%2Fpublication%2Fequitable-state-funding-for-school-facilities%2F.

95. *See* David Levinson et al., Education and Sociology: An Encyclopedia 513 (2002).

96. Handbook of Research in Education Finance and Policy ch. 20 (Helen F. Ladd & Edward B. Fiske eds., 2007).

requiring payment of a fee calculated based on square footage, number of bedrooms, or similar criteria), school districts and cities often rely upon developers to fund the shortfall between the mitigation payment and the cost of adequate facilities to house the students. Where such disagreements arise, school mitigation agreements are frequently in the nature of settlement agreements under which both parties agree to compromise their positions in order to avoid (or resolve) litigation. Cities and counties, which have land use approval authority over development, are often drawn into the debate regarding appropriate mitigation and may refuse to grant development approvals unless agreement on school mitigation is reached. Thus, school mitigation agreements may arise from a general or specific directive from the land use approval authority to the developer to resolve school mitigation issues as a condition of project approval.

Structure and Content of School Mitigation Agreements

The scope and complexity of school mitigation agreements varies depending on the size or extent of the development, ranging from payment of a specified per-unit fee to multifaceted programs involving dedication of land and financing or construction of all elementary and secondary school facilities and administrative facilities necessary to serve a master-planned community. However, most school mitigation agreements typically contain some or all of the following elements:

- A description of the development project(s) for which the mitigation is required
- The amount and timing of payment of fees, exactions, or contributions, and whether such payments are in lieu of or in addition to any mitigation requirements established under state or local laws or policies
- A description (either categorical or specific) of the facilities to be funded by the mitigation payments or the geographic area(s) in which the funds are to be used
- A description of any public financing (such as bonds secured by assessments or special taxes to be paid by the developer and/or by future residents of the development;[97] or payments or

97. In some states, special tax or assessment areas may be formed around the proposed development project for the purpose of funding the project's school mitigation obligations. The school district (or the special-purpose entity formed to administer the tax or assessment

reimbursements from the state for school facilities[98]) that is part of the mitigation package

- Delineation of the school district's responsibilities (if applicable) to seek available federal, state, or local funding,[99] and whether such funding will be additional to or in lieu of the funding provided for in the agreement
- Confirmation that by complying with the terms of the agreement, the developer will have fulfilled and mitigated its entire obligation to assist in funding or construction of school facilities to serve project students
- Whether and to what extent the agreement may be affected—if at all—by subsequent changes in laws governing school facilities mitigation

Agreements that include conveyance of land for school sites and/or construction and dedication of school buildings are more complex and are generally structured like real estate purchase contracts and/or construction contracts. Thus an agreement that contemplates conveyance of land for a school site will generally include provisions regarding title, escrow, due diligence, representations and warranties, and closing details. In some cases, the agreements will provide that any reimbursement from the state or other sources for land acquisition will be paid to the developer.[100]

---

district) can be authorized to issue tax-exempt bonds with a term of 20 or more years to fund school facilities. The bonds are repaid from taxes or assessments levied annually on the property tax bills of the property owners within the development project boundary.

98. New school facilities in California, for example, are financed under the School Facility Program. Under this program, state funding for new school construction is provided in the form of per-pupil grants for construction costs with supplemental grants for site development and site acquisition. New school construction projects are funded on a 50/50 state and local matching basis. Local school districts finance their 50 percent share of school facility projects with funding obtained from local general obligation bonds, developer fees or other mitigation fees, or other sources. Many school mitigation agreements in California are structured around available state funding, with the developer covering the gap between state funds and the cost of the school facilities. LAFORTUNE ET AL., *supra* note 94.

99. Nearly all public capital outlay funding for elementary and secondary facilities is from state and local taxes or assessments, with the federal share at less than 10 percent. MARY FILARDO & SEAN O'DONNELL, 21ST CENTURY SCHOOL FUND AND NATIONAL CLEARINGHOUSE FOR EDUCATIONAL FACILITIES, FEDERAL SPENDING ON PK–12 SCHOOL FACILITIES (2010), https://files.eric.ed.gov/fulltext/ED516064.pdf.

100. For example, in California, under the state's School Facility Program, the state will reimburse eligible school districts up to 50 percent of the cost of school sites. CAL. CODE REGS. tit. 2, § 1859.74.

School mitigation agreements that contemplate construction of school facilities by the developer take different forms depending upon whether the district will take the property in fee or under a lease.[101] Under a sale/lease-back arrangement, the school district sells the land to the developer, which constructs school facilities on the property. The developer then leases the property and buildings back to the school district for a nominal rent ($1 per year), with the district having the right to purchase the property at the end of the lease for a nominal amount. Under the lease/leaseback model (which may include the developer selling or dedicating the land to the district at the outset), the school district leases the land to the developer (for a nominal amount).

The developer then occupies the property for the period needed to build the school facilities and then leases the property and completed facilities back to the district under a facilities lease. Included in the facilities lease is the difference (if any) between the developer's mitigation obligation and the cost of the facilities (with the developer sometimes proceeding at the risk that anticipated state funding will not be received). Ownership is transferred to the district at the end of the lease.

The provisions of a school mitigation agreement will also vary depending upon the method chosen for project delivery. The agreements are often structured around a variant of the design-bid-build system, under which the parties select design professionals to prepare the complete set of construction documents (plans, specifications, and bidding requirements), the project is advertised for bids, and the contract is awarded to the lowest responsible bidder. The developer remains responsible for the construction costs (or its share of them) and may have a supervisory role but does not participate directly in the construction. Increasingly, however, districts and developers are using some form of the construction manager model, under which a design professional is selected and paid to oversee all aspects of the design and construction of the facilities. Under a variant of this model—the construction-manager-at-risk—the construction manager submits a guaranteed maximum price, including all construction costs and an agreed-upon profit percentage. The construction manager then bids and holds the contracts for the construction and manages the schedule

101. The lease model may be employed for various reasons, including to avoid cash-flow problems, to allocate risks, and/or to avoid certain public bidding or other public contracting requirements. This structure may also reduce the level of public agency risk associated with design issues, delays, and costs overruns.

and subcontractors. Regardless of the chosen project delivery method, the school mitigation agreement generally contains only the provisions necessary to specify the method and process of implementation, with details of the construction and management responsibility contained in separate construction agreements or construction management contracts.

Subdivision Improvement Agreement (California)

For decades, cities and counties in various states have required commercial and residential property developers to construct at their own expense subdivision improvements, including streets, curbs, gutters, sidewalks, drainage facilities, sewers, water systems, landscaping, utilities, fire protection equipment, and street signs.[102] In California,[103] if a project is conditioned on the developer's completion of subdivision improvements, and those improvements will not be completed until after the final map is filed, the subdivider must enter into a "subdivision improvement agreement" with the agency.[104] Such an agreement must provide that the subdivider will complete the required improvements at the subdivider's expense.[105] The developer has no right to a final map until the parties have entered into the agreement.[106]

---

102. *See* Richard Kelley & Michael M. Shultz, *"... Or Other Adequate Security": Using, Structuring, and Managing the Standby Letter of Credit to Ensure the Completion of Subdivision Improvements*, 19 URB. LAW. 39 (1987); Michael M. Shultz & Richard Kelley, *Subdivision Improvement Requirements and Guarantees: A Primer*, 28 WASH. U. J. URB. & CONTEMP. L. 3, 39 (1985); Comment, *Allocating the Burden of Increased Community Costs Caused by New Developments*, 1967 U. ILL. L.F. 318, 318 n.1, 321 n.13 (1967).

103. This section focuses on examples of subdivision improvement agreements entered into under California law due to the comprehensiveness of California's statutory framework and the extent to which issues related to subdivision improvement agreements have been litigated in California courts. Subdivision improvement agreements are also authorized under state law in Arizona, Colorado, Florida, Illinois, Montana, Pennsylvania, and Utah. *See, e.g.*, ARIZ. REV. STAT. § 11-821 (2011); COLO. REV. STAT. §§ 30-28-133, 31-23-214 (2011); FLA. STAT. § 177.091 (2011); 65 ILL. COMP. STAT. 5/9-5-1 (1992); MONT. CODE ANN. § 76-3-507 (2011); 53 PA. CONS. STAT. § 22770 (2011); UTAH CODE ANN. §§ 10-9a-103, 57-11-11[JAT Note: Text corrected.] (2011).

104. For ease of reference, cities, towns, and counties will be referred to as "agency" throughout this section.

105. CAL. GOV'T CODE § 66462(a).

106. *See, e.g.*, S. Cent. Coast Reg'l Comm'n v. Charles A. Pratt Constr. Co., 128 Cal. App. 3d 830, 834 (Cal. Ct. App. 1982).

Improvement Security Requirements

A subdivision improvement agreement requires that performance be guaranteed by security. By ordinance, an agency can require a subdivider to post bonds, cash deposits, instruments of credit, a lien upon the property, or any other form of security acceptable to the agency to secure completion of subdivision improvements.[107] The security ensures the performance of the terms of the agreement and payment for labor, materials, and improvements, along with a guaranty and warranty for one year, plus costs, including reasonable attorneys' costs.[108] Courts will not interfere with an agency's exercise of discretion in accepting or rejecting the security unless there is a showing of fraud, arbitrary action, or a clear abuse of discretion. Also, an agency may adopt financial size criteria for insurers with respect to performance bonds.[109] In addition, an agency may have the obligation to ensure that the surety is sufficient.[110]

An agency will determine the specific amount of security required for performance of an agreement to complete improvements.[111] However, California law requires (1) the amount for faithful performance must be no less than 50 percent or more than 100 percent of the total estimated cost of the improvement or the act to be performed; (2) the amount for payment to the contractor, subcontractors, laborers, and anyone providing equipment must be no less than 50 percent or more than 100 percent of the total estimated cost of the improvement or the performance of the required act; and (3) the amount must equal the amount determined by the agency to fulfill the obligations for one year after completion of the improvement arising under a guaranty and warranty against defective work, labor, and materials.[112] In addition, the security must be sufficient to cover any costs, reasonable expenses, and fees the agency would have if it successfully enforced the security.[113] Some nonprofit organizations are exempt from the first two

107. Cal. Gov't Code § 66499.

108. *Id.* §§ 66499.3, 66499.4.

109. 74 Op. Cal. Att'y Gen. 89 (1991).

110. Walt Rankin & Assocs., Inc. v. City of Murrieta, 84 Cal. App. 4th 605, 627–28 (Cal. Ct. App. 2000).

111. Cal. Gov't Code § 66499.3.

112. *Id.*

113. *Id.* § 66499.4.

requirements listed above if certain letter-of-credit payment or contractor payment conditions are met.[114]

Rights and Liabilities under a Subdivision Improvement Agreement

Once the improvement work begins, the subdivider and the entity furnishing the security (surety) are liable until all subdivision improvements are completed and accepted by the agency. Therefore, subdividers and sureties must maintain and repair improvements after completion until the agency accepts all improvements guaranteed.[115] Modifications to an improvement agreement do not necessarily affect an agency's right to damages against a subdivider and the surety.[116]

A local agency is entitled to damages under a performance bond when a subdivider responsible for constructing public improvements fails to perform, even if the agency incurs no out-of-pocket expense. In *City of Merced v. American Motorists Insurance Co.*, a developer entered into a subdivision agreement with the agency under which it agreed to obtain a performance bond for deferred work identified in the agreement.[117] After completing construction of numerous residential units, the developer became insolvent. The insolvent developer then conveyed the remaining undeveloped property to another developer, who agreed to perform the first developer's deferred work. The agency promised to obtain the bond proceeds and pay them to the second developer to defray the costs of completing the first developer's obligations. The agency then sued to enforce the first developer's deferred work obligations.

The bonding company argued the agency should not be able to enforce the performance bond against it since the agency was not damaged by the first developer's refusal to perform because the second developer agreed to timely perform the deferred work at no cost to the agency.[118] The appellate court disagreed and held that the agency's damages were not limited

---

114. *Id.* § 66499.3(c).

115. *See* Cnty. of Kern v. Edgemont Dev. Corp., 222 Cal. App. 2d 874, 879–80 (Cal. Ct. App. 1963).

116. City of Sacramento v. Trans Pac. Indus., Inc., 98 Cal. App. 3d 389, 400–01 (Cal. Ct. App. 1979).

117. 126 Cal. App. 4th 1316, 1318–19 (Cal. Ct. App. 2005).

118. *Id.* at 1323.

to its actual costs. The agency maintained a contractual right to expect the first developer to perform the deferred work, despite the agency's agreement with the second developer. According to the court, the agency was damaged once the first developer refused to perform. Thus, its damages are measured by the first developer's share of the uncompleted portion of the deferred work, and the surety is liable under the performance bond up to the bond amount.[119]

There is conflicting authority over whether the surety is liable under an improvement agreement when the subdivider has not actually commenced construction. In *County of Yuba v. Central Valley National Bank, Inc.*, the court held that if the project is abandoned after a final map has been recorded, even though the subdivider and the agency have entered into an improvement agreement, the surety is exonerated as long as no construction has begun.[120] If this occurs, the agency cannot collect the amount of the bond or force the surety to install the improvements. The agency may be able to proceed under California Government Code section 66499.11 *et seq.* and "revert the subdivision to acreage," which has the practical effect of rescinding the subdivision map.

Conversely, in *City of Los Angeles v. Amwest Surety Insurance Co.*, the court held the surety remained liable on the bond after the subdivider abandoned the project even though very minimal construction actually began.[121] The court distinguished *Yuba* based on the language of the security instrument, the fact that in *Amwest* the improvements were needed because another developer was going to develop the parcel, the money derived from the bond would be used to benefit the new development, and the parcel would not automatically revert to acreage because such a reversion is a discretionary, not a ministerial, action. It appears that the courts are limiting *Yuba* to its facts; thus, a surety will likely remain liable under an improvement agreement even if the subdivider has not begun construction.[122]

---

119. *Id.*

120. 20 Cal. App. 3d 109, 113 (Cal. Ct. App. 1971).

121. 63 Cal. App. 4th 378 (Cal. Ct. App. 1998).

122. *See, e.g., id., review denied* (June 17, 1998); *Am. Motorists Ins. Co.*, 126 Cal. App. 4th 1316.

Releasing Security

Under California law, the Subdivision Map Act (Map Act)[123] allows partial or complete release of the security for public improvements.[124] The security given for the faithful performance of an act must be released once the improvement is completed and accepted. Additionally, an agency may establish rules that permit a partial release of the security as the work progresses.[125] The Map Act sets forth a detailed process for such partial release of performance security.

For example, the subdivider may provide written notice to the agency when it believes the required work has been completed.[126] The agency then has 45 days to review and comment or approve the completion of the work.[127] If the agency concludes that all required work has not been completed, it must provide a list of outstanding obligations to the subdivider.[128] The subdivider has 45 days from the date of receipt of the list to provide the agency cost estimates for all remaining work.[129] The agency then has 45 days to review, comment, and approve, modify, or disapprove the cost estimates.[130] If the agency approves the cost estimates, it shall release all performance security except for security in an amount up to 200 percent of the cost estimates of the remaining work. Unless the agency allows for earlier release, the process of partially releasing performance security must take place when the cost estimate of the remaining work does not exceed 20 percent of the original performance security.[131]

If the obligation must be approved by another agency other than the agency holding the security, the agency cannot release the security until the obligation is performed to the other agency's satisfaction. The other agency has two months after completion to determine its satisfaction or dissatisfaction. If it reaches no decision after two months, the obligation shall be deemed to be satisfied.[132] The security given for labor and materials

123. Cal. Gov't Code § 66410 *et seq.*
124. *Id.* § 66499.7.
125. *Id.* § 66499.7(a).
126. *Id.* § 66499.7(b).
127. *Id.*
128. *Id.*
129. *Id.* § 66499.7(c).
130. *Id.* § 66499.7(d).
131. *Id.*
132. *Id.* § 66499.8.

must be released if no liens have been filed and the time has expired for a lien to be recorded pursuant to California Civil Code section 3114 *et seq.*, and the agency has accepted the work.[133] If liens have been filed, upon expiration of the period for recording of liens, the agency will hold an amount equal to the amount of the liens and release the remainder, provided the lien holders have given the agency written notice.[134] However, the release provisions do not apply to the portion of security that covers any warranty or guaranty by the subdivider or reasonable costs and attorneys' fees pursuant to California Government Code section 66499.9.[135]

Remedies

If a developer does not satisfy its obligations under the agreement, the method of recovery depends on the type of security furnished. If the security is cash or negotiable bonds and is conditioned on payments to the contractor, subcontractor, and other persons furnishing labor, materials, or equipment, an agency may recover from the holder of the deposit. If the security is a surety bond, an agency may recover from the surety and sue to enforce the bond. If an irrevocable standby letter of credit is used, an agency may draw on the letter of credit.[136]

The liability of a surety that issues a labor and materials bond for public improvements may extend to the benefit of contractors in addition to the agency.[137] This is because provisions of the California Civil Code that would provide an appropriate remedy are not applicable to privately funded public improvements.[138]

Tax Increment Financing Agreement

A tax increment financing (TIF) agreement is an agreement between a developer and a local government to use future gains in taxes to finance

133. *Id.* § 66499.7(h).
134. *Id.*
135. *Id.* § 66499.7(i).
136. *Id.* § 66499.10.
137. Sukut-Coulson, Inc. v. Allied Canon Co., 85 Cal. App. 3d 648, 651 (Cal. Ct. App. 1978).
138. *Id.* at 654; *see also* CAL. CIV. CODE §§ 3109 *et seq.*, 3179 *et seq.*

current improvements.[139] These improvements will lead, at least in theory, to increased tax revenues in the future. TIF agreements provide for the issuance of bonds to redevelop a blighted district. These bonds are repaid by capping the city's collection of property taxes at the pre-redevelopment levels and using the excess revenue from the higher property taxes. The process is a closed circuit where increased public investment into a TIF district induces private investment, which then increases property tax revenues that pay for this increased public investment. Once the TIF bonds are paid off, all of the property tax revenue will again go to the city.

Authority for municipalities to use TIF agreements must be granted by the state legislature.[140] TIF agreements have withstood attacks based on equal protection, due process, and uniformity of taxation clauses.[141] TIF enabling statutes usually exempt TIF bonds from municipal debt limitations.

Development of the Tax Increment Financing Agreement Model

TIF agreements started in California in 1952 and have subsequently been utilized in thousands of districts throughout the United States.[142] In fact, until 2011, when California amended its redevelopment laws to dissolve redevelopment agencies, every state except Arizona had enabling legislation for TIF agreements.[143] They have increased in popularity as the federal government has withdrawn funding for urban development and local governments have encountered difficulty raising tax revenues.[144] TIF agreements have expanded from redeveloping blighted areas to simply creating development, often on lands that are vacant or lightly developed, or even

139. For a comprehensive overview of TIF, see TAX INCREMENT FINANCING (David L. Callies & W. Andrew Gowder, Jr. eds., 2012).

140. EUGENE MCQUILLIN, LAW OF MUNICIPAL CORPORATIONS § 44.20 (3d ed. 2003).

141. For an analysis of the various constitutional challenges to TIF, see Michael Newman, *Tax Increment Financing for Development and Redevelopment*, 61 OR. L. REV. 123, 139–43 (1982).

142. COMMUNITY REDEVELOPMENT AGENCIES ANNUAL REPORT (2007–2008), https://sgf.senate.ca.gov/sites/sgf.senate.ca.gov/files/redevelopmentfacts2007-08.pdf.

143. *See* COUNCIL OF DEVELOPMENT FINANCE AGENCIES ET AL., TAX INCREMENT FINANCE: BEST PRACTICES REFERENCE GUIDE 1 (2007), https://www.cdfa.net/cdfa/cdfaweb.nsf/ord/TIFGuide.htmlf.

144. This was particularly true in California, where Proposition 13 has made raising property taxes difficult.

undeveloped farm lands.[145] In many states, TIF agreements have become all-purpose local government tools for financing public investment in market-oriented development, rather than simply a mechanism for combating blight.

Issues with Tax Increment Financing Agreements

A certain amount of risk is associated with entering into TIF agreements. TIF redevelopment commissions have broad power to direct huge projects and divert millions of dollars with little oversight or community input. This freedom may allow for deals that serve private interests and do not benefit the community as a whole. In fact, research suggests that some TIF projects may have been pursued in Chicago for political reasons that were not in the interest of the city as a whole.[146]

Furthermore, when TIF agreements are employed in areas that are prosperous or unsuitable for the type of development proposed, they may cause economic problems for the community by promoting an inefficient allocation of resources. Prosperous areas are already likely to receive private investment, and therefore a TIF agreement in these areas would cause the city to lose property tax revenue.

TIF may also cause financial trouble for the community in which it is implemented. TIF limits the amount of money that a redevelopment area will contribute in property taxes while increasing the number of services it will need due to increases in population. Since the redevelopment agency or TIF district is a separate corporate entity from the local government, all additional TIF revenue will be automatically funneled to the agency or district until all bonds have been paid off. This may force the city to raise other taxes or seek subsidies from federal or state sources to keep up with rising costs.[147]

---

145. Richard Briffault, *The Most Popular Tool: Tax Increment Financing and the Political Economy of Local Government*, 77 U. Chi. L. Rev. 65, 71 (2010).

146. *See The Chicago Reader TIF Archive*, Chi. Reader (Aug. 13, 2009), http://www.chicagoreader.com/chicago/the-chicago-reader-tif-archive/Content?oid=1180567.

147. For criticism of TIF, *see* George Lefcoe, *Competing for the Next Hundred Million Americans: The Uses and Abuses of Tax Increment Financing*, 43 Urb. Law. 427 (2011).

Transient Occupancy Tax Sharing Agreements

Transient Occupancy Tax Revenue

Taxes generated on hotel rooms and other temporary lodging facilities in which guests typically stay for 30 days or fewer can represent a significant source of revenue for local governments. The rate of tax levied on hotel rooms varies by state and locality, and some states consider stays as long as 180 days to be transient and subject to occupancy taxes. In areas where the state-levied occupancy tax rate is low, such as in California and New York where the state-levied rates are 0 and 4 percent, respectively, there are significant opportunities for local governments to raise significant revenue. Indeed, local occupancy tax rates in such states generally range from 8 to 15 percent.

As a result of the revenue-generating opportunities created by hotels, as well as the other economic benefits that result from guests spending time and money in the local area, local governments frequently are motivated to facilitate development of hotels within their communities. Such facilitation may take the form of providing an easier or expedited path to receiving development approvals, as well as one or more economic incentives, including the provision of public infrastructure, development fee waivers, reduced land costs, and/or contribution of local revenue to support the developer's land acquisition and development costs.

Form of Transient Tax Sharing Agreement

One approach frequently used to incentivize hotel development is for the developer and local government to enter into a transit occupancy tax sharing agreement, wherein the local government pledges to share portions of future transient occupancy tax (TOT) revenue with the developer. The shared TOT might be used as a direct economic incentive to defray the developer's costs of development, as well as to reimburse the developer for various development fees and/or land acquisition costs incurred in connection with development of a hotel project. Such agreements may be stand-alone TOT sharing agreements, or they may be imbedded in other agreements, such as a development agreement or an agreement addressing a package of economic incentives.

Key Terms to Include in a Transient Occupancy Tax Sharing Agreement

While there are many details that might be addressed in a TOT sharing agreement, it is important the agreement address at least the following key terms:

- *When the tax sharing will commence* (typically the date upon which the first increment of TOT is received from a guest)
- *How amounts to be shared will be determined* (lump sum or percentage of TOT received)
- *How frequently TOT will be paid and accounted for* (typically on a quarterly basis, but shorter or longer intervals may be appropriate)
- *When the tax sharing will terminate* (on a date certain, for a term certain, or after a fixed amount of TOT has been paid to the developer)

The TOT should be paid first by the developer to the local government in accordance with local law governing payment of TOT. Thereafter, the local government will pay a portion of the collected TOT to the developer in accordance with the TOT agreement.

Illustrative Example

It can be very beneficial to include an illustrative example of the TOT sharing as an attachment or exhibit to the agreement, to ensure the parties have a clear understanding of how the TOT sharing agreement will work and also to assist others who may be implementing the agreement in the future. As part of the negotiations it also may be beneficial for the local government (or developer) to retain an experienced fiscal consultant to assist in preparation of one or more illustrative examples of how the TOT will be shared based upon various assumptions about the size of the project and future room and occupancy rates.

APPENDIX 1

Checklist for Drafting Annexation Agreements

Agreements between property owners and municipalities regarding the use and development of land are an increasingly popular way to provide each party to the agreement certain guarantees about the development of a particular parcel of land. The property owner generally wishes to ensure that the municipality's zoning and land use regulations, conditions, and exactions remain fixed during the development of his property. The municipality typically seeks as many land development conditions as possible beyond what it could reasonably require through subdivision exactions, impact fees, and other conditions under the normal exercise of its regulatory authority or police power. Whether an annexation agreement will provide the security and control that both parties seek will depend, in part, on how well the approved draft of the agreement expresses the interests, intentions, and expectations of both parties. The following checklist describes the basic issues that an annexation agreement might address.

1. Definitions

All technical terms that will be used in the annexation agreement should be precisely defined in a table of definitions. Terms that have been defined in any applicable statute or ordinance should be defined the same way in the agreement.

2. Parties

All parties to the agreement should be named and their capacities to enter into the agreement clearly stated. In the case of developers/owners, their equitable or legal interests in the property should be stated. In the case of government entities, their authority to enter into development agreements should be recited.

3. Relationship of the Parties

The relationship between the parties to the agreement should be stated clearly. Typically, the statement will specify that the relationship is contractual and that the owner/developer is an independent contractor and not an agent of the local government.

4. Property

The property that is the subject of the agreement should be clearly and thoroughly identified and described in the agreement. This typically means including a legal description and often a parcel or tax identification number. It also might be helpful for the parties to include in the agreement a depiction of the property, particularly for larger parcels that may be annexed to develop mixed-use or industrial developments. In prospective developments with multiple owners or developers, the agreement should separately describe each property that is subject to the agreement, particularly where the owners or developers may have different responsibilities, obligations, and rights under the agreement.

5. Authorization

If applicable, the state enabling statute that authorizes the agreement should be referenced. The ordinance or resolution that is adopted by the corporate authorities to approve the agreement should also be cited.

6. Intent of the Parties

The intent of the parties to be bound by the terms of the agreement should be clearly stated.

7. Recitation of Benefits and Burdens

The parties should recite the benefits each expects to gain from entering into the agreement, as well as the burdens each agrees to bear. Because the agreement will be treated as a contract, the consideration each party is to receive from the other should be stated clearly in order to ensure enforceability. It is especially important that the benefits to the municipality and community be expressed in terms that exhibit the agreement as consistent with (or as an exercise of) the police power.

8. Notice and Hearings

The date on which the public hearing was held should be noted, as well as all relevant findings resulting from that hearing. All other pertinent notice and hearing requirements should be recited.

9. Annexation of the Property

The agreement should include language setting forth the process for annexing the property to the municipality.

10. Applicable Land Use Regulations

The agreement should contain a statement of all land use regulations to which the development project will be subject. The agreement should specify which regulations will apply to the project regardless of future changes or will otherwise be affected by the agreement. The statement should make clear that regulations not specifically identified as "frozen" will not be affected by the terms of the agreement and will be subject to enforcement and change under the same criteria that would apply if there were no agreement.

11. Approval and Permit Requirements

The parties should specify all discretionary approvals and permits that will have to be obtained before the development can proceed beyond its various stages. Permits and approvals obtained prior to execution of the agreement should be specified. Any and all conditions that must be met before obtaining permits and approvals should be listed.

12. Zoning and Development of the Property

The agreement should specifically identify the permitted uses of the property, the density of use, and the bulk, yard, and height regulations for the property. The agreement should also specify any zoning relief required for the development of the property, as well as all development approvals that the developer/owner intends to apply for and obtain prior to the development, including subdivision, zoning, and other approvals.

13. Plan Approvals

In addition to approval of the zoning and use, the parties also should reference the process for approval of all required plans for the proposed development, which might include subdivision, engineering, and architectural design, for example. In some cases, the parties might also include as attachments to the agreement the preliminary or concept plans, although typically the formal approval will be done by separate ordinance or another approval document. The parties should explain that the final approved plans will control over any preliminary or concept plans. The parties also might explain how minor or major changes to plans will be handled.

14. Dedications and Reservations

The agreement should provide, where appropriate, a statement of all reservations or dedications of land for public purposes that are required by law, ordinance, or any policy in effect at the time of entering into the agreement.

15. Fees

The parties typically will include a reference to applicable development or project fees (application, impact, building permit, design review, etc.). If fees are to remain frozen for the term of the agreement (or part thereof), it might be helpful to attach a fee schedule to the agreement identifying those fees.

16. Utility Connections

All water and sewer service, to be provided either by the developer or by the local government, should be described in detail, together with schedules of construction completion (if not existing), cost allocation (among developers, government, and later developers), and hookup or connection schedules.

17. Public Improvements

The parties should specify in the agreement which improvements are required to be constructed by the property owner/developer and ultimately dedicated to the municipality when completed. These improvements might include water and sewer improvements, storm water drainage and detention facilities, streets, sidewalks, and other public infrastructure. The parties also should detail the process for completion, inspection, and acceptance of the public improvements as well as the type of performance and payment security that must be posted by the developer to secure completion and to guarantee the improvements. If the municipality will require that the public improvements be oversized to benefit other properties and developments, the parties might want to include provisions for recapture.

18. Declaration of Covenants

If there will be a declaration of covenants to govern the potential development, the parties should note in the agreement any terms that the municipality wants to be incorporated into the declaration such as, for example, a requirement that private storm water detention and drainage facilities be maintained.

19. Duration of the Agreement

The agreement should state a termination date that cannot be more than 20 years from the date of execution of the agreement. It also should specify project commencement and completion dates, either for the project on the whole or for its various phases.

20. Amendment, Cancellation, or Termination

The agreement should recite the conditions and procedures required to amend, cancel, or terminate the agreement. That provision might also include a reference to any applicable statutes. If there are multiple owners or if the property is contemplated for partial sale in the future, the agreement might include a provision authorizing amendments to the agreement by the owner of the property to which the amendment would apply and the municipality, rather than requiring all owners to amend, if this is allowed by state law.

21. Periodic Review

The parties might provide in the agreement for periodic reviews of the project in order to determine compliance with the terms of the agreement. Procedures should be developed and specified for dealing with situations in which minor and major noncompliance is discovered.

22. Remedies

Remedies for breach on the part of either party should be provided. Specific remedies for specific breaches should be stated, if possible. The agreement should include a statement clarifying whether the remedies stated in the agreement are to be exclusive, or whether other statutory or common law remedies will also be available.

23. Enforcement; Successors

The agreement should specify that it will be enforceable, unless lawfully terminated or canceled, by any party to the agreement or any party's successor in interest, notwithstanding any subsequent changes in any applicable law adopted by the municipality entering into the agreement that alter or amend the laws, ordinances, resolutions, rules, or policies frozen by the agreement.

24. Indemnification; Hold Harmless Clause

The agreement should contain a provision that the developer/property owner holds the municipality and its agents harmless from liability for damages, injury, or death that may arise from the direct or indirect operations of the owner, developer, contractors, and subcontractors that relate to the project.

25. Insurance and Bonds

The agreement should specify the insurance coverage required by the developer/owner for the development project. Performance security requirements should be listed in detail. Applicable ordinances relating to bond or other security requirements should be cited. The agreement should also cite to any applicable statutes or ordinances that require bond or other security requirements. In some cases, the parties might want to include a form of acceptable surety bond or letter of credit as an attachment to the agreement.

26. Severability Clause

The agreement should include a clause specifying that the provisions of the agreement are severable, if the parties so agree. Any limitations on the severability of any particular clause or clauses should be clearly stated.

27. Merger Clause

A merger clause or other statement should be provided specifying that the terms of the agreement as stated in the written document are both a final and complete expression of the parties' intentions.

28. Statements of Incorporation by Reference

All documents related to the agreement or otherwise attached or appended to the agreement should be expressly stated to be incorporated into the agreement by reference. These might include lists of conditions, schedules of completion for public facilities, imposition of dedications, impact fees, and development plans and specifications. To the extent the agreement includes recitals or background or historical information, the parties should include an express statement that these are incorporated into the agreement by reference.

29. Cooperation

The agreement should include a statement of the extent to which the municipality will cooperate with the owner in his efforts to secure required permits from nonparty government agencies.

30. Subsidiary or Collateral Agreements

If the owner has obtained additional agreements relating to the development project from any nonparty agencies or persons (i.e., county, state, or other governmental agency), those agreements and the parties should be specified.

31. Notices

The parties should include in the agreement a notice provision for all parties and their representatives.

APPENDIX 2

Simple Annexation Agreement

ANNEXATION AGREEMENT

This Annexation Agreement ("*Agreement*") is made and entered into this _____ day of __________, _____ by and among the Village of __________, an _________ Municipal Corporation located in ______ County, Illinois ("*Village*") and ___________________________ ("*Owner*").

RECITALS

A. Owner is the owner of record of approximately _____ acres of real property located in ________ County, ________, which property is legally described on **Exhibit "A"** attached hereto and incorporated herein by reference ("Property").

B. The Property that is the subject matter of this agreement is located generally at __________ with common street addresses of ___________ with PINs ___________. The Property is depicted on the plat of annexation attached hereto as **Exhibit "B"** and incorporated herein by reference.

C. The parties desire to enter into this Agreement pursuant to the provisions of 65 ILCS 5/11-15.1-1 *et seq.* in accordance with the terms and conditions hereinafter set forth.

D. The Property is not presently located within the corporate limits of any municipality but is contiguous to and may be annexed to the Village as provided in 65 ILCS 5/7-1-1 *et seq.*

E. Owner seeks to annex the Property into the Village for future development in the ____ and ____ zoning districts, subject to approval of a planned unit development for any use or development of the Property. All zoning, development, and use of the Property shall be subject to the terms of this Agreement and shall comply with all zoning, building, planned unit development, and other applicable Village Code requirements.

F. The Village has agreed to annex the property into the Village, to zone the property as herein described, and to grant the requested rezoning of the Property to the ___ and ___ zoning districts as set forth herein, in accordance with all applicable building and zoning procedures and processes under the Zoning Code and applicable Village Code regulations.

G. Owner has filed with the Village Clerk a proper Annexation Petition ("Annexation Petition") pursuant to 65 ILCS 5/7-1-8, signed by the owner(s) of record of the Property. [There are no electors residing on the Property.] [The elector has also signed the Annexation Petition.]

H. Pursuant to the applicable provisions of the Illinois Municipal Code, a proposed Annexation Agreement similar in substance and in form to this Agreement was submitted to the Mayor and Village Trustees (hereinafter collectively referred to as the "Corporate Authorities") and a public hearing was held thereon pursuant to notice, as provided by statute.

I. Pursuant to notice, as required by all applicable statutes and ordinances, public hearings were held by the Village Plan Commission and Village Board related to the requested rezoning and with respect to the annexation of the Property and the findings of fact and recommendations made by the Plan Commission have been forwarded to the Corporate Authorities.

J. Any required notices have been given, as required by statute.

K. All other and further notices, publications, procedures, public hearings, and other matters attendant to the consideration and approval of this Agreement and the annexation and zoning of the Property have been given, made, held, and performed, or will be made, as required by 65 ILCS 5/7-1-8 and 5/11-15.1-1 *et seq.*, and all other applicable statutes, and all applicable ordinances, regulations, and procedures of the Village. This Agreement is made and entered into by the parties pursuant to these statutes.

L. The Corporate Authorities have duly considered all necessary petitions to enter into this Agreement, have considered the recommendations of the Plan Commission in connection with the proposed zoning for the Property, have further duly considered the terms and provisions of this Agreement, and have, by an ordinance duly adopted by a vote of two-thirds (2/3) or more of the Corporate Authorities then holding office, authorized the Mayor to execute, and the Village Clerk to attest, this Agreement on behalf of the Village.

NOW THEREFORE, in consideration of the foregoing recitals and the mutual covenants and agreements herein made, the parties hereby agree as follows:

ARTICLE I

RECITALS

The Parties acknowledge that the statements and representations contained in the foregoing recitals are true and accurate and incorporate such recitals into this Agreement as if fully set forth in this Article I.

ARTICLE II

ANNEXATION OF THE PROPERTY

A. Upon execution of this Agreement by all Parties, the Corporate Authorities shall proceed, subject to the terms and conditions set forth in this Agreement, to consider the question of annexing the Property to the Village and do all things necessary or appropriate to cause the Property to be validly annexed to the Village, including adoption of an ordinance annexing the Property to the Village ("Annexation Ordinance").

B. This Agreement in its entirety, at the option of the Owner, shall be null, void, and of no force and effect unless the Property is validly annexed to the Village and validly zoned and classified in accordance with and as contemplated by this Agreement at the times specified herein. Without Owner's written consent, no action should be taken by the Corporate Authorities to annex the Property to the Village unless this Agreement has been fully executed by all Parties.

ARTICLE III

ZONING OF THE PROPERTY

Immediately after the adoption of the Annexation Ordinance, the Village agrees to consider the adoption of an ordinance ("Rezoning Ordinance") amending the Village's zoning map to classify the Property into the ___ and ___ zoning districts. The Rezoning Ordinance shall not be effective until the recordation of the Annexation Ordinance.

Except as expressly authorized by Article V of this Agreement, no use, development, or construction shall be permitted on the Property unless and until Owner or any subsequent owner or developer of the Property has (1) applied for and obtained planned unit development approval for any proposed development or construction, which approval shall be subject to, and processed in accordance with, the Village's planned unit development standards and procedures contained in Village ordinances in effect at the time approval is requested and (2) entered into a development agreement with the Village to govern the use and development of the Property.

If no principal building has been constructed on the Property in accordance with the terms of this Agreement within ____ years after the effective date of this Agreement, then the Village shall be authorized to rezone the Property to the _____ zoning district.

ARTICLE IV

DEVELOPMENT AND USE OF THE PROPERTY

Subject to the provisions and procedures of this Agreement and the Zoning Code, the Property may be developed only with those uses that are specifically authorized pursuant to an ordinance approving a planned unit development for the Property, as required by Article III of this Agreement. Development of the Property shall be pursuant to and in accordance with the following:

1. This Agreement.
2. The Ordinance approving a planned unit development for the Property and all plans approved by that Ordinance.
3. The Zoning Code.
4. The Subdivision Code.
5. The Building Code.
6. All other applicable state or federal statutes and Village codes, ordinances, and regulations.

Unless otherwise provided in this Agreement, in the event of a conflict between or among any of the above plans or documents, the plan or document that provides the greatest control and protection for the Village, as determined by the Village Administrator, shall control. All of the above plans and documents shall be interpreted so that the duties and requirements imposed by any one of them are cumulative among all of them, unless otherwise provided in this Agreement.

ARTICLE V

USE OF THE PROPERTY PRIOR TO DEVELOPMENT

Notwithstanding any provision of this Annexation Agreement or the Village Code to the contrary, Owner shall be permitted to continue the existing agricultural uses on the Property as legal nonconforming uses until such time as those portions of the Property are developed.

ARTICLE VI

MUTUAL ASSISTANCE

The Parties shall do all things necessary or appropriate to carry out the terms and provisions of this Agreement and to aid and assist each other in carrying out the terms and objectives of this Agreement and the intentions of the Parties as reflected by these terms including without limitation the giving of notices, the holding of public hearings, the enactment by the Village of resolutions and ordinances, and the taking of such other actions as may be necessary to enable the Parties' compliance with the terms and provisions of this Agreement and as may be necessary to give effect to the terms and objectives of this Agreement and the intentions of the Parties as reflected by said terms. The Village shall not be required to do anything that is not reasonable or customarily done by the Village in similar circumstances, nor shall the Village be required to incur any liability or expenditure that is not reimbursed by Owner.

ARTICLE VII

REMEDIES

Upon a breach of this Agreement, any of the Parties, in any court of competent jurisdiction, by an action or proceeding at law or in equity, may secure the specific performance of the covenants and Agreements herein contained. No action taken by any Party hereto pursuant to the provisions of this Article VII or pursuant to the provisions of any other Article of this Agreement shall be deemed to constitute an election of remedies and all remedies set forth in this Agreement shall be cumulative and non-exclusive of any other remedy either set forth herein or available to any Party at law or in equity. In the event of a material breach of this Agreement, the parties agree that the Party alleged to be in breach shall have thirty (30) days after written notice of the breach to correct the same prior to the non-breaching Party's seeking of any remedy provided for herein (provided, however, that said thirty (30) day period shall be extended if the defaulting Party has initiated the cure of said default and is diligently proceeding to cure the same, not to exceed an additional sixty (60) days). If any of the Parties shall fail to perform any of its obligations hereunder, and the Party affected by such default shall have given written notice of such default to the defaulting Party, and such defaulting Party shall have failed to cure such default within thirty (30) days of such default notice (provided, however, that said thirty (30) day period shall be extended if the defaulting Party has initiated the cure of said default and is diligently proceeding to cure the same, not to exceed an additional sixty (60) days); then, in addition to any and all other remedies that may be available, either in law or equity, the Party affected by such default shall have the right (but not the obligation) to take such action as in its reasonable discretion and judgment shall be necessary to cure such default; provided, however, that the Owner agrees that it will not seek, and does not have the right to seek, to recover a judgment for monetary damages against the Village, or any of its elected or appointed officials, officers, employees, agents, representatives, engineers, or attorneys, on account of the negotiation, execution, or breach of this Agreement. The failure of the Parties to insist upon the strict and prompt performance of the terms, covenants, Agreements, and conditions herein contained, or any of them, upon any other Party imposed, shall not constitute or be construed as a waiver or relinquishment of any Party's right thereafter to enforce any such term, covenant, Agreement, or condition, but the same shall continue in full force and effect. If the performance of any covenant to be performed hereunder by any Party is delayed as a result of circumstances that are beyond the reasonable control of such Party (which circumstances may include acts of God, war, acts of civil disobedience, strikes, or similar acts), the time for such performance shall be extended by the amount of time of such delay.

ARTICLE VIII

TERM

This Agreement shall be binding upon the Parties and their respective successors and assigns for twenty (20) years, commencing as of the date hereof.

ARTICLE IX

MISCELLANEOUS

A. **Notices.** Any notice or communication required or permitted to be given under this Agreement shall be in writing and shall be delivered (i) personally, (ii) by a reputable overnight courier, (iii) by certified mail, return receipt requested, and deposited in the U.S. mail, postage prepaid, (iv) by facsimile, or (v) by electronic mail ("e-mail"). Facsimile notices shall be deemed valid only to the extent that they are (a) actually received by the individual to whom addressed and (b) followed by delivery of actual notice in the manner described in either (i), (ii), or (iii) above within three (3) business days thereafter at the appropriate address set forth below. E-mail notices shall be deemed valid only to the extent that they are (a) opened by the recipient on a business day at the address set forth below, and (b) followed by delivery of actual notice in the manner described in either (i), (ii), or (iii) above within three (3) business days thereafter at the appropriate address set forth below. Unless otherwise provided in this Agreement, notices shall be deemed received after the first to occur of (a) the date of actual receipt; or (b) the date that is one (1) business day after deposit with an overnight courier as evidenced by a receipt of deposit; or (c) the date that is three (3) business days after deposit in the U.S. mail, as evidenced by a return receipt. By notice complying with the requirements of this Section, each Party to this Agreement shall have the right to change the address or the addressee, or both, for all future notices and communications to them, but no notice of a change of addressee or address shall be effective until actually received.

[INSERT NOTICES]

B. **Entire Agreement**. This Agreement sets forth all Agreements, understandings, and covenants between and among the Parties. This

Agreement supersedes all prior Agreements, negotiations, and understandings, written and oral, and is a full integration of the entire Agreement of the Parties.

C. **Amendment**. This Agreement, and the exhibits attached hereto, may be amended only by the mutual consent of the Parties by adoption of an ordinance by the Village approving said amendment as provided by law and by the execution of said amendment by the Parties or their successors in interest.

D. **Severability**. If any provision, covenant, Agreement, or portion of this Agreement or its application to any person, entity, or Property is held invalid, such invalidity shall not affect the application or validity of any other provisions, covenants, Agreements, or portions of this Agreement, and to that end, all provisions, covenants, Agreements, and portions of this Agreement are declared to be severable.

E. **Survival**. The provisions contained herein shall survive the annexation and rezoning of the Property and shall not be merged or expunged by such action.

F. **Successors and Assigns**. This Agreement shall inure to the benefit of, and be binding upon, successors of Owner and its respective successors, grantees, lessees, and assigns, and upon successor Corporate Authorities of the Village and shall constitute a covenant running with the land.

G. **Time Is of the Essence**. Time of the essence of this Agreement and of each and every provision hereof.

H. **Rights Cumulative**. Unless expressly provided to the contrary in this Agreement, each and every one of the rights, remedies, and benefits provided by this Agreement shall be cumulative and shall not be exclusive of any other rights, remedies, and benefits allowed by law.

I. **Non-Waiver**. The Village shall be under no obligation to exercise any of the rights granted to it in this Agreement. The failure of the Village to exercise at any time any right granted to the Village shall not be deemed or construed to be a waiver of that right, nor shall the failure void or affect the Village's right to enforce that right or any other right.

J. **Consents**. Unless otherwise provided in this Agreement, whenever the consent, permission, authorization, approval, acknowledgment, or similar indication of assent of any Party to this Agreement, or of any duly authorized officer, employee, agent, or representative of any Party to this Agreement, is required in this Agreement, the consent, permission, authorization, approval, acknowledgement, or similar indication of assent shall be in writing.

K. **Governing Law**. This Agreement shall be governed by, and enforced in accordance with, the internal laws, but not the conflicts of laws rules, of the State of Illinois.

L. **Village Approval**. Wherever any approval or consent of the Village, or of any of its departments, officials, or employees, is called for under this Agreement, the same shall not be unreasonably withheld or delayed.

M. **Interpretation**. This Agreement shall be construed without regard to the identity of the Party who drafted the various provisions of this Agreement. Moreover, each and every provision of this Agreement shall be construed as though all parties to this Agreement participated equally in the drafting of this Agreement. As a result of the foregoing, any rule or construction that a document is to be construed against the drafting Party shall not be applicable to this Agreement.

N. **No Third-Party Beneficiaries**. No claim as a third-party beneficiary under this Agreement by any Person shall be made, or be valid, against the Village or the Owner.

O. **Recording**. After Owner has paid to the Village an amount sufficient to cover the cost of recording this Agreement, all necessary plats, the affidavit of service of notice as required by Section 7-1-1 of the Illinois Municipal Code, 65 ILCS 5/7-1-1, and the Annexation Ordinance, the Village shall promptly cause this Agreement to be recorded in the office of the Recorder of _____ County.

P. **Authority to Execute**. The Village hereby warrants and represents to Owner that the persons executing this Agreement on its behalf have been properly authorized to do so by the Corporate Authorities. Owner hereby warrants and represents to the Village (i) that it is the record and beneficial owner of fee simple title to the Property, (ii) that no other Person has any legal, beneficial, contractual, or security interest in the Property, (iii) that it has the full and complete right, power, and authority to enter into this Agreement, to agree to the terms, provisions, and conditions set forth in this Agreement, and to bind the Property as set forth in this Agreement, (iv) that all legal actions needed to authorize the execution, delivery, and performance of this Agreement have been taken, and (v) that neither the execution of this Agreement nor the performance of the obligations assumed by Owner will (a) result in a breach or default under any agreement to which Owner is a party or to which it or the Property is bound or (b) violate any statute, law, restriction, court order, or agreement to which Owner or the Property are subject.

IN WITNESS WHEREOF, the parties hereto have executed this Agreement on the date first above written and, by so executing, each of the Parties warrants that it possesses full right and authority to enter in to this Agreement.

SIGNATURE BLOCKS

APPENDIX 3

Model Annexation and Development Agreement (Residential)

ANNEXATION, SUBDIVISION, AND DEVELOPMENT AGREEMENT

THIS ANNEXATION AND DEVELOPMENT AGREEMENT ("Agreement") is dated as of the ____ day of ________, _____ ("Effective Date"), and is by and between the **VILLAGE OF** __________, an Illinois municipal corporation ("Village") and ________________ ("Owner").

IN CONSIDERATION OF the recitals and the mutual covenants and agreements set forth in this Agreement, the parties agree as follows:

SECTION 1. RECITALS.*

WHEREAS, the Village and Owner desire to enter into this annexation and development agreement ("Annexation Agreement" or "Agreement") to set forth the terms and conditions for annexation, zoning, subdivision, development, and use of the property consisting of approximately _____ acres ("Property"), located generally at ______________, and legally described on **Exhibit A** attached to this Agreement; and

*All defined terms initially appear in bold and italics and thereafter as capitalized words and phrases throughout this Agreement. They shall have the meanings set forth in the preamble, in Section 2, and elsewhere in this Agreement.

WHEREAS, as of the Effective Date, the Owner is the owner of record of the Property; and

WHEREAS, [there are no electors residing within the Property] [at least 51% of the electors residing within the Property join in the Annexation Petition]; and

WHEREAS, the Owner desires and proposes to have the Property annexed to the Village pursuant to and in accordance with Section 7-1-8 of the Illinois Municipal Code, 65 ILCS 5/7-1-8, and this Agreement; and

WHEREAS, the Property is contiguous to the corporate limits of the Village and is not within the corporate limits of any municipality; and

WHEREAS, the Owner has filed a plat of annexation and an annexation petition with the Village requesting that the Village annex the Property pursuant to and in accordance with Section 7-1-8 of the Illinois Municipal Code, 65 ILCS 5/7-1-8, and this Agreement; and

WHEREAS, the Owner has also presented to the Village a plan for development of the Property, which development plan is shown in more detail on the Preliminary Plans attached as **Exhibit B**; and

WHEREAS, the Owner has requested that the Village approve a rezoning to the ______ zoning district and grant a special use permit for a planned unit development to allow the development of [DESCRIBE DEVELOPMENT], subject to the development standards, departures, and conditions as set forth in this Agreement; and

WHEREAS, upon annexation of the Property, the Owner desires to have the Property rezoned into the zoning district described above and to have the Village approve the Preliminary Planned Unit Development Plan, Preliminary Engineering Plans, and Preliminary Plat of Subdivision; and

WHEREAS, all notices, publications, procedures, public hearings and other matters required for the consideration and approval of this Agreement have been made, given, held, and performed by the Village as required by 65 ILCS 5/11-15.1-1 *et seq.* and the Zoning Enabling Act, 65 ILCS 5/11-13-1 *et seq.*; and

WHEREAS, the proposed Agreement was submitted pursuant to the applicable provisions of the Illinois Municipal Code, to the Corporate Authorities of the Village (hereinafter referred to as the "Corporate Authorities") and a public hearing was held on _________, ______ with an opportunity for public comment, pursuant to proper notice, as provided by statute; and

WHEREAS, the Corporate Authorities of the Village have considered this Agreement and determined that this Agreement is in the best interests of the Village and its residents; and

WHEREAS, by a favorable vote of two-thirds of the Corporate Authorities of the Village then holding office, the Village has considered the question of the Agreement and has adopted an ordinance approving this Agreement and authorizing execution thereof; and

WHEREAS, upon the adoption of this Agreement, the Corporate Authorities agree to consider the zoning and development approvals for the Property; and

WHEREAS, the Village and Owner, consistent with Illinois law, have agreed to the terms and conditions set forth in this Agreement as evidenced by the signatures affixed hereto.

SECTION 2. DEFINITIONS; RULES OF CONSTRUCTION.

A. Definitions. Whenever used in this Agreement, the following terms shall have the following meanings unless a different meaning is required by the context:

"Annexation Petition": The petition, executed by the Owner as the owner of the Property [and by at least 51% of the electors residing within the territory of the Property], and dated as of ______________, seeking annexation of the Property to the Village. The original is on file with the Village Clerk.

"Annexation Plat": The annexation plat prepared by ______________, consisting of ___ sheets, with latest revision date of ______________, a copy of which is attached to this Agreement as **Exhibit C**.

"Building Code": The Village of ______ building regulations, as they have been and may in the future be amended.

"Corporate Authorities": The President and Board of Trustees of the Village.

"Final Engineering Plan": The engineering plan that receives the approval of the Village Engineer pursuant to Section 5.B of this Agreement and in accordance with the Requirements of Law. After that approval, the Final Engineering Plan shall, automatically and without further action by the Corporate Authorities, be deemed to be incorporated in, and made a part of, this Agreement and shall, for all purposes in this Agreement, supersede the Preliminary Engineering Plan.

"Final Landscaping Plan": The landscaping plan that receives the approval of the Village Engineer pursuant to Section 5.B of this Agreement and in accordance with the Requirements of Law. After that approval, the Final Landscaping Plan shall, automatically and without further action by the Corporate Authorities, be deemed to be incorporated in, and made a part of, this Agreement and shall, for all purposes in this Agreement, supersede the Preliminary Landscaping Plan.

"Final PUD Plans": The final planned unit development plans that receive the approval of the Corporate Authorities pursuant to Section 5.B of this Agreement and in accordance with the Requirements of Law. After that approval, the Final PUD Plans shall, automatically and without further action by the Corporate Authorities, be deemed to be incorporated in, and made a part of, this Agreement and shall, for all purposes in this Agreement, supersede the Preliminary Planned Unit Development Plan.

"Final Subdivision Plat": The final subdivision plat that receives the approval of the Corporate Authorities pursuant to Section 5.B of this Agreement and in accordance with the Requirements of Law. After that approval, the Final Subdivision Plat shall, automatically and without further action by the Corporate Authorities, be deemed to be incorporated in, and made a part of, this Agreement and shall, for all purposes in this Agreement, supersede the Preliminary Subdivision Plat.

"Force Majeure": Strikes, lockouts, acts of God, or other factors beyond a party's reasonable control and reasonable ability to remedy; provided, however, that Force Majeure shall not include delays caused by weather conditions, unless those conditions are unusually severe or abnormal considering the time of year and the particular location of the Property.

"Improvements": All of the public and private improvements and facilities necessary to serve the Property, including without limitation the improvements shown on the Preliminary Subdivision Plat or the Final Subdivision Plat and the Preliminary Engineering Plan or the Final Engineering Plan, the improvements set forth on the list attached to this Agreement as **Exhibit G**, all other storm water detention and retention facilities, water mains, storm sewers, sanitary sewers, streets, lighting, sidewalks, parkways, rough and final grading, trees, sod, seeding, and other landscaping, and all other improvements required pursuant to this Agreement, the Preliminary Subdivision Plat or the Final Subdivision Plat, the Preliminary Engineering Plan or the Final Engineering Plan, the Preliminary Landscaping Plan or the Final Landscaping Plan, and the Requirements of Law.

"Person": Any corporation, partnership, individual, joint venture, trust, estate, association, business, enterprise, proprietorship, or other legal entity of any kind, either public or private, and any legal successor, agent, representative, or authorized assign of the above.

"Preliminary Engineering Plan": The preliminary engineering plan prepared by ____________, consisting of ______ sheets, with latest revision date of ____________, which plan has been approved by the Village Engineer, a copy of which is attached to this Agreement as **Exhibit B.**

"Preliminary Landscaping Plan": The preliminary landscaping plan prepared by ____________, consisting of ______ sheets, with latest revision date of ____________, a copy of which is attached to this Agreement as **Exhibit B.**

"Preliminary Planned Unit Development Plan": The preliminary planned unit development plan of the Property prepared by __________, consisting of ______ sheets, with latest revision date of ____________, a copy of which is attached to this Agreement as **Exhibit B.**

"Preliminary Subdivision Plat": The preliminary subdivision plat prepared by _______, consisting of ______ sheets, with latest revision date of ____________, a copy of which is attached to this Agreement as **Exhibit B.**

"Property": The tract of land consisting of approximately ___ acres of territory, generally located at the ________ corner of __________ in unincorporated __________ County, and legally described in **Exhibit A** to this Agreement.

"Requirements of Law": All applicable federal, state, and local laws, statutes, codes, ordinances, resolutions, orders, rules, and regulations.

"Subdivision Code": The Village of __________ subdivision regulations, as they have been and may in the future be amended.

"Zoning Code": The Village of __________ zoning ordinances, as they have been and may in the future be amended.

B. Rules of Construction.

1. Grammatical Usage and Construction. In construing this Agreement, pronouns include all genders, and the plural includes the singular and vice versa.
2. Headings. The headings, titles, and captions in this Agreement have been inserted only for convenience and in no way define, limit, extend, or describe the scope or intent of this Agreement.
3. Calendar Days. Unless otherwise provided in this Agreement, any reference in this Agreement to "day" or "days" shall mean calendar

days and not business days. If the date for giving of any notice required to be given, or the performance of any obligation, under this Agreement falls on a Saturday, Sunday, or federal holiday, then the notice or obligation may be given or performed on the next business day after that Saturday, Sunday, or federal holiday.

SECTION 3. ANNEXATION OF THE PROPERTY.

A. Adoption of Annexation Ordinance. Immediately after the execution of this Agreement, the Corporate Authorities agree to approve an ordinance ("Annexation Ordinance") in substantially the form of **Exhibit D** attached to this Agreement annexing the Property (and any contiguous rights-of-way) to the Village pursuant to Section 7-1-8 of the Illinois Municipal Code, 65 ILCS 5/7-1-8; provided, however, that the Annexation Ordinance will not be effective unless the following conditions are satisfied:

1. The Owner has paid to the Village the amounts due pursuant to Section 11 of this Agreement.
2. The Owner has paid to the Village an amount sufficient to cover the cost of recording this Agreement, all necessary plats, the affidavit of service of notice as required by Section 7-1-1 of the Illinois Municipal Code, 65 ILCS 5/7-1-1, and the Annexation Ordinance.

After the Annexation Ordinance becomes effective, the Village will record the Annexation Ordinance in the office of the Recorder of __________ County.

B. Effective Date of Annexation. The annexation of the Property (and any contiguous rights-of-way) will occur on, but not before, the date of recordation of the Annexation Ordinance, all necessary plats, and the affidavit of service of notice as required by Section 7-1-1 of the Illinois Municipal Code, 65 ILCS 5/7-1-1.

SECTION 4. ZONING OF THE PROPERTY.

A. Rezoning. Immediately after the adoption of the Annexation Ordinance, the Village agrees to adopt an ordinance, substantially in the form of **Exhibit E** to this Agreement ("Rezoning Ordinance"), amending the Village's zoning map to classify the Property into the ______ zoning district as generally depicted on the Preliminary Plans. The Rezoning Ordinance will not be effective until the recordation of the Annexation Ordinance in accordance with Section 3.A of this Agreement.

B. PUD. Immediately after the approval of this Agreement, the Village agrees to take all steps necessary to adopt a valid and binding ordinance substantially in the form of **Exhibit F** ("PUD Ordinance"), to grant a special use permit for a planned unit development and approving the Preliminary Plans for the Property. The PUD Ordinance will not be effective until the recordation of the Annexation Ordinance in accordance with Section 3.A of this Agreement.

SECTION 5. APPROVAL OF SUBDIVISION, ENGINEERING, AND LANDSCAPING PLANS/PLATS.

A. Preliminary Subdivision, Preliminary Planned Unit Development, Preliminary Landscaping, and Preliminary Engineering Plans. Immediately after the adoption of the Rezoning Ordinance, the Village agrees to approve the Preliminary Subdivision Plat, Preliminary Planned Unit Development Plan, Preliminary Landscape Plan, and the Preliminary Engineering Plan ("Preliminary Plans"), which Preliminary Plans are attached to this Agreement as **Exhibit B**. The Owner acknowledges and agrees that no construction, improvement, or development of any kind will be permitted on any portion of the Property until the Final Engineering Plan, the Final Landscaping Plan, Final PUD Plans, and the Final Subdivision Plat are approved by the Village in accordance with the Subdivision Code and this Agreement.

B. Final Plans. Prior to the development of the Property and within two years after the effective date of the PUD Ordinance, which time period may be extended by the Village Board by Resolution and will not require an amendment to the Annexation Agreement, the Owner will prepare and submit to the Village a Final PUD Plans, Final Subdivision Plat, Final Landscaping Plans, and Final Engineering Plans (collectively, "Final Plans") all prepared in substantial conformity with the Preliminary Plans. The Village acknowledges and agrees that the Final PUD Plans and the Final Subdivision Plat may be incorporated into one and the same document.

1. Approval if Substantially Conform to General Development Plans. After the Final Plans have been submitted to the Village, the Village will cause the same to be promptly reviewed and shall cause such meetings to be conducted as may be necessary for approval of the Final PUD Plans and Final Subdivision Plat. The approval of the Final PUD Plans and Final Subdivision Plat will require a meeting before the Plan Commission and Board of Trustees, but does not require

a public hearing before the Plan Commission so long as the Final PUD Plans and Final Subdivision Plat substantially conform to the Preliminary Plans. Following the required review and meetings, the Village Board agrees to promptly adopt an ordinance approving the Final PUD Plans and Final Subdivision Plat and directing all required Village signatures and certifications to be affixed to the Final PUD Plans and Final Subdivision Plat provided that the Final PUD Plans and Final Subdivision Plat are in substantial conformance with the Preliminary Plans (modifications approved by the Village Engineer to accommodate changes required to obtain required permits for the sewer improvements, wetlands, water facilities, stormwater detention and drainage improvements, and the roadway improvements shall not be deemed to impact the determination of substantial conformance). However, no such signatures and certifications will be affixed by the Village until the Owner has (A) obtained all other approvals, sworn statements, signatures, and certifications required for the Final PUD Plans and Final Subdivision Plat; (B) paid the Village its legal, engineering, consulting, and administrative fees, costs, and expenses; and (C) deposited with the Village Clerk a sufficient sum, in current funds, to reimburse the Village for the actual cost of recording the Final PUD Plans and Final Subdivision Plat.

2. Recordation. After final approval, execution, and certification of the Final PUD Plans and Final Subdivision Plat by the Village, the Village will record the Final Subdivision Plat with the Lake County Recorder of Deeds.

C. Changes in the Final Plans during Development.

1. Minor Adjustments. During the construction and development of the Property, the Village Administrator in consultation with the Village Engineer may authorize minor adjustments to any of the Final Plans when the adjustments are necessary in light of technical or engineering considerations. The determination as to whether an adjustment is a minor adjustment or major adjustment will be in the sole discretion of the Village Administrator.
2. Major Adjustments. Any major adjustment to any of the Final Plans not specifically listed in or approved pursuant to this Agreement shall be considered to be a major adjustment and will be granted only after application to, and approval by, the Corporate Authorities

by amendment to the approvals granted in this Agreement and the Zoning and Development Approval Ordinance.

SECTION 6. USE AND DEVELOPMENT OF THE PROPERTY.

A. Use Restrictions. Subject to the provisions and procedures of this Development Agreement and the Zoning Code, the Property may be developed with the uses listed in the PUD Ordinance.

B. General Restrictions. Subject to the particular terms for development set forth in Section 6.D of this Agreement, and the restrictive covenants set forth in Section 9 of this Agreement, development of the Property, except for minor alterations due to final engineering and site work approved by the Village Engineer, as appropriate, will be pursuant to and in accordance with the following:

1. This Agreement.
2. The Preliminary Plans.
3. The Final PUD Plans.
4. The Final Subdivision Plat.
5. The Final Engineering Plan.
6. The Final Landscaping Plan.
7. The Zoning Code.
8. The Subdivision Code.
9. The Building Code.
10. The other Requirements of Law.

Unless otherwise provided in this Agreement, in the event of a conflict between or among any of the above plans or documents, the plan or document that provides the greatest control and protection for the Village, as determined by the Village Administrator, will control. All of the above plans and documents are to be interpreted so that the duties and requirements imposed by any one of them are cumulative among all of them, unless otherwise provided in this Agreement.

C. Easements. The owner agrees to grant such utility and enforcement easements to the Village and other governmental bodies and utility services over, on, and across the Property for the purposes of enforcing applicable laws, making repairs, installing and servicing utilities, and providing public and emergency services.

D. Particular Terms for Development. Notwithstanding any use or development right that may be applicable or available to the Property pursuant to the Zoning Code or any other Requirement of Law, the Property will be used and developed only as follows: [add special restrictions].

E. Damage to Public Property. The Owner must maintain the Property and all streets, sidewalks, and other public property in and adjacent to the Property in a good and clean condition at all times during development of the Property and construction of the Improvements. Further, the Owner shall promptly clean all mud, dirt, or debris deposited on any street, sidewalk, or other public property in or adjacent to the Property by the Owner or any agent of or contractor hired by, or on behalf of, the Owner, and shall repair any damage that may be caused by the activities of the Owner or any agent of or contractor hired by, or on behalf of, the Owner. If, within one hour after the Village gives the Owner notice to clean all mud, dirt, or debris deposited on any street, sidewalk, or other public property in or adjacent to the Property by the Owner or any agent of or contractor hired by, or on behalf of, the Owner, the Owner neglects to clean, or undertake with due diligence to clean, the affected public property, then the Village shall be entitled to clean, either with its own forces or with contract forces, the affected public property and to recover from the Owner the costs incurred in performing the cleaning.

SECTION 7. IMPROVEMENTS.

A. Owner Duty to Construct Improvements. In connection with the development of the Property, the Owner shall, at its sole cost and expense, design, construct, and install all of the Improvements on and serving the Property that are identified on the Preliminary Plans and in the approved Final Engineering Plans and Final PUD Plans.

B. Standards Applicable to Improvements.

1. General Standards. All Improvements must be designed and constructed pursuant to, and in accordance with, the Final Engineering Plan, the Final Landscaping Plan, and the Subdivision Code, and to the satisfaction of the Village Engineer. All work performed on the Improvements must be conducted in a good and workmanlike manner and in accordance with the schedule established in Section 7.C of this Agreement. All materials used for construction of the Improvements must be new and of first-rate quality.
2. Special Standards.
   i. Landscaping. Landscaping on the Property must be installed pursuant to the Final Landscape Plans, which Plans must be in

substantial conformance with the Preliminary Landscape Plans included as part of the Preliminary Plans and will be subject to Village review and approval. The Owner will be required to maintain the landscaping on the Property in accordance with good arboricultural and landscaping practices and as detailed in the Declaration of Covenants. If, for whatever reason, any of the plantings depicted on any approved landscaping plan are removed, destroyed, or fail to survive two years following (i) the issuance of a certificate of occupancy for the improvements on a particular lot or (ii) initial installation of such plantings, whichever is later, the Owner must, not later than the next planting season occurring at least 30 days after the Owner receives notice from the Village, replace such plantings with substitute plantings that substantially conform to the size and type of the original plantings, as depicted on the Final Landscape Plans. For purposes of this Subsection, a "planting season" shall be either the period between 15 April and 15 June or the period between 1 September and 1 November in any calendar year.

ii. Screening along Boundaries. The Owner must install [**fence/berm/other screening**] along the [**describe boundary**] of the Property. The height, location, and materials for the screening will be subject to the review and approval of the Village Administrator.
iii. Stormwater Detention. The Owner must design and install the stormwater detention facilities for the Property, which stormwater detention facilities will be constructed and completed in accordance with the Final Engineering Plans.
iv. Sanitary Sewer. Sanitary sewer service must be provided to the Property by [describe service], which sanitary sewer facilities will be constructed and completed in accordance with the Final Engineering Plans.
v. Water. Water service must be provided to the Property [describe service]. The extensions and upgrades to the water system will be constructed and completed in accordance with the Final Engineering Plans.
vi. Roadway Improvements. All roads within the Property, as well as access improvements to and from the Property, must be constructed and completed in accordance with the Final

Engineering Plans. The Owner must also construct and complete any necessary off-site roadway improvements in accordance with the Final Engineering Plans.

vii. Sidewalks and Bike Path. The Owner must construct and complete, at its sole cost and expense, all sidewalks within the Property in the locations depicted on the Preliminary Plans, which sidewalks must be constructed and completed in accordance with the Final Engineering Plans.

viii. Dumpsters. All dumpsters and other trash enclosures must be installed, maintained, and screened in accordance with Village ordinances and regulations.

ix. Lighting. Final exterior lighting plans must be included in and approved as part of the Final Engineering Plans.

x. Signage. All signage will be subject to the Village's sign regulations. Owner must submit to the Village for its review and approval, which approval will not be unreasonably withheld, a comprehensive sign package including all proposed signage for the Property.

xi. Parking. Parking areas for the Property must be installed and maintained on the Property substantially in accordance with the Preliminary Plans and the Final Engineering Plans, and must comply with the parking requirements for the ____ zoning district.

3. Contract Terms; Prosecution of the Work. The Owner and all of its contractors must prosecute the work diligently, continuously, in full compliance with, and as required by or pursuant to, this Agreement, until the work is properly completed. Each Owner's contract with a contractor must provide that the Owner may take over and prosecute the work if the contractor fails to do so in a timely and proper manner.

4. Engineering Services. The Owner must provide, at its sole cost and expense, all engineering services for the design and construction of the Improvements, including without limitation full inspection services of a professional engineer responsible for overseeing the construction of the Improvements. The Owner must promptly provide the Village with the name of the resident engineer and a telephone number or numbers at which the engineer can be reached at all times.

5. Village Inspections and Approvals. Village representatives have the full right, permission, and authority to inspect and approve all work on the Improvements at all times.
6. Other Approvals. If the construction and installation of any Improvement require the consent, permission, or approval of any Person, then the Owner must take all steps required to obtain the required consent, permission, or approval. No work requiring the consent, permission, or approval of any Person may commence without that prior consent, permission, or approval.

C. Schedule for Completion of Improvements. All Improvements must be completed and made ready for inspection, approval, and any required acceptance by the Village pursuant to the construction schedule approved by the Village Engineer as part of the Final Engineering Plan. The Owner will be allowed extensions of time beyond the completion dates set forth in the construction schedule only for delay caused by Force Majeure. The Owner must, within two days after any unavoidable delay commences and again within two days after the delay terminates, give notice to the Village for its review and approval of the delay, the cause for the delay, the period or anticipated period of the delay, and the steps taken by the Owner to mitigate the effects of the delay. Any failure of the Owner to give the required notice shall be deemed a waiver of any right to an extension of time for any the delay.

D. Final Inspections and Approvals. When the Owner determines that an Improvement has been properly completed, the Owner must request final inspection, approval, and, as appropriate, acceptance of the Improvement by the Village. The notice and request must comply with all requirements of the Subdivision Code and must be given sufficiently in advance to allow the Village time to inspect the Improvement and to prepare a punch list of items requiring repair or correction and to allow the Owner time to make all required repairs and corrections prior to the scheduled completion date. The Owner must promptly make all necessary repairs and corrections as specified on the punch list. The Village will not be required to approve or accept any Improvement until all of the Improvements, including without limitation all punch list items, have been fully and properly completed.

E. Dedication and Acceptance of Specified Improvements. The Owner must dedicate to the Village the Improvements set forth in the schedule attached to this Agreement as **Exhibit G**. Nothing whatsoever will constitute an acceptance by the Village of any Improvement except only express acceptance by the Village in compliance with the requirements of the Subdivision Code. Prior to acceptance of the Improvements to be accepted by the Village, the Owner must execute, or cause to be executed, all documents that the Village requests to transfer ownership of the Improvements to, and to evidence ownership of the Improvements by, the Village, free and clear of all liens, claims, encumbrances, and restrictions unless otherwise approved by the Village. The documents transferring ownership of the Improvements to, and to evidence ownership of the Improvements by, the Village will be acceptable in form and substance to the Village Attorney. Owner must, simultaneously, grant, or cause to be granted, to the Village all insured easements or other property rights as the Village may require to install, operate, maintain, service, repair, and replace the Improvements that have not previously been granted to the Village, free and clear of all liens, claims, encumbrances, and restrictions, unless otherwise approved by the Village.

F. Owner's Guaranty and Maintenance of Improvements. The Owner hereby guarantees the prompt and satisfactory correction of all defects and deficiencies in the Improvements that occur or become evident within two years after approval and any required acceptance of the Improvements by the Village pursuant to this Agreement. If any defect or deficiency occurs or becomes evident during the two-year period, then the Owner must, after 10 days' prior written notice from the Village (subject to Force Majeure), correct it or cause it to be corrected. In the event any Improvement is repaired or replaced pursuant to the demand of the Village, the Guaranty provided by this Section 7.F will be extended, as to the repair or replacement, for two full years from the date of the repair or replacement. If an owners' association is required to be created pursuant to a declaration meeting the requirements of Section 9 of this Agreement, then, unless the owners' association has assumed all responsibility for maintenance, and, in all events, for a period of at least two years after Village approval, the Owner must, at its sole cost and expense, maintain, without any modification, except as specifically approved by the Village Engineer, in a first-rate condition, at all times, the Improvements. In the event the Village Engineer determines, in the Village Engineer's sole and absolute discretion, that the Owner is not adequately maintaining, or has not adequately maintained, any Improvement, the Village may, after 10 days' prior written notice to the Owner, enter on any or all of the Property for the purpose of performing maintenance work on and to any affected Improvement. In the event that the Village causes to be performed any work pursuant to this Section 7.F the Village has the right to draw from the performance securities deposited pursuant to Section 12 of this Agreement, or the right to demand immediate payment directly from the Owner, based on costs actually incurred or on the Village's reasonable estimates of costs to be incurred, an amount of money sufficient to defray the entire costs of the work, including without limitation legal fees and administrative expenses. The Owner must, after demand by the Village, pay the required amount to the Village.

G. Issuance of Permits and Certificates.

1. Performance Security. The Village is not required to issue any permits in connection with any Improvements or other development activities relating to the Property until the Owner has delivered to the Village the performance securities required under Section 12 of this Development Agreement.
2. Right to Withhold Permits and Certificates. The Village has the absolute right to withhold any building permit or certificate of occupancy at any time the Owner is in breach of the terms of this Agreement, subject to the Village providing written notice of the violation and providing the Owner with an opportunity for the Owner to cure the violation within 30 days of the notice or such longer period as may be provided in this agreement.
3. Completion of Improvements. The Village has no obligation to issue certificates of occupancy for any buildings or structures located on the Property until the applicable Improvements are completed by the Owner in accordance with the schedule approved by the Village Engineer as referenced in Section 9.C of this Agreement or until other arrangements satisfactory to the Village Engineer, in the Engineer's reasonable discretion, shall have been made. The issuance of any building permit or certificate of occupancy by the Village at any time prior to completion of all the Improvements and approval and, where appropriate, acceptance thereof by the Village will not confer on the Owner any right or entitlement to any other building permit or certificate of occupancy.

H. Abandonment of Proposed Development. Subject to Force Majeure, if the Owner fails to diligently pursue all construction as required in, or permitted by, this Agreement to completion within the time period prescribed in the building permit or permits issued by the Village for such construction, and if the building permit or permits are not renewed within three months after the expiration thereof, the Owner must, within 60 days after notice from the Village, remove any partially constructed or partially completed Improvements from the Property and take any other actions necessary in order to secure and/or and make safe the Property. In the event the Owner fails or refuses to remove the Improvements or secure or make safe the Property, as required, the Village has, and is hereby granted, in addition to all other rights afforded to the Village in this Agreement and by law, the right, at its option, to secure and/or make safe the Property, including, if necessary, demolishing and/or removing any unsafe Improvements, and the Village has the right to apply any applicable security or otherwise charge the Owner for an amount sufficient to defray the entire cost of the work, including reasonable legal and administrative costs. If the amount charged is not paid by the Owner within 30 days following a demand in writing by the Village for payment, the charge, together with interest and costs of collection (including reasonable attorneys' fees), will become a lien against the Property, and the Village has the right to collect the charge, with interest and costs, and to enforce the lien in the same manner as mortgage foreclosure proceedings.

SECTION 8. CONSTRUCTION TRAFFIC AND PARKING; STREETS.

A. Designated Traffic Routes. The Village may designate routes of access to the Property for construction traffic to protect pedestrians and to minimize disruption of traffic and damage to paved street surfaces; provided, however, that the designated routes shall not unduly hinder or obstruct direct and efficient access to the Property for construction traffic. The Owner must keep all routes used for construction traffic free and clear of mud, dirt, debris, obstructions, and hazards and shall repair all damage caused by the construction traffic. The Village also may designate from time to time temporary construction haul roads on and to the Property that will be located and constructed in a manner acceptable to the Village Engineer.

B. Parking. All construction vehicles, including passenger vehicles, and construction equipment must be parked within the Property or in areas designated by the Village.

C. Streets.

1. Owner Requirement. All streets designated to be dedicated to the Village must be constructed and dedicated to the Village in accordance with this Agreement.
2. Protection of Final Surface Course. Except with the prior express consent of the Village, no construction traffic is permitted to utilize any street to be dedicated to the Village after installation of the final surface course of that street. If the Owner uses the street for construction traffic, the Owner must keep the street free and clear of mud, dirt, debris, obstructions, and hazards and shall, after the use is no longer necessary, restore and repair that street to the standards established in the Subdivision Code.
3. Dedication and Acceptance. No street will be deemed to be accepted by the Village, and the Village shall have no obligation or liability in respect of the street, until the street has been completed, approved, and accepted by the Village in accordance with Section 7.E of this Agreement. The Owner acknowledges and agrees that (a) the Village will not be obligated to accept any street until all construction traffic on the street has ceased and the street has been completed and, if necessary, restored and repaired as required by this Agreement and (b) the Village will not be obligated to keep any street cleared, plowed, or otherwise maintained until the street has been completed, approved, and accepted by the Village in accordance with this Agreement, or until other arrangements satisfactory to the Village Engineer, in the Village Engineer's sole and absolute discretion, shall have been made.

SECTION 9. DECLARATION OF COVENANTS.

Concurrent with the recordation of the Final Subdivision Plat, a declaration of covenants, acceptable in form and substance to the Village Attorney, must be recorded against the Property. The declaration must be approved by the Corporate Authorities prior to becoming effective and shall provide, at a minimum, for the following:

A. The protection and maintenance (including prohibitions on the removal or relocation of such improvements unless otherwise approved by the Village), by the property owners, in perpetuity, of the following private

Improvements and common areas on the Property: [describe improvements]; and

B. The right (but not the obligation) of the Village to take action to cure any failure of the property owners to properly maintain and repair the common areas and private Improvements or to otherwise fail to abide by the provisions of the declaration or declarations following reasonable notice and cure periods and the right of the Village to be reimbursed for all costs and expenses incurred by the Village related thereto, including without limitation the right of the Village to perfect a lien to recover such costs and expenses against any or all of the parcels of property within the Property, all subject to notice and cure periods reasonably acceptable to the parties.

SECTION 10. RECAPTURES.

A. Recapture Fees. The Owner must pay all costs, including interest if any, due from the Owner as a benefited property owner pursuant to the recapture agreements and ordinances described in the schedule attached to this Agreement as **Exhibit H** and pursuant to all other recapture agreements and ordinances previously entered into or adopted by the Village pursuant to Section 9-5-1 of the Illinois Municipal Code. In addition, if the Village at any time in the future enters into a recapture agreement or adopts a recapture ordinance pursuant to Section 9-5-1 in which the Owner is determined to be a benefited property owner, then the Owner does hereby unconditionally agree to pay its proportionate share of the costs, including interest if any, set forth in that agreement or ordinance.

B. Right to Recapture Costs of Oversized Improvements [IF APPLICABLE]. The Village hereby finds and agrees that, as a result of the construction of [describe oversized improvements] by the Owner as required by this Agreement ("Recapture Improvement[s]"), substantial benefit will be provided to certain properties ("Benefited Properties") that lie outside the Property. The Village further finds that the Property and the Benefited Properties will be benefited by the Recapture Improvement[s] in proportion to their respective [total areas] [frontages along ________] [projected water demands] [projected sewage flows]. Within 60 days following completion and acceptance of the Recapture Improvement[s] pursuant to Sections 7.D and 7.E of this Agreement, the Village agrees to adopt an ordinance substantially in the form attached to this Agreement as **Exhibit I** to establish such charges as are necessary to allow the Owner to recover from each Benefited Property its proportionate share of the actual cost of construction of the Recapture Improvement[s] ("Recapture Ordinance"), calculated, for each Benefited Property, on the basis of [square feet of area] [lineal feet of frontage] [projected average daily water demand] [projected average daily sewage flow] ("Recapture Fee"). The Owner shall, not later than the time it gives the notice of completion and request for acceptance required pursuant to Section 7.D of this Agreement, submit to the Village documentation of the actual cost of construction of the Recapture Improvement[s] for review and approval by the Village and for the Village's use in preparation of the Recapture Ordinance. The Village will pay to the Owner, within 30 days after collection, the amount of any Recapture Fee collected. The adoption of the Recapture Ordinance and the payment to the Owner of any Recapture Fees collected by Village shall be the only responsibilities of the Village with respect to the collection or payment of any Recapture Fee, and the Village has no other or further obligation to the Owner with respect to the collection or payment of any Recapture Fee. The Village will, at the Owner's expense, cause a copy of this Agreement to be recorded in the office of the Recorder of __________ County as notice to the owners of the Benefited Properties and required by Section 9-5-2 of the Illinois Municipal Code.

SECTION 11. FEES, DEDICATIONS, DONATIONS, AND CONTRIBUTIONS.

A. Annexation Fee. The Owner must pay to the Village, in addition to all other specific sums required to be paid pursuant to this Agreement or the Requirements of Law, the total sum of ______________ Dollars ($______________) to be used at the sole and absolute discretion of the Village for the general purposes of the Village.

B. Negotiation and Review Fees. In addition to all other costs, payments, fees, charges, contributions, or dedications required by this Agreement or by the Requirements of Law, the Owner must pay to the Village, immediately after presentation of a written demand or demands for payment, all legal, engineering, and other consulting or administrative fees, costs, and expenses incurred or accrued in connection with the review and processing of plans for the development of the Property and in connection with the negotiation, preparation, consideration, and review of this Agreement. Payment of all fees, costs, and expenses for which demand has been made, but payment has not been received, by the Village prior to execution of this Agreement, must be made by a certified or cashier's check contemporaneous with the execution of this Agreement by the Village. Further, the Owner agrees that it will continue to be liable for and to pay, immediately after presentation of a written demand or demands for payment, the fees, costs and expenses incurred in connection with any applications, documents, or proposals, whether formal or informal, of whatever kind submitted by the Owner during the term of this Agreement in connection with the use and development of the Property. Further, the Owner agrees that it shall be liable for and will pay after demand all fees, costs, and expenses incurred by the Village for publications and recordings required in connection with the above matters.

C. Recapture Fees. The Owner must pay to the Village the amounts due pursuant to Section 10.A of this Agreement.

D. Other Village Fees. In addition to all other costs, payments, fees, charges, contributions, or dedications required by this Agreement, the Owner must pay to the Village all application, inspection, and permit fees, all water and sewer general and special connection fees, tap-on fees, charges, and contributions, and all other fees, charges, and contributions pursuant to the Requirements of Law.

E. Dedications, Donations, and Contributions to the Village. The Owner must dedicate sites, easements, and rights-of-way as required by this Agreement, including without limitation [add description of any dedication, donation, or contribution not otherwise required by this Agreement].

F. Impact Fees for Residential Development. Any residential development of the Property must be in compliance with the provisions of the Village Code requiring payment of impact fees applicable at the time of development.

SECTION 12. PERFORMANCE SECURITY.

A. Performance and Payment Letter of Credit. As security to the Village for the performance by the Owner of the Owner's obligations (1) to construct and complete the Improvements pursuant to and in accordance with this Agreement, (2) to pay all Village costs, fees, and charges due from the Owner pursuant to this Agreement, (3) to maintain and repair streets, sidewalks, and other public property pursuant to this Agreement, and (4) to otherwise faithfully perform its undertakings pursuant to this Agreement, the Owner must, prior to the recordation of the Final Subdivision

Plat, deposit with the Village Administrator a letter of credit ("Performance and Payment Letter of Credit"), in an amount equal to either (a) 125% of the Approved Cost Estimate or (b) in cases where executed contracts for construction and installation of an Improvement have been filed with the Village Clerk pursuant to this Agreement, 110% of the amount of the contracts. The Performance and Payment Letter of Credit must be maintained and renewed by the Owner, and must be held in escrow by the Village, until any required acceptance of the Improvements by the Village pursuant to this Agreement and the posting of the Guaranty Letter of Credit as required by Section 12.B of this Agreement. After any required acceptance of the Improvements and posting of the Guaranty Letter of Credit, the Village will release the Performance and Payment Letter of Credit.

B. Guaranty Letter of Credit. Immediately after any required acceptance by the Village of the Improvements pursuant to this Agreement, the Owner must post a new letter of credit in the amount of ten percent of the actual total cost of the Improvements as security for the performance of the Owner's obligations under this Agreement ("Guaranty Letter of Credit"). The Guaranty Letter of Credit will be held by the Village in escrow until the last to occur of (i) the date that is the end of the two-year guaranty period set forth in this Agreement or (ii) the date that is two years after the proper correction of any defect or deficiency in the Improvements pursuant to this Agreement and payment of the cost of correction. If the Village is required to draw on the Guaranty Letter of Credit by reason of the Owner's failure to fulfill its obligations under this Agreement, then the Owner shall within 10 days thereafter cause the Guaranty Letter of Credit to be increased to its full original amount.

C. Costs. The Owner bears the full cost of securing and maintaining the Performance and Payment Letter of Credit and the Guaranty Letter of Credit.

D. Form of Letters of Credit. The Performance and Payment Letter of Credit and the Guaranty Letter of Credit each must be in a form satisfactory to the Village Attorney and substantially in the form attached as **Exhibit J**. Each shall be from a bank (i) acceptable to the Village, (ii) having capital resources of at least Fifty Million Dollars ($50,000,000), (iii) with an office located in the Chicago Metropolitan Area, and (iv) insured by the Federal Deposit Insurance Corporation. Each letter of credit shall, at a minimum, provide that (1) it will not be canceled without the prior consent of the Village; (2) it will not require the consent of the Owner prior to any draw on it by the Village; and (3) if at any time it will expire within 45 or any lesser number of days, and if it has not been renewed, and if any applicable obligation of the Owner for which it is security remains uncompleted or unsatisfactory, then the Village may, without notice and without being required to take any further action of any nature whatsoever, call and draw down the letter of credit and thereafter either hold all proceeds as security for the satisfactory completion of the obligations or employ the proceeds to complete the obligations and reimburse the Village for any and all costs and expenses, including without limitation legal fees and administrative costs, incurred by the Village, as the Village determines. The Performance and Payment Letter of Credit may provide that the aggregate amount of the letter of credit may be reduced, but only after joint direction by the Owner and the Village, either to reflect a reduction in the total amount of the deposit required pursuant to Section 12.A of this Agreement from 125% of the Approved Cost Estimate to 110% of the amount of an executed contract or to reimburse the Owner for payment of Improvement work satisfactorily completed. No reduction for payment of Improvement work satisfactorily completed will be allowed except after presentation by the Owner of proper contractors' sworn statements, partial or final waivers of lien, as may be appropriate, and any additional documentation that the Village may reasonably request to demonstrate satisfactory completion of the Improvement in question and full payment of all contractors, subcontractors, and material suppliers. The Guaranty Letter of Credit shall not be reduced by reason of any cost incurred by the Owner to satisfy its obligations under this Agreement.

E. Replenishment of Letters of Credit. If at any time the Village determines that the funds remaining in the Performance and Payment Letter of Credit are not, or may not be, sufficient to pay in full the remaining unpaid cost of all Improvements and all unpaid Village fees, or that the funds remaining in the Guaranty Letter of Credit are not, or may not be, sufficient to pay all unpaid costs of correcting any and all defects and deficiencies in the Improvements, then, within 10 days after a demand by the Village, the Owner must increase the amount of the appropriate letter of credit to an amount determined by the Village to be sufficient to pay the unpaid costs and fees. Failure to increase the amount of the security will be grounds for the Village to draw down the entire remaining balance of the letters of credit.

F. Replacement of Letters of Credit. If at any time the Village determines that the bank issuing either the Performance and Payment Letter of Credit or the Guaranty Letter of Credit is without capital resources of at least Fifty Million Dollars ($50,000,000), is unable to meet any federal or state requirement for reserves, is insolvent, is in danger of becoming any of the foregoing, or is otherwise in danger of being unable to honor the appropriate letter of credit at any time during its term, or if the Village otherwise reasonably deems itself to be insecure, then the Village has the right to demand that the Owner provide a replacement letter of credit from a bank satisfactory to the Village. The replacement letter of credit must be deposited with the Village not later than 10 days after the demand. After deposit of the replacement letter of credit, the Village will surrender the original letter of credit to the Owner.

G. Use of Funds in the Event of Breach of Agreement. If the Owner fails or refuses to complete the Improvements in accordance with this Agreement, or fails or refuses to correct any defect or deficiency in the Improvements as required by Section 7.F of this Agreement, or fails or refuses to restore property in accordance with a demand made pursuant to Section 7.H of this Agreement, or in any other manner fails or refuses to meet fully any of its obligations under this Agreement, then the Village may, in its sole and absolute discretion, draw on and retain all or any of the funds remaining in either the Performance and Payment Letter of Credit or the Guaranty Letter of Credit. The Village thereafter will have the right to exercise its rights under Sections 7.F and 7.H of this Agreement, to take any other action it deems reasonable and appropriate to mitigate the effects of the failure or refusal, and to reimburse itself from the proceeds of the letters of credit for all of its costs and expenses, including without limitation legal fees and administrative expenses, resulting from or incurred as a result of the Owner's failure or refusal to fully meet its obligations under this Agreement. If the funds remaining in the letters of credit are insufficient to repay fully the Village for all its costs and expenses, and to maintain a cash reserve equal to the required Guaranty Letter of Credit during the entire time the Guaranty Letter of Credit should have been maintained by the Owner, then the Owner must, after demand of the Village, immediately deposit with the Village additional funds as the Village determines are necessary to fully repay the Village's costs and expenses and to establish the required cash reserve.

H. Village Lien Rights. If any money, property, or other consideration due from the Owner to the Village pursuant to this Agreement is not either recovered from the performance security deposits required in this Section 12 or paid or conveyed to the Village by the Owner within 10 days after a demand for payment or conveyance, then the money, or the Village's reasonable estimate of the value of the property or other consideration, together with interest at the maximum rate permitted by law and costs of collection, including without limitation legal fees and administrative expenses, shall become a lien on the Property, and the Village will have the right to collect the amount or value, with applicable interest and costs, including without limitation legal fees and administrative expenses, and the right to enforce the lien in the manner provided by law for mortgage foreclosure proceedings. The lien will be subordinate to the lien of any first mortgage now or hereafter placed on the Property; provided, however, that the lien subordination shall apply only to charges that have become due and payable prior to a sale or transfer of the Property pursuant to a decree of foreclosure, or any other proceeding in lieu of foreclosure, but the sale or transfer shall not relieve the Property from liability for any charges thereafter becoming due, nor from the lien of any subsequent charge.

SECTION 13. LIABILITY AND INDEMNITY OF VILLAGE.

A. Village Review. The Owner acknowledges and agrees that the Village is not, and will not be, in any way liable for any damages or injuries that may be sustained as the result of the Village's review and approval of any plans for the Property or the Improvements, or the issuance of any approvals, permits, certificates, or acceptances for the development or use of the Property or the Improvements, and that the Village's review and approval of those plans and the Improvements and issuance of those approvals, permits, certificates, or acceptances does not, and shall not, in any way, be deemed to insure the Owner, or any of its heirs, successors, assigns, tenants, and licensees, or any other Person, against damage or injury of any kind at any time.

B. Village Procedure. The Owner acknowledges and agrees that notices, meetings, and hearings have been properly given and held by the Village with respect to the approval of this Agreement and agrees not to challenge the Village's approval on the grounds of any procedural infirmity or of any denial of any procedural right.

C. Indemnity. The Owner agrees to, and does hereby, hold harmless and indemnify the Village, the Corporate Authorities, the Plan Commission, and all Village elected or appointed officials, officers, employees, agents, representatives, engineers, and attorneys, from any and all claims that may be asserted at any time against any of them in connection with (i) the Village's review and approval of any plans for the Property or the Improvements; (ii) the issuance of any approval, permit, certificate, or acceptance for the Property or the Improvements; and (iii) the development, construction, maintenance, or use of any portion of the Property or the Improvements.

D. Defense Expense. The Owner must, and does hereby agree to, pay all expenses, including without limitation reasonable legal fees and administrative expenses, incurred by the Village in defending itself with regard to any and all of the claims referenced in Section 13.C of this Agreement.

SECTION 14. NATURE, SURVIVAL, AND TRANSFER OF OBLIGATIONS.

All obligations assumed by the Owner under this Agreement will be binding on the Owner personally, on any and all of the Owner's heirs, successors, and assigns, and on any and all of the respective successor legal or beneficial owners of all or any portion of the Property. To assure that the Owner's heirs, successors, and assigns, and successor owners of all or any portion of the Property have notice of this Agreement and the obligations created by it, the Owner will:

A. Deposit with the Village Clerk, contemporaneously with the Village's approval of this Agreement, any consents or other documents necessary to authorize the Village to record this Agreement in the office of the Recorder of __________ County; and

B. Notify the Village in writing at least 30 days prior to any date after which the Owner transfers a legal or beneficial interest in any portion of the Property to any Person not a party to this Agreement; and

C. Incorporate, by reference, this Agreement into any and all real estate sales contracts entered into for the sale of all or any portion of the Property to any Person not a party to this Agreement; and

D. Require, prior to the transfer of all or any portion of the Property, or any legal or equitable interest in the Property to any Person not a party to this Agreement, the transferee to execute an enforceable written agreement, in a form approved by the Village Attorney, agreeing to be bound by this Agreement ("Transferee Assumption Agreement"), and to provide the Village, after request, with reasonable assurance of the financial ability of the transferee to meet those obligations as the Village may require.

The Village agrees that after a successor becoming bound to the personal obligation created in the manner provided in this Agreement and providing the financial assurances required in this Section 14, the personal liability of the Owner will be released to the extent of the transferee's assumption of liability. The failure of the Owner to provide the Village with a fully executed copy of a Transferee Assumption Agreement required above by the transferee to be bound by this Agreement and, if requested by the Village, with the transferee's proposed assurances of financial capability before completing the transfer will result in the Owner remaining fully liable for all of the Owner's obligations under this Agreement but will not relieve the transferee of its liability for those obligations as a successor to the Owner.

SECTION 15. TERM.

This Agreement will be in full force and effect from and after the Effective Date for 20 years, or for the longest term allowed under Section 11-15.1-5 of the Illinois Municipal Code, 65 ILCS 5/11-15.1-5, or its successor statute; provided, however, that this Agreement will be of no force or effect until the Owner has first paid in full the amounts due to the Village as a condition precedent to the execution of this Agreement by the Village, pursuant to Section 11 of this Agreement, but no delay in payment shall serve to extend the date of termination of this Agreement.

SECTION 16. ENFORCEMENT.

The parties to this Agreement may, in law or in equity, by suit, action, mandamus, or any other proceeding, including without limitation specific performance, enforce or compel the performance of this Agreement; provided, however, that the Owner agrees that it will not seek, and does not have the right to seek, to recover a judgment for monetary damages against the Village, or any of its elected or appointed officials, officers, employees, agents, representatives, engineers, or attorneys, on account of the negotiation, execution, or breach of this Agreement. In addition to every other remedy permitted by law for the enforcement of the terms of this Agreement, the Village will be entitled to withhold the issuance of building permits or certificates of occupancy for any and all buildings and structures within the Property at any time when the Owner has failed or refused to meet fully any of its obligations under this Agreement.

SECTION 17. GENERAL PROVISIONS.

A. Notice. Any notice or communication required or permitted to be given under this Agreement must be in writing and shall be delivered (i) personally, (ii) by a reputable overnight courier, (iii) by certified mail, return receipt requested, and deposited in the U.S. Mail, postage prepaid, (iv) by facsimile, or (v) by electronic mail ("e-mail"). Facsimile notices will be deemed valid only to the extent that they are (a) actually received by the individual to whom addressed and (b) followed by delivery of actual notice in the manner described in either (i), (ii), or (iii) above within three business days thereafter at the appropriate address set forth below. E-mail notices shall be deemed valid only to the extent that they are (a) opened by the recipient on a business day at the address set forth below, and (b) followed by delivery of actual notice in the manner described in either (i), (ii), or (iii) above within three business days thereafter at the appropriate address set forth below. Unless otherwise provided in this Agreement, notices will be deemed received after the first to occur of (a) the date of actual receipt; or (b) the date that is one (1) business day after deposit with an overnight courier as evidenced by a receipt of deposit; or (b) the date that is three (3) business days after deposit in the U.S. mail, as evidenced by a return receipt. By notice complying with the requirements of this Section 17.A, each party to this Agreement has the right to change the address or the addressee, or both, for all future notices and communications to them, but no notice of a change of addressee or address will be effective until actually received.

Notices and communications to the Village must be addressed to, and delivered at, the following address:

____

____

____

____

With a copy to:

____

____

____

____

Notices and communications to the Owner must be addressed to, and delivered at, the following address:

____

____

____

____

With a copy to:

____

____

____

____

B. Time of the Essence. Time is of the essence in the performance of this Agreement.

C. Rights Cumulative. Unless expressly provided to the contrary in this Agreement, each and every one of the rights, remedies, and benefits provided by this Agreement are cumulative and are not exclusive of any other rights, remedies, and benefits allowed by law.

D. Non-Waiver. The Village will be under no obligation to exercise any of the rights granted to it in this Agreement. The failure of the Village to exercise at any time any right granted to the Village will not be deemed or construed to be a waiver of that right, nor will the failure void or affect the Village's right to enforce that right or any other right.

E. Consents. Unless otherwise provided in this Agreement, whenever the consent, permission, authorization, approval, acknowledgement, or similar indication of assent of any party to this Agreement, or of any duly authorized officer, employee, agent, or representative of any party to this Agreement, is required in this Agreement, the consent, permission, authorization, approval, acknowledgement, or similar indication of assent will be in writing.

F. Governing Law. This Agreement will be governed by, and enforced in accordance with, the internal laws, but not the conflicts of laws rules, of the State of Illinois.

G. Severability. It is hereby expressed to be the intent of the parties to this Agreement that should any provision, covenant, agreement, or portion of this Agreement or its application to any Person or property be held invalid by a court of competent jurisdiction, the remaining provisions of this Agreement and the validity, enforceability, and application to any Person or property will not be impaired thereby, but the remaining provisions shall be interpreted, applied, and enforced so as to achieve, as near as may be, the purpose and intent of this Agreement to the greatest extent permitted by applicable law.

H. Entire Agreement. This Agreement constitutes the entire agreement between the parties and supersedes any and all prior agreements and negotiations between the parties, whether written or oral, relating to the subject matter of this Agreement.

I. Interpretation. This Agreement will be construed without regard to the identity of the party who drafted the various provisions of this Agreement. Moreover, each and every provision of this Agreement will be construed as though all parties to this Agreement participated equally in the drafting of this Agreement. As a result of the foregoing, any rule or construction that a document is to be construed against the drafting party will not be applicable to this Agreement.

J. Exhibits. Exhibits A through J attached to this Agreement are, by this reference, incorporated in, and made a part of, this Agreement. In the event of a conflict between an exhibit and the text of this Agreement, the text of this Agreement shall control.

K. Amendments and Modifications. No amendment or modification to this Agreement will be effective until it is reduced to writing and approved and executed by all parties to this Agreement in accordance with all applicable statutory procedures.

L. Changes in Laws. Unless otherwise provided in this Agreement, any reference to the Requirements of Law will be deemed to include any modifications of, or amendments to, the Requirements of Law that may occur in the future.

M. Authority to Execute. The Village hereby warrants and represents to the Owner that the Persons executing this Agreement on its behalf have been properly authorized to do so by the Corporate Authorities. The

Owner hereby warrants and represents to the Village (i) that it is the record and beneficial owner of fee simple title to the Property, (ii) that no other Person has any legal, beneficial, contractual, or security interest in the Property, (iii) that it has the full and complete right, power, and authority to enter into this Agreement and to agree to the terms, provisions, and conditions set forth in this Agreement and to bind the Property as set forth in this Agreement, (iv) that all legal actions needed to authorize the execution, delivery, and performance of this Agreement have been taken, and (v) that neither the execution of this Agreement nor the performance of the obligations assumed by the Owner will (a) result in a breach or default under any agreement to which the Owner is a party or to which it or the Property is bound or (b) violate any statute, law, restriction, court order, or agreement to which the Owner or the Property are subject.

N. No Third-Party Beneficiaries. No claim as a third-party beneficiary under this Agreement by any Person will be made, or be valid, against the Village or the Owner.

O. Recording. After the Owner has paid to the Village the amounts due pursuant to Section 11 of this Agreement and the Owner has paid to the Village an amount sufficient to cover the cost of recording this Agreement, all necessary plats, the affidavit of service of notice as required by Section 7-1-1 of the Illinois Municipal Code, 65 ILCS 5/7-1-1, and the Annexation Ordinance, the Village shall promptly cause this Agreement to be recorded in the office of the Recorder of ________ County.

ATTEST: VILLAGE OF ________________________________

By: ________________________________

Village Clerk Village President

OWNER

By: ________________________________

Its: ________________________________

Table of Exhibits

Exhibit	Title or Description
A	Legal Description of Property
B	Preliminary Plans
C	Annexation Plat
D	Annexation Ordinance
E	Rezoning Ordinance
F	PUD Ordinance
G	Description of Required Improvements
H	Recapture Schedule
I	Form of Recapture Ordinance
J	Form of Letter of Credit or Performance/Payment Bond

APPENDIX 4

Sample Development Agreement (California)

RECORDING REQUESTED BY AND WHEN RECORDED MAIL TO: ____________________ ____________________ ____________________ ____________________ ____________________	

SPACE ABOVE THIS LINE FOR RECORDER'S USE

DEVELOPMENT AGREEMENT NO. _________
CONCERNING THE PROPERTY LOCATED
AT ______________________________

THIS DEVELOPMENT AGREEMENT (this "Agreement") is dated for reference as of this ____ day of _______________ and is entered into by and between ____________________ ("Developer"), and the CITY _________________, a ______________________ municipal corporation and charter city existing under the laws of the State of California ("City"). The Developer and the City may at times be referred to individually as a "Party" and jointly as the "Parties."

WITNESSETH:

A. Recitals.

(i) California Government Code Section 65864 *et seq.* ("Development Agreement Law") authorizes cities to enter into binding development agreements with persons having legal or equitable interests in real property for the development of such property.

(ii) Developer owns that certain real property located entirely within the City consisting of approximately _______ acres located at _________________ with Assessor Parcel Number ___________, as further described in Exhibit "A" attached hereto and incorporated herein by this reference (hereinafter the "Site" or "Property").

(iii) Developer desires to demolish the improvements, commercial structures and associated parking facilities currently existing on the Site and subsequently redevelop the Site with approximately _________________________ (_____) total residential units to be comprised of approximately ________ multifamily units and approximately ____ townhomes, together with publicly accessible open space and approximately ______ parking spaces (as more specifically defined herein, the "Project").

(iv) Subject to the Existing Approvals (as defined in Recital (vi) below), by way of this Agreement, the City and Developer desire to provide specific controls for development of the Project on the Site and provide for efficient utilization of the Site in a manner that is consistent with sound land use and planning principles, and to advance the State and local goals of increasing the number of market rate and affordable housing units available in the community.

(v) In addition to other public and private benefits flowing to the Parties by virtue of this Agreement, the Developer desires to secure the benefits afforded by the Development Agreement Law and receive the assurance that they may proceed with the Project on the Site in accordance with and subject to the Existing Approvals, this Agreement, and other laws and regulations of the City in effect as of the Effective Date (as defined in Section B.1(c) below).

(vi) The Project and this Agreement are subject to and conditioned upon the following land use entitlements (collectively the "Existing Approvals"), each of which has been granted or otherwise issued by the City prior to or concurrently with the City Council's approval of this Agreement and which are expressly incorporated into and made a part of this Agreement:

a) Environmental Compliance. The potential environmental impacts of the Project have been properly reviewed and evaluated by the City pursuant to the California Environmental Quality Act ("CEQA"), Public Resources Code Section 21000 *et seq.* Pursuant to CEQA and in accordance with the recommendation of the City's Planning Commission, the City Council approved an Addendum to the ________________ General Plan Environmental Impact Report ("General Plan EIR") finding that the Project will not result in new or more significant environmental impacts than those previously identified in the General Plan EIR and further determined that the Project and this Agreement will, as a whole, be consistent with the objectives, policies, and general land uses and programs specified in the General Plan.

b) General Plan Amendment. Following review and recommendation by the Planning Commission, and after a duly noticed public hearing and approval of the Addendum, on ____________________, the City Council adopted Resolution No. ______ approving minor amendments to the General Plan ("GPA") to establish that density can be calculated cumulatively across multiple, adjacent parcels that are in common ownership and to clarify that high-density residential uses and townhomes are consistent with the vision and desired urban form in the Entertainment Mixed-Use land use designation and Entertainment Corridor.

c) General Mixed-Use Rezoning. Following review and recommendation by the Planning Commission, and after a duly noticed public hearing and approval of the Addendum, on ____________, the City Council, adopted Ordinance No. ______ approving a zoning amendment rezoning the Site from "Regional Commercial" to "General Mixed-Use" (GMU) (the "Zoning Amendment").

d) Vesting Tentative Map. Following review and recommendation by the Planning Commission, and after a duly noticed public hearing and approval of the Addendum, on ______________, the City Council adopted Resolution No. ______ approving a vesting tentative map for the Project.

e) Site Plan Review. Following review and recommendation by the Planning Commission, and after duly noticed public hearing and approval of the Addendum, on ________________, the City Council adopted Ordinance No. ______ approving a site plan for the Project pursuant to Section ____________ of the ___________ Municipal Code.

f) Enacting Ordinance. The Enacting Ordinance as defined in Recital (ix).

(vii) Prior to the City Council's consideration of the Existing Approvals and this Agreement, and after a duly noticed public hearing on ________________, the Planning Commission adopted a Resolution recommending that the City Council approve the Addendum to the General Plan EIR and adopt the Existing Approvals.

(viii) The City has given notice of its intention to adopt this Agreement, conducted public hearings thereon pursuant to Government Code Section 65867, and the City Council hereby finds that: (1) the provisions of this Agreement and its purposes are consistent with the General Plan as amended by the GPA; (2) the Project and this Agreement are compatible with the uses authorized in, and the regulations prescribed for in the General Plan as amended by the GPA; (3) this Agreement will not be detrimental to the health, safety, and general welfare of the community; (4) this Agreement will not adversely affect the orderly development of the Site; (5) this Agreement will facilitate development of the Site in a timely, efficient, and economical manner; and (6) this Agreement is consistent with and advances the public convenience, general welfare, and good land use practices, and otherwise advances and serves the best interests of the City and its residents.

(ix) On _____________, the City Council held a duly noticed public hearing and adopted Ordinance No. _____ ("Enacting Ordinance") approving this Agreement with Developer, and the Enacting Ordinance became effective as of __________.

B. Agreement.

NOW, THEREFORE, the City and Developer hereto agree as follows:

1. Definitions. In this Agreement, unless the context otherwise requires and in addition to the capitalized terms and phrases defined elsewhere herein, the following capitalized terms shall have the following meaning:

a. "City" is the City of ____________.

b. "Developer" is ________________, a California ______________.

c. "Effective Date" means the later of i) the date of the recording of this Agreement on the Site in the Official Records of the County of ___________, as required by Section 31 hereof, and ii) the effective date of the Enacting Ordinance, which date is set forth in Recital (ix).

d. "Development Plan" are those plans, specifications, and images for the Project attached hereto as Exhibit "B" and incorporated herein by this reference.

e. "Project" means and refers to the development approved for the Site as provided in this Agreement and the Existing Approvals consisting of the construction of approximately ____ total residential units, including approximately ____ multifamily units and approximately ____ townhomes, publicly accessible open space, approximately ____ parking spaces, and related site improvements on approximately __ acres of land located at ____________________________ (APN No. ________________) within the General Mixed Use (GMU) zone, all as reflected in the Development Plan.

2. Recitals. The recitals are true, correct, and a part of this Agreement and shall be enforceable as any other provision of this Agreement.

3. Interest of Developer. Developer warrants and represents that: (a) it has a legal interest in the Site; (b) that it has full legal right to enter into this Agreement; and (c) that the persons executing this Agreement on behalf of Developer have been duly authorized to do so.

4. Binding Effect of Agreement. Developer hereby subjects the Project and the Site to the covenants, reservations and restrictions as set forth in this Agreement. The City and the Developer hereby declare their specific intent that the covenants, reservations and restrictions as set forth herein shall be deemed covenants running with the land and shall pass to and be binding upon Developer's successors and assigns in title or interest to the Project for the Term (as defined in Section 6 below) of this Agreement. Each and every contract, deed or other instrument hereinafter executed, covering or conveying the Project or any portion thereof shall conclusively be held to have been executed, delivered and accepted subject to the covenants, reservations and restrictions expressed in this Agreement, regardless of whether such covenants, reservations and restrictions are set forth in such contract, deed or other instrument.

The City and Developer hereby further declare their understanding and intent that the benefit of such covenants touch and concern the land by enhancing and increasing the enjoyment and use of the Site by Developer and the future occupants of the Project, as the intended beneficiaries of such covenants, reservations and restrictions, and by furthering the public purposes for which this Agreement is adopted.

5. Relationship of Parties. It is understood that the contractual relationship between City and Developer is such that Developer is an independent party and is not and shall not be considered the agent of City for any purpose whatsoever.

6. Term of Agreement. The term of this Agreement shall commence on the Effective Date and shall continue in full force and effect for twenty (20) years and expire at 12:00 p.m. on the day that is twenty (20) years after the Effective Date ("Term"); unless such term is extended or earlier terminated pursuant to the terms or conditions of this Agreement, or upon the mutual written agreement or consent of the Parties and subject to compliance with the Development Agreement Law.

7. Vested Rights. Developer shall have the vested right to develop the Project on the Site in accordance with and subject to the provisions of this Agreement, the Existing Approvals (defined in Recitals (vi), the Existing Standards (defined in Section 13.1 below), and conditioned upon Developer's receipt of any Subsequent Approvals (defined in Section 8 below) necessary to develop the Project and operate the Permitted Uses (defined in Section 14 below) on the Site. Notwithstanding the foregoing or anything to the contrary in this Agreement, Developer's rights under this Agreement shall automatically expire if construction is not commenced within the time required by Section 9 hereof, subject to any extensions permitted under this Agreement.

a. Vesting Tentative Subdivision Map and Other Entitlement Extensions. Pursuant to Government Code Section 65863.9 and 66452.6(a) and this Agreement, the life of the Existing Approvals, including but not limited to the rezone of the Property to a General Mixed-Use zone, approval of the Vesting Tentative Map, and Site Plan Review, any Subsequent Approval (defined in Section 8), which may be approved by the City in connection with the development of the Project, shall automatically be extended to be coterminous with the Term of this Agreement.

8. Affordable Housing. Developer shall develop approximately _____ multifamily units on Parcels A, B, C, and D as depicted on the Development Plan. Of the approximately _____ total multifamily units developed on Parcels A, B, C, and D, _____ percent (__%) of such units shall be restricted for Low Income Households and _____ percent (__%) shall be restricted for Moderate Income Households, as those terms are defined in this Section, for a total of ________ percent (__%) of the units deed restricted for affordable. The deed restricted affordable units on Parcels A, B, C, and D shall be: (a) located and spread across buildings on Parcels A, B, C, and D and comingled with the non-restricted (market rate) units, such that approximately ______ percent (__%) of the units located in any such building, and approximately ______ percent (__%) of the units on Parcels A, B, C, and D, shall be restricted for Low Income Households or Moderate Income Households; and (b) developed in the same time or phases as non-restricted (market rate) units, such that approximately ______ percent (__%) of the units developed in each development phase (and receiving a Certificate of Occupancy), excluding Parcel E, shall be Low Income Households or Moderate Income Households. The "Moderate Income Households" shall mean persons and families whose income does not exceed one hundred twenty percent (120%) of the then-current median income of the County of _______ adjusted for family size by the State Department of Housing and Community Development in accordance with adjustment factors adopted and amended from time to time by the United States Department of Housing and Urban Development pursuant to Section 8 of the United States Housing Act of 1937, as amended, and California Health and Safety Code Section 50093, as it may be amended from time-to-time. "Low Income Households" shall mean persons and families whose income is between fifty percent (50%) and eighty percent (80%) of the area median income of the County of ________ adjusted for family size by the State Department of Housing and Community Development in accordance with adjustment factors adopted and amended from time to time by the United States Department of Housing and Urban Development pursuant to Section 8 of the United States Housing Act of 1937, as amended, and California Health and Safety Code Section 50093, as it may be amended from time-to-time. Developer represents and warrants that it has not entered into any agreement that would restrict or compromise its ability to comply with the requirements and restrictions set forth in this Section, and Developer covenants that it shall not enter into any agreement that is inconsistent with such requirements and restrictions without the express written consent of the City.

8A. Subsequent Approvals. Certain subsequent permits and approvals, in addition to the Existing Approvals, will be necessary for Developer's development and operation of the Project on the Site as contemplated by this Agreement and the Existing Approvals ("Subsequent Approvals").

Subsequent Approvals include all ministerial actions, permits, and approvals and discretionary actions, permits, and approvals that are approved, granted, or issued for the Project after the Effective Date, including, without limitation: (i) final maps, (ii) demolition permits, excavation permits, grading permits, building permits, sewer and water connection permits, certificates of occupancy, and similar permits and approvals, or any amendments to, or repealing of, any of the foregoing, (iii) use permits and other similar discretionary permits and approvals, and (iv) amendments to the Existing Approvals. The conditions, terms, restrictions, and requirements associated with any such Subsequent Approvals shall be consistent with the Existing Standards (except as otherwise provided in Section 13) and, if Developer submits a completed application for any such Subsequent Approvals for the Project or Permitted Use that is consistent with this Agreement and provided that Developer is not in default of this Agreement, such application shall not be unreasonably delayed or denied by the City. The City shall review, consider, and make a final determination on applications from Developer for Subsequent Approvals in accordance with and subject to the provisions of this Agreement, the Approvals, and the Existing Standards (defined in Section 13.1 below).

9. Construction. The Parties acknowledge that Developer cannot at this time predict when, or the rate at which, the Project would be developed. Such decisions depend upon numerous factors which are not all within the control of Developer. Developer, subject to the terms of this Agreement, shall have the right to develop the Project in such order and at such rate and times as Developer deems appropriate within the exercise of its sole and subjective business judgment. Such right is consistent with, and necessary to, the purpose and understanding of the Parties to this Agreement. Because the California Supreme Court held in Pardee Construction Co. v. City of Camarillo, 37 Cal.3d 465 (1984), that failure of the Parties to provide for the timing of development resulting in a later adopted initiative restricting the timing of development to prevail over such Parties' agreement, it is the Parties' intent to cure that deficiency by acknowledging and providing that Developer shall have the right (without obligation), subject to the provisions of this Agreement, to complete the Project in such order and at such rate and at such times as Developer deems appropriate within the exercise of its subjective business judgment.

a. Expiration. Notwithstanding the foregoing or any contrary term or provision under the City's Zoning Code, this Agreement and Developer's vested right to proceed with construction and operation of the Project on the Site shall expire if construction of the Project is not commenced within five (5) years after the Effective Date, unless such time is extended pursuant to Section 9(b) or Section 10 below. The commencement of construction for purposes of this Section is satisfied by the issuance of a grading permit or building permit.

b. Extensions. Developer may request extensions to the deadline to commence construction of the Project before expiration of the original deadline. The Director of Community and Economic Development may grant one or more extensions if such extension would not be materially detrimental to the public health, safety, and welfare in light of the facts and circumstances existing at the time.

10. Permitted Delays. Performance by either Party of its obligations under this Agreement shall be excused, and the Term shall be extended, for periods equal to the duration of any of the following:

10.1 Force Majeure. The Term, as set forth in Section 6, and the time within which either Party shall be required to perform any act under this Agreement shall be extended by a period of time equal to the number of days during which performance of such act is delayed unavoidably and beyond the reasonable control of the Party seeking the delay by strikes, lockouts, and other labor difficulties; Acts of God; unusually severe weather, but only to the extent that such weather or its effects (including, without limitation, dry-out time) result in delays that cumulatively exceed twenty (20) days for any winter season occurring after commencement of construction of the Project; failure or inability to secure materials or labor by reason of priority or similar regulations or order of any governmental or regulatory body; changes in local, State, or Federal laws or regulations; any development moratorium or any action of other public agencies that regulate land use, development, or the provision of services that prevents, prohibits, or delays construction of the Project; enemy action; civil disturbances; wars; terrorist acts; fire; unavoidable casualties; or mediation, arbitration, litigation, or other administrative or judicial proceeding involving the Existing Approvals or this Agreement; a local, state, or federal declaration of emergency based on an epidemic or pandemic, including any quarantine or other health-related orders, directives, regulations, laws or other requirements implemented in response to such epidemic or pandemic (each a "Force Majeure Delay"). An extension of time for any such cause shall be for the period of the Force Majeure Delay and shall commence to run from the time of the commencement of the cause, if notice by the Party claiming such extension is sent to the other Party within sixty (60) days of the commencement of the cause. If notice is sent after such sixty (60) day period, then the extension shall commence to run no sooner than sixty (60) days prior to the giving of such notice. Times of performance under this Agreement may also be extended in writing by the mutual agreement of the City Manager and Developer. Developer's inability or failure to obtain financing shall not be deemed to be a cause outside the reasonable control of the Developer and shall not be the basis for a Force Majeure Delay.

10.2 Extension of Term Due to Legal Action or Referendum. If any litigation is filed challenging this Agreement or any Existing Approval or Subsequent Approval having the direct or indirect effect of delaying this Agreement or any Existing Approval or Subsequent Approval, including any challenge to the validity of this Agreement or any of its provisions, or if this Agreement or an Existing Approval or Subsequent Approval is suspended pending the outcome of an electoral vote on a referendum, then the Term of this Agreement and all Existing Approvals or Subsequent Approvals shall be extended for the number of days equal to the period starting from the commencement of the litigation or the suspension to the date of final disposition of such litigation or suspension, including any applicable periods of appeal. The Parties shall document the start and end of an extension pursuant to this Section within thirty (30) days of the applicable dates.

10.3 Economic Delay. A recession, as defined by the National Bureau of Economic Research.

10.4 Administrative Delay. Actions of the City or other governmental agency beyond the control of the Developer that prevent, prohibit, or unreasonably delay the Developer's ability to proceed with development of the Project within the time required by this Agreement. Delays in processing and acting on applications for ministerial permits or approvals by the City or other governmental agencies shall be deemed to be unreasonable if they exceed the average time it normally takes the agency to process and act on similar applications by more than thirty (30) days.

11. Assignment.

11.1 Subject to Section 11.3, Developer shall have the right to sell, mortgage, hypothecate, assign or transfer this Agreement, and any and all of its rights, duties and obligations hereunder, to any person, partnership, joint venture, firm or corporation at any time during the Term of this Agreement, provided that any such sale, mortgage, hypothecation, assignment or transfer must be pursuant to a sale, assignment or other transfer of the interest of Developer in the Property, or a portion thereof. In the event of any such sale, mortgage, hypothecation, assignment or transfer, (a) Developer shall notify City of such event and the name of the transferee, together with the corresponding entitlements being transferred to such transferee, and (b) the agreement between Developer and such transferee shall provide that either Developer or the transferee or both shall be liable for the performance of all obligations of Developer pursuant to this Agreement. Such transferee and/or Developer shall notify City in writing which entity shall be liable for the performance of such obligations, and upon the express written assumption of any or all of the obligations of Developer under this Agreement by such assignee, transferee or purchaser, Developer shall be relieved of its legal duty to perform said obligations under this Agreement with respect to the Property or portion thereof, so transferred, except to the extent Developer is in default under the terms of this Agreement and/or City's consent to the assignment is required pursuant to Section 11.3.

11.2 Subject to Section 11.3, all or a portion of the Site may be sold, mortgaged, hypothecated, assigned or transferred to persons for development by them in accordance with the provisions of this Agreement. Effective upon such sale, mortgage, hypothecation, assignment or transfer, the obligations of Developer shall become several and not joint. Upon the sale, transfer, or assignment of Developer's rights and interests under this Agreement as permitted pursuant to this Section of the Agreement, Developer shall be released from its obligations under this Agreement with respect to the Property, or portion thereof so transferred, provided that (a) Developer is not then in default under this Agreement, (b) Developer has provided to City the notice of such transfer specified in Section 11.1 of this Agreement, and (c) the transferee executes and delivers to City a written agreement in which (i) the name and address of the transferee is set forth and (ii) the transferee expressly and unconditionally assumes all the obligations of Developer under this Agreement with respect to the Property, or portion thereof, so transferred. Non-compliance by any such transferee with the terms and conditions of this Agreement shall not be deemed a default hereunder or grounds for termination hereof or constitute cause for City to initiate enforcement action against the other Party or persons then owning or holding interest in the Property or any portion thereof and not themselves in default hereunder. The provisions of this Section shall be self-executing and shall not require the execution or recordation of any further document or instrument. Any and all successors, assigns and transferees of Developer shall have all of the same rights, benefits and obligations of Developer as used in this Agreement and the term "Developer" as used in this Agreement shall refer to any such successors, assigns and transferees unless expressly provided herein to the contrary.

11.3 City's Consent. The City's consent shall not be required to a transfer or assignment between Developer(s). Moreover, the City's consent to a transfer or assignment pursuant to this Section 11 shall not be required unless, at the time of the transfer or assignment, Developer is in default under the terms of this Agreement. If Developer is in default under the terms of this Agreement, City shall consent in writing to any transfer or assignment which provides adequate security to City, in the reasonable exercise of the City's discretion, to guarantee the cure of the default upon completion of the transfer or assignment.

12. General Standards and Restrictions Pertaining to Development of the Site. The following specific restrictions shall apply to the Site pursuant to this Agreement:

a. Developer shall have the right to develop the Project and operate the Permitted Uses on the Site in accordance with and subject to the terms and conditions of this Agreement, the Existing Approvals, Existing Standards, and other applicable laws and regulations, and City shall have the right to control development and use of the Site in accordance with the foregoing.

b. The type, density, intensity, and configuration of use allowed, size, and location of the building and other improvements and provisions for the reservation or dedication of land for public purposes, location of public improvements, together with other terms and conditions of development applicable to the Site, shall be as set forth in this Agreement and the Existing Approvals and any Subsequent Approvals.

c. The Development Plan establishes the standards and requirements applicable to development of the Site. The City agrees and acknowledges that the design regulations and standards set forth in the Development Plan shall govern development of the Site notwithstanding any contrary provision in the City's Zoning Code, including but not limited to any greater restrictions on use of buildings or the Site, parking requirements, and building heights.

d. Park Fee. The Developer shall pay to the City a park fee mandated by City Ordinance No. 1416 in the amount of $_________ per dwelling unit ("Park Fee"), which includes adjustment for credits received for the Project's publicly accessible private open space. Pursuant to Section 18.64.080 of the City's Code, the population per dwelling unit used to determine the Park Fee shall be based on the average number of persons that will occupy the dwelling units for this Project which shall be 2.20. Developer's payment of the Park Fee shall be phased during the development of the Project. Developer shall pay the portion of the Park Fee applicable to the residential units in each building upon the issuance of a Certificate of Occupancy for each building.

e. Community Benefit Fee. Developer shall pay a "Community Benefit Fee" in the amount of $________ per residential unit to the City. Developer's payment of the Community Benefit Fee shall be phased during the development of the Project. Developer shall pay the portion of the Community Benefit Fee applicable to the residential units in each Parcel prior to the issuance of a vertical building permit for each Parcel.

f. The Parties acknowledge and agree that the development of the Project in accordance with this Agreement provides substantial community benefits to the City, including but not limited to the development of publicly accessible open space as generally depicted in the Development Plan.

g. Developer shall install public improvements including an underground drainage pipe and water main along ___________ Avenue as set forth in the Development Plan, attached hereto as Exhibit "B."

h. Traffic Fee. Pursuant to ____________________ Resolution No. 9726, Developer shall pay to the City a Traffic Impact Fee in the amount of $________ per net new PM peak hour trip generated by the Project. Developer shall pay the applicable portion of the Traffic Impact Fee for a building upon the issuance of a Certificate of Occupancy for such building.

i. Art Installation. Developer shall provide an art installation within the Project's publicly accessible open space. The selection of materials used for the art installation shall be subject to review and approval by the City Manager and approval of such materials shall not be unreasonably withheld unless the City Manager determines that the materials pose a safety hazard to residents or vehicles. The Parties agree and acknowledge that the total cost for the design, materials, and installation of the art installation shall not exceed ______________________ ($________).

j. Off-Site Improvements. Developer shall pay to the City a fee in the amount of $________ upon the issuance of a vertical building permit for the first residential building in consideration for the installation of traffic light cameras at the intersection of ____________ and ____________. The traffic light cameras shall be per specifications provided by the Chief of Police and consistent with the type of camera technology used by the ________________ Police Department at other intersections within the City.

13. Effect of City Regulations on Development of Project.

13.1 Existing Standards. Except as expressly provided in this Agreement, all substantive and procedural requirements and provisions contained in the City's ordinances, specific plans, rules and regulations, including but not limited to the Existing Approvals, Municipal Code, and Zoning Code in effect as of the Effective Date of this Agreement, shall apply to the construction and development of the Project and Site ("Existing Standards").

a. The provisions of this Section 13 shall not preclude the application to the development of the Site those changes in City ordinances, regulations, plans or specifications which are specifically mandated and required by changes in state or federal laws or regulations as provided in California Government Code Section 65869.5 or any successor provision or provisions. In the event such changes in the law prevent or preclude compliance with one or more of the provisions of the Agreement, such provisions of the Agreement shall be modified or suspended or performance thereof delayed, as may be necessary to comply with such changes in the law.

b. The payment of fees associated with the construction of the Project, including land use approvals, development fees, building permits, etc., shall be pursuant to those fees in effect at the time of the Effective Date of the Agreement. The Parties further agree that the fees owed pursuant to Section 12 shall be in the amount reflected in Section 12 and shall not be subject to escalation based on the Consumer Price Index or otherwise.

c. Nothing herein shall prevent the application of health and safety regulations (i.e., fire, building, seismic, plumbing and electric codes) that become applicable to the City on a Citywide basis.

13.2 Future Changes to Existing Standards. Developer may, at its option, develop the Site in accordance with new City ordinances, development regulations and other policies, technologies, or guidelines adopted by the City after the Effective Date ("Future Changes to Existing Standards"), without obligation to bring other portions of the Site into conformance with Future Changes to Existing Standards. Application of any Future Changes to Existing Standards under this Section shall be on a Project-phase basis.

14. Permitted Uses. The uses allowed on the Site, the density and intensity of such uses, the maximum height and size of proposed buildings, and other terms and conditions applicable to the Site ("Permitted Uses") shall be those set forth in this Agreement, the Existing Approvals, and any Subsequent Approvals.

15. Annual Review. During the term of this Agreement, City shall annually review the extent of good faith compliance by Developer with the terms of this Agreement. Without request or demand from the City, Developer shall file an annual report with the City regarding compliance with the terms of this Agreement no later than the anniversary of the Effective Date. Developer shall have the right to cause the annual report to be filed by any lessee then occupying the Site provided, however, that Developer shall remain primarily responsible for such filing. If Developer has effectuated an assignment, transfer, or conveyance permitted under this Agreement so that Developer's interest in the Site and obligations under this Agreement, or a portion or portions thereof, has/have been divided between Developer and each transferee, then the City's annual review hereunder shall be conducted separately with respect to Developer and each transferee.

16. Indemnification and Legal Challenge. To the maximum extent permitted by law, Developer agrees to, and shall, defend, indemnify and hold City and its elected officials, officers, contractors serving as City officials, agents, and employees ("Indemnitees") harmless from liability for damage and/or claims for damage for personal injuries, including death, and claims for property damage, and with respect to all other actions and liabilities for damages caused or alleged to have been caused by reason of Developer's activities in connection with the construction of the Project, and which may arise from the direct or indirect actions or inactions of Developer or of Developer's contractors, agents, employees or any other persons acting or failing to act on Developer's behalf, which relate to the construction of the Project. This defense and indemnity obligation includes payment of attorney's fees and all costs of litigation. This indemnity provision applies to all damages and claims for damage, as described above, regardless of whether or not the City prepared, supplied or approved the plans, specifications or other documents for the Project.

The City shall promptly notify the Developer of any claim, action, or proceeding within the scope of this Section 16. In the event of any legal action challenging the validity, applicability, or interpretation of any provision of this Agreement or the Approvals, the Developer shall indemnify, defend and hold harmless the Indemnitees, and each of them, with respect to all liability, costs and expenses, including reasonable attorney's fees, actually incurred by and/or awarded against any of the Indemnitees in relation to such legal action. Developer shall have the right to select counsel of its choice. The Parties hereby agree to cooperate in defending such action. The City will not voluntarily assist in any such third-party challenge or take any position adverse to the Developer in connection with such third-party challenge. In the event of any litigation challenging the effectiveness of this Agreement, or any portion hereof, this Agreement shall remain in full force and effect while such litigation, including any appellate review, is pending, unless otherwise ordered by the court. Absent issuance of an injunction, the Developer may elect to continue development under this Agreement pending completion of the litigation but it shall do so at its sole and exclusive risk, and the City shall not be liable for any loss of any kind or nature suffered as a result thereof.

17. Amendments. Subject to Section 18 below, this Agreement may be amended or canceled, in whole or in part, only by mutual written consent of the Parties and then in the manner provided for in California Government Code Section 65868 *et seq.*, or successor provisions thereto.

18. Minor Modifications to Development Plan and Agreement.

a. Minor modifications and changes to the Development Plan may be initiated by the application of the Developer and may be approved by the Director of Community and Economic Development pursuant to the interdepartmental review process under Section 19.128.100 as of the Effective Date, without requiring public notice or hearing or approval by City Council. The Director's determination may be appealed pursuant to Section 19.128.020(H).

b. Minor modifications to conditions may be initiated only by the application of the Developer and shall be processed pursuant to Section 19.128.100(J) as of the Effective Date. Pursuant to Section 19.128.100(J), minor modifications to conditions may be approved by the Director of Community and Economic Development without requiring further procedure including public notice or hearing and shall be processed pursuant to the interdepartmental review process under Section 19.128.100 as of the Effective Date.

c. Minor modifications and changes include, without limitation, modifications to the building design or footprint affecting setbacks, parking layout and design, and landscape design. Minor modifications are not intended to constitute a substantive change or an amendment to this Agreement and public notices and hearings shall not be required. Modifications or changes shall be deemed minor if they do not result in, for example: i) an increase in density or intensity of use; ii) a change in permitted uses; or iii) an increase in the maximum height and size of buildings.

d. Changes to the Development Plan and Agreement, other than minor modifications and changes as determined by the Director of Community and Economic Development, shall be processed as an amendment to this Agreement pursuant to Section 17 above.

19. Enforcement.

19.1 Developer Default. In the event of a default under the provisions of this Agreement by Developer, City shall give written notice to Developer (or its successor) by registered or certified mail addressed at the address stated in this Agreement, and if such violation is not corrected to the reasonable satisfaction of City within thirty (30) days after such notice is given, or if not corrected within such reasonable time as may be required to cure the breach or default if said breach or default cannot be cured within thirty (30) days (provided that acts to cure the breach or default must be commenced within said thirty (30) days and must thereafter be diligently pursued by Developer), then City may refuse to issue any permits or other approvals which Developer would otherwise have been entitled to pursuant to this Agreement. In the event Developer defaults on an obligation to pay any fee at the time required pursuant to Section 12 of this Agreement, City shall be entitled to pursue whatever legal or equitable remedies are available to collect any such amounts due subject to the meet and confer, notice, and cure provisions in this Section. The City shall have no right to seek specific performance to cause Developer to otherwise proceed with the development of the Project in any manner.

19.2 City Default. In the event of a default under the provisions of this Agreement by City, Developer shall give written notice to the City, by registered or certified mail addressed at the address stated in this Agreement, and if such violation is not corrected to the reasonable satisfaction of Developer within thirty (30) days after such notice is given, or if not corrected within such reasonable time as may be required to cure the breach or default if said breach or default cannot be cured within thirty (30) days (provided that acts to cure the breach or default must be commenced within said thirty (30) days and must thereafter be diligently pursued by City), then Developer may avail itself of the rights and remedies under this Section. Developer has invested significant time and resources and performed extensive planning and processing of the Project and will be investing significant time in implementing the Project in reliance upon the terms of this Agreement. It is therefore not possible to determine the sum of money which would adequately compensate Developer for such efforts and City and Developer agree that damages would not be an adequate remedy if City fails to carry out its obligations under this Agreement. Therefore, specific performance of this Agreement is the only remedy which would compensate Developer if City fails to carry out its obligations under this Agreement, and City hereby agrees that Owner shall be entitled to specific performance in the event of a default by City hereunder.

19.3 Meet and Confer. Before sending a notice of default in accordance with this Section, the Party asserting that the other Party has failed to perform or fulfill its obligations under this Agreement shall first attempt to meet and confer with the other Party to discuss the alleged failure and shall permit such Party a reasonable period, but not less than thirty (30) days, to respond to or cure such alleged failure.

20. Event of Default. Developer is in default under this Agreement upon the happening of one or more of the following events or conditions:

a. If a material warranty, representation or statement is made or furnished by Developer to City and is false or proved to have been false in any material respect when it was made;

b. If a finding and determination is made by City following an annual review pursuant to Section 15 hereinabove, upon the basis of substantial evidence, that Developer has not complied in good faith with any material terms and conditions of this Agreement, after notice and opportunity to cure as described in Section 16 hereinabove; or

c. A breach by Developer of any of the provisions or terms of this Agreement, after meet and confer, notice and opportunity to cure as provided in Section 19 above.

21. No Waiver of Remedies. City does not waive any claim of defect in performance by Developer if on periodic review City does not enforce this Agreement. Nonperformance by Developer shall not be excused because performance by Developer of the obligations herein contained would be unprofitable, difficult or expensive or because of a failure of any third party or entity, other than City. No waiver by City of any breach or default under this Agreement shall be deemed to be a waiver of any other subsequent breach thereof or default hereunder.

22. City Not Liable For Damages. It is acknowledged by the Parties that the City would not have entered into this Agreement if it could be held liable in damages under or with respect to this Agreement or the application thereof. Consequently, and except for the payment of attorney's fees in accordance with this Agreement, the City shall not be liable in damages to the Developer, or to any assignee, transferee or any other person, and the Developer covenants on behalf of itself and its successors in interest not to sue for or claim any damages:

a. For any breach of this Agreement, or any breach arising out of or relating to this Agreement;

b. For the taking, impairment or restriction of any right or interest conveyed or provided hereunder or pursuant hereto;

c. Arising out of or connected with any dispute, controversy or issue regarding the application or interpretation or effect of the provisions of this Agreement; or

d. For any injury to or interference with the rights of the property owner, allegedly or actually arising out of, or incurred in connection with, the Parties entering this Agreement, or their exercise of any rights under this Agreement.

Therefore, City and Developer agree that, in the event of a breach of this Agreement, each of the Parties hereto may pursue the following: (a) remedies set forth in Section 19; or (b) cancellation of this Agreement upon the mutual written consent of the Parties, each in their sole and absolute discretion.

23. Rights of Lenders under This Agreement. Should Developer place or cause to be placed any encumbrance or lien on the Project, or any part thereof, the beneficiary ("Lender") of said encumbrance or lien shall have the right at any time during the Term of this Agreement and the existence of said encumbrance or lien to:

a. Do any act or thing required of Developer under this Agreement, and any such act or thing done or performed by Lender shall be as effective as if done by Developer;

b. Realize on the security afforded by the encumbrance or lien by exercising foreclosure proceedings or power of sale or other remedy afforded in law or in equity or by the security document evidencing the encumbrance or lien (hereinafter referred to as "a trust deed");

c. Transfer, convey or assign the title of Developer to the Project to any purchaser at any foreclosure sale, whether the foreclosure sale be conducted pursuant to court order or pursuant to a power of sale contained in a trust deed; and

d. Acquire and succeed to the interest of Developer by virtue of any foreclosure sale, whether the foreclosure sale be conducted pursuant to a court order or pursuant to a power of sale contained in a trust deed.

e. Should any Lender require or request an amendment of this Agreement with respect to the rights and remedies granted to a Lender, City hereby agrees to execute and deliver such an amendment so long as the proposed amendment does not materially and adversely affect the rights, powers, and remedies of the City with respect to a default by Developer hereunder. In such event, Lender shall be responsible for paying City's actual costs, including attorney's fees, incurred by the City in accommodating such request.

24. Notice to Lender. City shall give written notice of any default or breach under this Agreement by Developer to Lender (if known by City) and afford Lender the opportunity after service of the notice to:

a. Cure the breach or default within thirty (30) days after service of said notice, where the default can be cured by the payment of money;

b. Cure the breach or default within thirty (30) days after service of said notice where the breach or default can be cured by something other than the payment of money and can be cured within that time; or

c. Cure the breach or default in such reasonable time as may be required where something other than payment of money is required to cure the breach or default and cannot be performed within thirty (30) days after said notice, provided that acts to cure the breach or default are commenced within a thirty (30) day period after service of said notice of default on Lender by City and are thereafter diligently continued by Lender.

25. Action by Lender. Notwithstanding any other provision of this Agreement, a Lender may forestall any action by City for a breach or default under the terms of this Agreement by Developer by commencing proceedings to foreclose its encumbrance or lien on the Project. The proceedings so commenced may be for foreclosure of the encumbrance by order of court or for foreclosure of the encumbrance under a power of sale contained in the instrument creating the encumbrance or lien. The proceedings shall not, however, forestall any such action by the City for the default or breach by Developer unless:

a. They are commenced within thirty (30) days after service on Developer of the notice described herein above;

b. They are, after having been commenced, diligently pursued in the manner required by law to completion; and

c. Lender keeps and performs all of the terms, covenants and conditions of this Agreement requiring the payment or expenditure of money by Developer until the foreclosure proceedings are complete or are discharged by redemption, satisfaction or payment.

26. Notice. Any notice required to be given by the terms of this Agreement shall be provided by certified mail, return receipt requested, at the address of the respective Parties as specified below or at any other such address as may be later specified by the Parties hereto.

To Developer: ______________________________________

With copy to: ______________________________________

To City: ______________________________________

27. Attorney's Fees. In any proceedings arising from the enforcement of this Agreement or because of an alleged breach or default hereunder, the prevailing Party shall be entitled to recover its costs and reasonable attorney's fees and experts' fees incurred during the proceeding (including appeals) as may be fixed within the discretion of the court.

28. Binding Effect. This Agreement shall bind, and the benefits and burdens hereof shall inure to, the respective Parties hereto and their legal representatives, executors, administrators, successors and assigns, wherever the context requires or admits.

29. Applicable Law and Venue. This Agreement shall be construed in accordance with and governed by the laws of the State of California. Venue for any action or litigation brought for breach or to enforce any provision of this Agreement shall be the Superior Court of the County of _______, California.

30. Partial Invalidity. If any provisions of this Agreement shall be deemed to be invalid, illegal or unenforceable, the validity, legality or enforceability of the remaining provisions hereof shall not in any way be affected or impaired thereby.

31. Recordation. This Agreement shall, at the expense of Developer, be recorded in the Official Records of the County Recorder of the County of _________ within ten (10) business days following the Agreement Date. Upon the expiration of the terms of this Agreement, upon the request of the Developer, the City will execute and deliver, in recordable form, an instrument confirming that the provisions of this Agreement have expired.

32. Time of Essence. Time is of the essence in every provision hereof in which time is a factor.

33. Integrated Agreement. This Agreement consists of this Agreement together with all Exhibits attached hereto, and referenced documents, and all of the same are hereby incorporated herein by reference. The provisions of this Agreement shall govern over any inconsistent or conflicting provisions set forth in the Exhibits or incorporated documents, or in any other agreement between the Parties. No representation or promise, verbal or written, not expressly set forth herein shall be binding or have any force or effect.

34. Surviving Provisions. In the event this Agreement is terminated, neither Party shall have any further rights or obligations hereunder, except for those obligations which by their terms survive expiration or termination.

35. Counterparts. This Agreement may be executed in one or more counterparts, each of which shall be deemed an original, but all of which together constitute one and the same instrument. Signature pages may be detached from the counterparts and attached to a single copy of this Agreement to physically form one document.

IN WITNESS WHEREOF, this Agreement has been executed by the Parties and shall be effective on the Effective Date set forth hereinabove.

CITY OF ______________________________, a Municipal Corporation

Dated:____________________ By:____________________________

Mayor

ATTEST:______________________

City Clerk, City of __________

Approved as to form:

City Attorney

DEVELOPER:

____

____

By: ________________________

____

Date: ____________________________ By: __________________________________

Name: ______________________________

Title: ________________________________

Exhibit A

LEGAL DESCRIPTION

Exhibit B

DEVELOPMENT PLAN

Exhibit C

FORM OF ASSIGNMENT AND ASSUMPTION AGREEMENT

RECORDING REQUESTED BY
CITY CLERK
OF THE CITY OF __________
(Exempt from Recording Fees Pursuant to Government Code Section 27383)
AND WHEN RECORDED MAIL TO:

ASSIGNMENT AND ASSUMPTION AGREEMENT

RELATIVE TO DEVELOPMENT AGREEMENT FOR [__________]

THIS ASSIGNMENT AND ASSUMPTION AGREEMENT (hereinafter, the "**Assignment**") is entered into this _____ day of ______________, 20__, by and between______________, a _________________ ("**Assignor**") and ______________________, a _______________ ("**Assignee**").

RECITALS

A. ______________________, a ______________ and the City of ______________, a California charter city and municipal corporation of the State of California (the "**City**"), entered into that certain Development Agreement (the "**Development Agreement**") dated as of ______, 20__ for reference purposes, with respect to certain real property owned by Assignor, as such property is more particularly described in the Development Agreement (the "**Project Site**"). The Development Agreement was recorded in the Official Records of the ________ County on ___________ as Document No. _________.

B. The Development Agreement provides that, subject to the terms and requirements set forth therein, Developer (Assignor) has the right to: (i) transfer all or a portion of the Property, (ii) assign all of its rights, title, interest and obligations under the Development Agreement to a transferee with respect to the portions of the Property transferred to the transferee, and (iii) upon the execution and delivery of an approved Assignment and Assumption Agreement, to be released from any prospective liability or obligation under the Development Agreement with respect to those rights, duties, obligations or interests and real property so Transferred, except as otherwise provided in the Development Agreement.

C. Assignor intends to convey certain real property as more particularly identified and described on Exhibit A attached hereto (hereinafter the "**Transferred Property**") to Assignee. The Transferred Property is subject to the Development Agreement.

D. Assignor desires to assign and Assignee desires to assume Assignor's right, title, interest, burdens and obligations under the Development Agreement with respect to and as related to the Transferred Property, as more particularly described below.

ASSIGNMENT AND ASSUMPTION

NOW, THEREFORE, for good and valuable consideration, the receipt and sufficiency of which are hereby acknowledged, Assignor and Assignee hereby agree as follows:

1. Defined Terms. Initially capitalized terms used herein and not otherwise defined shall have the meaning ascribed to them in the Development Agreement.
2. Assignment of Development Agreement. Assignor hereby assigns to Assignee, effective as of the later of (i) Assignor's conveyance of the Transferred Property to Assignee or (ii) the date on which City receives a copy of the fully executed Assignment and Assumption Agreement, all of the rights, title, interest, burdens and obligations of Assignor under the Development Agreement with respect to the Transferred Property (the "Assigned and Assumed Obligations"). Assignor retains all the rights, title, interest, burdens and obligations under the Development Agreement with respect to (i) the Transferred Property that are not Assumed and Assigned Obligations and (ii) all other portions of the Project Site owned by Assignor.
3. Assumption of Development Agreement. Assignee hereby assumes, effective as of Assignor's conveyance of the Transferred Property to Assignee, all of the Assigned and Assumed Obligations with respect to the Transferred Property and agrees to observe and fully perform, and to be subject to, all of the Assumed and Assigned Obligations. The Parties intend that, upon the execution of this Assignment and conveyance of the Transferred Property to Assignee, Assignee shall become the "Developer" under the Development Agreement with respect to the Transferred Property and the Assigned and Assumed Obligations.

4. Reaffirmation of Indemnifications. Assignee hereby consents to and expressly reaffirms any and all indemnifications of the City set forth in the Development Agreement, including without limitation Section ___ of the Development Agreement.
5. Binding on Successors. All of the covenants, terms and conditions set forth herein shall be binding upon and shall inure to the benefit of the Parties hereto and their respective heirs, successors and assigns.
6. Notices. The notice address for Assignee under Section ____ of the Development Agreement shall be:

   ____

   ____

   Attn: ____

   With copy to:

   ____

   ____

   Attn: ____

7. Counterparts. This Assignment may be executed in as many counterparts as may be deemed necessary and convenient, and by the different Parties hereto on separate counterparts, each of which, when so executed, shall be deemed an original, but all such counterparts shall constitute one and the same instrument.
8. Governing Law. This Assignment and the legal relations of the Parties hereto shall be governed by and construed and enforced in accordance with the laws of the State of California, without regard to its principles of conflicts of law.

IN WITNESS HEREOF, the Parties hereto have executed this Assignment as of the day and year first above written.

ASSIGNOR:
[insert signature block]

ASSIGNEE:
[insert signature block]

APPENDIX 5

Checklist for Drafting Community Benefits Agreements

The following are some of the issues that community groups and developers should consider in negotiating a Community Benefits Agreement (CBA):

Parties

- Developer obligations
- Community coalition obligations
- Individual agency obligations
- Is the municipality a party to the agreement?
- Who has the authority to speak for or sign for each party?

Benefits

- What are the benefits to all involved parties?
- Is a needs assessment or study required (relevant to environmental benefits)?
- What is the scope of the developer's responsibility or financial obligation?
- When does it begin and how long does it last?
- Does the obligation transfer to subsequent project owners, or other third parties such as subcontractors or on-site vendors?
- What is the implementation process?

- What is the implementation time line?
- Will an individual agency or a committee be responsible for the oversight?
- How will the process be monitored?
- How often will reports be made?
- Is there a process to amend the terms of the benefit or program?

Remedies

- What constitutes a breach on the part of the developer?
- What constitutes a breach on the part of the community?
- What are the remedies in the event of a breach?
- Are the remedies specific to each benefit?
- What type of notice is required before relief is sought?
- Will the right to request specific performance be included?
- Is equitable relief permitted in the event of an irreparable injury?
- Who is responsible for attorney's fees in the event of a court action?
- Will the other clauses of a CBA remain in effect in the event of a breach?
- Are there any intended third-party beneficiaries?
- Should a mediation process be pursued in the case of a breach (before taking legal action)?

APPENDIX 6

Sample Reimbursement and Processing Agreement

REIMBURSEMENT AND PROCESSING AGREEMENT
BETWEEN
THE CITY OF __________
AND
[Developer/Landowner]

THIS AMENDED AND RESTATED REIMBURSEMENT AND PROCESSING AGREEMENT ("**Agreement**") is made and entered into on the ____ day of ___________, 20__ by and between the ___________, a California municipal corporation ("**City**"), and ___________ ("**Developer**") (collectively, the "**Parties**").

RECITALS

A. Developer has a legal and/or equitable interest in approximately ______ contiguous acres of real property located within the City, located at ___________, as depicted in the attached *Exhibit A-1*, and as more particularly described in the attached *Exhibit A-2* (the "**Property**").

B. Developer has submitted to City applications (collectively, the "**Applications**") for certain planning approvals, including environmental review, required for a project that Developer proposes to develop on the

Property (the "**Project**"). The Applications request approval of a general plan amendment, rezoning, and associated amendments to the zoning code, specific plan, and development agreement (collectively, the "**Entitlements**"). In the event the Entitlements are approved by the City, several future land use approvals and entitlements will be required for the Project to proceed, including but not limited to tentative and final subdivision maps, design review approvals, and final development plans (collectively, "**Future Approvals**"). The Parties intend that cost recovery by the City for expenses associated with the review, evaluation, and processing of the Future Approvals will be governed either by a development agreement approved along with the Entitlements or, alternatively, by another reimbursement and processing agreement to address the Future Approvals. Such agreement also would cover reimbursement of expenses related to any City approval of the Applications.

C. City and Developer have entered into this Agreement to implement a reimbursement program pursuant to which City will review the Applications and Developer will fund that review. Nothing in this Agreement is or should be construed to control or limit the City's exercise of discretion with respect to any aspect of the Entitlements or to constitute a covenant, promise, or commitment by City (including, without limitation, any agency, board, or commission of the City) to grant any Entitlement or to make any final decision on any Application, nor shall it prevent City (including, without limitation, any agency, board, or commission of the City) from acting on any Application in any manner other than that deemed proper by City.

D. The City and Developer intend that as a result of this Agreement all costs and expenses associated with the City's review, evaluation, consideration, and processing of the Applications, including but not limited to compensation for all City employee staff time and payment of all third-party consultant contracts, shall be paid using funds deposited in advance with City by Developer for such purpose and that City shall not be required to advance City funds or incur any liability to cover such costs and expenses.

E. Prior to entering into this Agreement, the City incurred expenses for its review, evaluation, consideration, and processing of the Applications and Developer has deposited funds with City to reimburse City for such expenses. As of the date of this Agreement, the Parties anticipate there will be a balance remaining on deposit after payment of estimated expenses incurred through _________, 20__ and invoiced on _________, 20__, which deposit will be credited to the Evergreen Deposit described in Section 4.02.

AGREEMENT

ARTICLE 1. EFFECTIVE DATE AND TERM

Section 1.01. Effective Date. This Agreement shall become effective upon the later to occur of City Council approval of this Agreement or the date this Agreement is fully executed by the Parties (the "**Effective Date**").

Section 1.02. Term. The term of the Agreement (the "**Term**") shall begin on the Effective Date and shall terminate upon the earlier of (a) the date of termination pursuant to Section 5.04 herein or (b) the date the City Council takes final action on the Applications or otherwise concludes its review of the Applications.

ARTICLE 2. GENERAL

Section 2.01. In General. Developer acknowledges and agrees that the review, evaluation, consideration, and processing of the Applications and all related and supporting material, documentation, and data will not occur if Developer does not fund such work in advance, and that City may immediately suspend such work until adequate funds to meet processing costs are deposited with City and may terminate this Agreement pursuant to Section 5.04. The Parties acknowledge that the complexity and the expected duration of the processing of the Applications make it helpful to establish a reimbursement program that provides Developer with financial accountability for the money City is expending to review the Applications.

ARTICLE 3. PLANNING AND ENTITLEMENT IN GENERAL

Section 3.01. Process in General. The Parties agree that the permits and planning requests to be reviewed, evaluated, considered, and processed by City shall be those in the Applications. Developer agrees to provide the "Technical Reports" (defined below in Section 3.02) and any other information reasonably required for the City's environmental review process. City's processing of such Applications for which deposits shall be made pursuant to this Agreement shall include, without limitation, (a) all work that facilitates City's review, evaluation, consideration, and processing of (i) the Applications, (ii) the Project, (iii) Technical Reports submitted in support of the Applications or developed by City or its consultants, (iv) supplements or amendments to the Applications and any accompanying data, submittals, and materials, and (v) any supplementary or additional material provided by Developer or developed by City or its consultants;

(b) preparation by City and its consultants of Technical Reports and related material, documentation, and data relating to the Applications, including but not limited to supplemental or additional Technical Reports, as well as review, evaluation, consideration, and internal and external communication regarding such supplemental or additional Technical Reports; and (c) negotiation and preparation of a development agreement and/or other agreements deemed necessary by City to protect its interest in the event any of the Applications are approved. Expenses for which Developer shall deposit funds with the City pursuant to this and any other section of this Agreement may include (x) staff time and expenses at rates consistent with those charged to other applicants on major planning projects; (y) consultant fees and costs (including, without limitation, costs and fees of specialized legal counsel retained to assist City staff and City's consultants); and (z) any other items that are agreed to in writing by City and Developer.

Section 3.02. CEQA Review. City will act as lead agency under the California Environmental Quality Act ("**CEQA**"). Developer will prepare or commission, at its sole cost, and submit to City any and all studies and evaluations that may be requested as a part of the City's CEQA review and planning processes, including, without limitation, studies and evaluations covering issues such as air quality; energy and greenhouse gas emissions; biological resources; cultural resources; hazardous materials and related issues; hydrology and water quality; noise; transportation; water supply; wastewater and stormwater; fiscal reports; planning studies; and others that may be required in the City's discretion (collectively, the "**Technical Reports**"). City will review and consider the Technical Reports in the preparation of its environmental evaluation under CEQA and its consideration of the Applications. Developer acknowledges and agrees that City must independently review and exercise its independent judgment with respect to the content and conclusions of the Technical Reports and may in its discretion retain consultants or rely upon its own staff, at Developer's cost, to review and comment on the Technical Reports, or to provide such supplemental or additional Technical Reports, evaluations, analysis, and internal or external communications as City may deem necessary or desirable, during the environmental review and planning process.

Section 3.03. NEPA Review. If City concludes that its environmental review document should be prepared to address the requirements of the National Environmental Policy Act (i.e., as a joint EIR-EIS), then any additional work by the City or additional work by City's Consultants on behalf of the City in connection with such document shall be covered by this Agreement. However, this Agreement does not provide for reimbursement for work by agencies other than City.

Section 3.04. Lead Project Manager. The Lead Project Manager for Developer for purposes of receiving information, scopes of work, and invoices from City relating to its Consultants pursuant to Section 4 of this Agreement is identified in Section 5.06. Developer may replace its Lead Project Manager at any time, but shall within two (2) business days provide written notice to City containing the name and contact information of any replacement Lead Project Manager.

ARTICLE 4. SELECTION OF CONSULTANTS AND FUNDING OF PLANNING EFFORTS

Section 4.01. Consultants.

(a) Prior to selecting any consultant or subconsultant to be retained by City under this Agreement (each, a "**Consultant**"), City shall provide the Lead Project Manager for Developer with information relative to such Consultant, and the proposed scope and budget for such Consultant; provided, however, that the ultimate selection and retention of any Consultant shall be made by City in its sole discretion.

(b) City shall deliver to the Lead Project Manager for Developer copies of all proposed consultant contracts and subcontracts (collectively, "**Consultant Contracts**"), including budgets and scopes of work, and any proposed amendments of previously approved Consultant Contracts. All Consultants retained by City pursuant to this Agreement will report to City. Developer agrees that City will charge actual staff time and expenses attributable to the administration of Consultant Contracts entered into by City under this Agreement.

(c) City shall on a monthly basis deliver to the Lead Project Manager for Developer copies of invoices from all Consultants. Developer may review those invoices and inform City in writing of any dispute that it may have within fifteen (15) days of receipt of such invoice. Developer may ask City to withhold payment from the Consultant and, upon such request by Developer, City shall not be required to withhold payment of any invoice for more than ten (10) days following a request by Developer to withhold payment. During such ten- (10) day period, City shall (i) upon request by the Lead Project Manager meet in person with the Lead Project Manager up to two times to discuss the disputed invoice, and (ii) in good faith review and consider the objections by Developer regarding the disputed invoice. In the event that City and the Lead Project Manager for Developer are not able to agree within such ten- (10) day period on a course of action with respect to the invoice, it shall be within City's exclusive and sole discretion to pay the disputed invoice in full and Developer shall be responsible for the full cost of City's payment of the invoice so long as such invoice relates to City's review, evaluation, consideration, or processing of the Applications. In the event Developer has exercised its right to request withholding of payment pursuant to this Section 4.01(c) on three or more occasions during the Term of this Agreement, Developer shall have the right to retain, at its own expense, an independent third-party facilitator and to have such facilitator attend and participate in meetings with the Lead Project Manager regarding disputed invoices. Participation of the facilitator shall be advisory only and shall not constrain the City's exclusive and sole discretion to pay the disputed invoice in full or Developer's obligation to reimburse the full cost of City's payment of the invoice so long as such invoice relates to City's review, evaluation, consideration, or processing of the Applications.

(d) All proposed Consultant Contracts shall provide that (i) Consultants shall bill only for their actual costs, with no premiums or surcharges on costs, expenses, sub-consultants, or otherwise; (ii) copies of all invoices and appropriate supporting documentation, except those of outside counsel to City, shall be made available to Developer, subject to the exception described in Section 4.03(c); and (iii) Consultant invoices shall include sufficient detail regarding work performed and time incurred to allow reasonable review by City and Developer, and shall provide a calculation of how much Consultant has billed City to date and how much remains available for billing under the Consultant's then-approved scope of work.

(e) City shall, on a monthly basis, provide to the Lead Project Manager for Developer a summary report on the fees incurred by the City's team of Consultants and City staff, the percentage of work that has been completed by the City's team of Consultants on the then-current scopes of work, and how much remains available for billing under the then-approved scopes of work.

(f) Within thirty (30) days following termination of this Agreement pursuant to Section 1.02 or Section 5.04, City shall deliver to the Lead Project Manager for Developer electronic copies (or hard copies if electronic versions do not exist) of all work prepared to date by any Consultant, whether in draft or final form, and in City's files as of such date, including without limitation all studies, reports, plans, drawings, and similar work (the "**Consultant Work**"). With respect to work not in City's files as of the date for compliance with this section, City shall have no obligation beyond making a request that Consultant provide all work to City. If Consultant Work has not been approved or adopted by City staff in writing, Developer shall keep such work, including any documentation thereof in whatever form, confidential, and shall not share such work with any member of the public unless City consents to such disclosure or such disclosure is required by law. Developer shall hold City, its officers, and employees harmless from and against any and all costs, including attorneys' fees, damages, or liabilities incurred by Developer and arising from Developer reliance on any Consultant Work that is delivered to Developer in accordance with this Subsection (f). This obligation to hold the City harmless shall survive termination of this Agreement pursuant to Section 1.02 or Section 5.04.

Section 4.02. Evergreen Deposit.

(a) As of the date of this Agreement, City had incurred expenses for its review, evaluation, consideration, and processing of the Applications and Developer deposited funds with City to reimburse City for such expenses. The Parties anticipate that, as of the date of this Agreement, all invoices submitted as of ______ 1, 20__ have been reimbursed in full by Developer. The Parties anticipate that there will be a balance remaining on deposit after payment of all invoices submitted between ______ 1, 20__ and the date of this Agreement. In such event the balance on deposit will be credited by the City toward the Evergreen Deposit described below in Section 4.02(b).

(b) Developer shall establish and fund a deposit account designed to ensure that the City is never required to perform work for which reimbursement funds have not been previously deposited (the "**Evergreen Deposit**"). The Evergreen Deposit shall contain funds necessary to cover three (3) months' worth of budgeted expenditures by the City relating to processing of the Applications (i) the month in which work is being done, (ii) the month in which invoices are being prepared for the prior month's work, and (iii) the month those invoices are being reimbursed by Developer. Developer shall fund the Evergreen Deposit initially by depositing with the City on or before ______ 1, 20__ the sum of $1,000,000—an amount that anticipates approximate expenditures by the City of $333,333.33 per month for three months. Developer shall replenish the Evergreen Deposit on a monthly basis until termination of this Agreement pursuant to

Section 1.02 or Section 5.04 or as long as expenditures made by the City relating to the processing of the Applications remain unreimbursed, whichever is later. On or before ______ ___, 20__, Developer shall deposit the amount necessary to replenish the Evergreen Deposit to $1,000,000. Beginning on _________, 20__, Developer shall replenish the Evergreen Deposit by depositing on or before the last day of each month the full amount of all invoices delivered by the City to Developer within the previous month. Thus, for example, on or before ______ __, 20__, Developer would replenish the Evergreen Deposit by depositing the sum of all invoices submitted by the City to Developer during the month of ______ 20__.

(c) In the event the City determines that total invoices for any particular three- (3) month period are likely to exceed $1,000,000, City may request that Developer increase the total funds available in the Evergreen Deposit accordingly. If Developer does not agree to increase the deposited amount, the City may adjust its work schedule, including through the adjustment of Project deadlines, so as not to exceed $1,000,000 in expenditures over any three- (3) month period.

(d) The Parties acknowledge that deposits to the Evergreen Deposit are not a "source of income" within the meaning of the California Political Reform Act (pursuant to California Government Code Section 87103.6).

(e) In no event shall City or its Consultants be obligated to perform any work in connection with the Applications, including but not limited to City staff review, evaluation, analysis, or internal or external communication regarding such Applications where (1) Developer is delinquent in the initial funding of, or any required replenishment of, the Evergreen Deposit required by Section 4.02(b) & (c), above; (2) the actual costs associated with City staff time and/or Consultant Work has exceeded the amount being held by the City in the Evergreen Deposit to cover such costs; or (3) Developer is otherwise in breach of this Agreement in any respect.

(f) Upon termination of this Agreement, City shall have a reasonable time to seek and receive from Developer all remaining and outstanding reimbursements to which it is entitled under this Agreement. Once all remaining and outstanding reimbursements have been paid to City by Developer, City shall return to Developer any remaining unused portion of the Evergreen Deposit.

Section 4.03. Recordkeeping and Audits.

(a) City shall maintain records with respect to the services performed by City and its Consultants under this Agreement (the "**Records**") in accordance with City's current procedures. City shall retain such Records for the period required by law, or, for Records that are the subject of audit findings, until such audit findings have been resolved. The Records shall include official documentation evidencing the charges to support all costs.

(b) At any time during normal business hours, but on no less than forty-eight (48) hours, prior notice by Developer to City, City shall make available to Developer for examination all Records. City shall permit Developer to audit, examine, duplicate, and make excerpts or transcripts of the Records. If any audit reveals inaccuracies in billings or payments, the necessary adjustments to correct the inaccuracies shall be made.

(c) Nothing in this Agreement shall be construed to require City to provide Developer with documents or portions of documents that are privileged, attorney work product, or attorney-client privileged.

ARTICLE 5. MISCELLANEOUS PROVISIONS

Section 5.01. Excusable Delays; Extension of Time of Performance. In the event of delays due to strikes, inability to obtain materials, civil commotion, fire, war, terrorism, lockouts, riots, floods, earthquakes, epidemic, quarantine, freight embargoes, failure of contractors to perform, or other circumstances beyond the reasonable control of the Parties and that substantially interfere with the ability of either Party to perform its obligations under this Agreement, then the time for performance of any such obligation shall be extended for such period of time as the cause of such delay shall exist but in any event not longer than for such period of time ("**Excusable Delay**"). In the event an Excusable Delay results in the delay of payment by Developer of a deposit or other compensation meant to pay for the actual or estimated costs incurred by City and its Consultants in processing the Applications, then City shall have the option of suspending processing of the Applications for the duration of such Excusable Delay.

Section 5.02. California Law. This Agreement shall be governed by, and construed in accordance with, the laws of the State of California.

Section 5.03. Nature of Commitment. Nothing in this Agreement is or should be construed to be a covenant, promise, or commitment by City (including, without limitation, any agency, board, or commission of the City) to grant any Entitlement or to make a final decision on any Application, nor shall it prevent City (including, without limitation, any agency, board, or commission of the City) from acting, or electing not to act, on any Application in any manner other than that deemed proper by City.

Section 5.04. Early Termination.

(a) *By Developer.* Developer or its successors shall have the right, upon ten (10) days' prior written notice to City, to terminate this Agreement, provided Developer has withdrawn each of the Applications and has provided written notice of such withdrawal to City. City shall have two (2) business days following Developer's termination to terminate all substantive Consultant Work. Developer shall remain liable for expenses incurred by City and its Consultants following Developer's termination in order to terminate contractual relationships and to conduct clerical, logistical, or other non-substantive work required to efficiently wrap up the consulting relationship.

(b) *By City.* City shall have the right to terminate both this Agreement and its review, evaluation, consideration, and processing of the Applications (1) at any time during which the City has suspended processing of the Applications pursuant to any provision of this Agreement, or (2) in the event of any breach by Developer of the terms of this Agreement. To terminate this Agreement, City shall provide written Notice of Intent to Terminate to Developer and shall include reference to either the grounds upon which processing has been suspended or the breach upon which the termination is based. Developer shall have ten (10) days to commence cure of the grounds upon which processing has been suspended or the breach. Where Developer has commenced its cure within ten (10) days, it shall have an additional thirty (30) days, or longer upon mutual agreement of the Parties, to complete its cure; provided, however, that the partial reimbursement of funds or partial replenishment of deposits in an amount less than what is required by this Agreement does not qualify as the commencement of a cure. In the event Developer has not commenced its cure within ten (10) days of City's Notice of Intent to Terminate or has not completed its cure within an additional thirty (30) days where cure was timely commenced, City shall have the right to provide Developer a Notice of Termination, which shall have the effect of immediately terminating the Agreement. City shall not be required to do any work relating to the review, evaluations, consideration, or processing of the Applications during the notification and correction or cure periods described in this Section 5.04(b).

(c) *Ongoing Obligation*. Developer shall remain obligated following termination of this Agreement pursuant to Section 1.02 or this Section 5.04 to reimburse the City for all City or Consultant Work performed consistent with this Agreement.

Section 5.05. No Agency, Joint Venture, or Partnership. It is understood that Developer is not an agent of City. City and Developer hereby renounce the existence of any form of joint venture or partnership between them and agree that nothing contained herein or in any document executed in connection therewith shall be construed as making City and Developer joint venturers or partners.

Section 5.06. Notices. Any notice or communication required hereunder between the Parties must be in writing, and may be given either personally, by telefacsimile (with original forwarded by regular United States mail), by registered or certified mail (return receipt requested), or by Federal Express or other similar courier promising overnight delivery. If personally delivered, a notice shall be deemed to have been given when delivered to the Party to whom it is addressed. If given by facsimile transmission, a notice or communication shall be deemed to have been given and received upon actual physical receipt of the entire document by the receiving Party's facsimile machine. Notices transmitted by facsimile after 5:00 p.m. on a normal business day or on a Saturday, Sunday, or holiday shall be deemed to have been given and received on the next normal business day. If given by registered or certified mail, such notice or communication is deemed to have been given and received on the first to occur of (i) actual receipt by any of the addressees designated below as the Party to whom notices are to be sent; or (ii) five (5) days after a registered or certified letter containing such notice, properly addressed, with postage prepaid, is deposited in the United States mail. If given by Federal Express or similar courier, a notice or communication shall be deemed to have been given and received on the date delivered as shown on a receipt issued by the courier. Any Party hereto may at any time, by giving ten (10) days' written notice to the other Party hereto, designate any other address in substitution of the address to which such notice or communication shall be given. Such notices or communications shall be given to the Parties at their addresses set forth below:

CITY:	City Manager
	____________________
	____________________
	____________________
with copies to:	City Attorney
	____________________
	____________________
	____________________
DEVELOPER:	____________________
	____________________
	____________________
with copies to:	____________________
	____________________
	____________________

Section 5.07. Incorporation of Recitals. The recitals contained in this Agreement, and the introductory paragraph preceding the recitals, are hereby incorporated into this Agreement as is fully set forth herein.

Section 5.08. Severability. If any term or provision of this Agreement, or the application of any term or provision of this Agreement to a particular situation, is held by a court of competent jurisdiction to be invalid, void, or unenforceable, the remaining terms and provisions of this Agreement, or the application of this Agreement to other situations, shall continue in full force and effect unless amended or modified by mutual consent of the Parties. Notwithstanding the foregoing, if any material provision of this Agreement, or the application of such provision to a particular situation, is held to be invalid, void, or unenforceable, either City or Developer may (in their sole and absolute discretion) terminate this Agreement by providing written notice of such termination to the other Party, provided, however, that Developer's obligations to pay all processing costs of City and its Consultants pursuant to this Agreement, including any Excess Amounts identified by City, shall survive termination of this Agreement.

Section 5.09. Assignment and Transfer. It is contemplated that Developer may assign or transfer all or any portion of its interest in the Project or the Property to one or more third parties. In the event Developer transfers all of the Property and the Project to a person or entity, the transferee shall automatically succeed to all of Developer's rights and obligations under this Agreement past, present, and future. Developer shall remain jointly and severally liable for all obligations pursuant to this Agreement alongside such new transferee until such time as Developer delivers to City an Assignment and Assumption Agreement executed by such transferee in a form reasonably approved by the City Attorney. In the event Developer proposes to transfer some portion of either the Project or the Property to one or more third parties but retains an interest in either the Property or the Project itself, Developer and such transferee or transferees shall be jointly and severally liable for all obligations pursuant to this Agreement until such time as Developer, the transferee or transferees, and the City execute a Reimbursement and Processing Agreement that supersedes this Agreement and sets forth, among other things, allocation of responsibilities for various costs among Developer and its transferees and City's rights to suspend or terminate processing of Applications in the event of default by fewer than all of the parties to such Reimbursement and Processing Agreement.

Section 5.10. Indemnification, Cooperation in the Event of Challenge.

(a) *Developer Processing Challenge.* A "**Developer Processing Challenge**" is any claim, demand, proceeding, application, petition, complaint, or action filed, brought, or otherwise commenced by Developer seeking to review, challenge, set aside, modify, overturn, supersede, or annul City's review, evaluation, consideration, processing, or disposition of or decisions regarding the Applications or Entitlements or a portion thereof and any combination thereof. As to a Developer Processing Challenge, Developer and City shall each remain liable for their respective attorneys' fees and costs of litigation and costs of experts and consultants retained in such litigation.

(b) *Indemnification for Project-Related Challenges.* A "**Project-Related Challenge**" is: (i) any claim, demand, proceeding, application, petition, complaint, or action filed, brought, or otherwise commenced by a third party seeking to review, challenge, set aside, modify, overturn, supersede, or annul any provision of this Agreement or City's performance hereunder, or City's review, evaluation, consideration, processing, or disposition of or decisions regarding the Applications or Entitlements or a portion thereof and any combination thereof; (ii) any other claim, demand, proceeding, application, petition, complaint, or action filed, brought, or otherwise commenced by Developer (other than a Developer

Processing Challenge) or by a third party concerning the Project or aimed at precluding development of the Project or a portion thereof and any combination thereof, including those actions where City determines, in its sole discretion, that it is obligated to defend the challenged action even if the effect of such action would be to impede development of all or a portion of the Project. As to any Project-Related Challenge by Developer, Developer shall be liable for, and shall reimburse to City, City's attorneys' fees and costs of litigation and costs of experts and consultants retained in such litigation. As to any Project-Related Challenge by a third party, Developer shall fully indemnify, defend, release, and hold harmless City, its officers, its employees, its consultants, and their agents from all financial and other liability related to such Project-Related Challenge, including but not limited to attorneys' fees and costs of litigation and costs of experts and consultants.

(c) *Cooperation in the Event of a Project-Related Challenge.* In the event of any Project-Related Challenge by a third party, the Parties shall cooperate in defending against such challenge. Each Party shall promptly notify the other of any Project-Related Challenge by a third party of which it becomes aware. Developer shall assist and cooperate at its expense with City in connection with any Project-Related Challenge by a third party.

(d) *Reimbursement Relating to Project-Related Challenge.* City may use its own legal staff or outside counsel in connection with defense of any Project-Related Challenge, at the City Attorney's sole discretion, and City shall have the right to select outside counsel of its choice, in its sole discretion. All costs to City associated with its defense of any Project-Related Challenge, including but not limited to the time and expenses of City Attorney's Office, other City staff, any Consultants or experts retained in connection with the Project-Related Challenge, attorneys' fees of City's selected outside counsel, and litigation costs shall be fully reimbursed to City by Developer, provided Developer shall have the right to monthly invoices for all such costs in the case of a Project-Related Challenge by a third party. Developer shall make payment to City for any costs covered by this Section 5.10 within thirty (30) days of receipt of an invoice from City for such costs.

(e) *Limitation on Remedies.* In any action at law or equity or other legal or administrative proceeding arising out of or relating to this Agreement, the Applications, or City's review, evaluation, consideration, processing, or disposition of the Applications, including but not limited to any Developer Processing Challenge or Project-Related Challenge, neither City nor Developer shall be entitled to damages or other remedies or relief except as expressly set forth in this Section 5.10(e). Permitted remedies shall include (i) mandatory or injunctive relief, (ii) writ of mandate, (iii) specific performance or termination of this Agreement, or (iv) a claim for reimbursement of unexpended funds advanced by Developer to City. Without limiting the generality of the foregoing, neither City nor Developer shall be liable, under any circumstances, for any direct, indirect, special, compensatory, consequential, punitive, or exemplary damages, regardless of whether the claim for such damages is based on contract, tort, statute, or other basis liability.

(f) *Continuing Rights, Obligations.* The rights and obligations set forth in this Section 5.10 shall survive termination of this Agreement.

Section 5.11. Integration; Counterparts; Exhibits. This Agreement may be executed in two (2) duplicate originals, each of which is an original, but all of which taken together are considered one and the same instrument. This Agreement consists of Articles 1 through 5, including the recitals, and **Exhibits A-1** and **A-2**, both inclusive, attached hereto, and incorporated by reference herein, which constitute the entire understanding and agreement of the Parties. The exhibits are as follows:

Exhibit A-1 Map of Property
Exhibit A-2 Description of Property

Section 5.12. Amendment of This Agreement. This Agreement may be amended from time to time, in whole or in part, only by written amendment executed by all Parties to the Agreement or their successors in interest subject to the same process by which the Agreement was originally executed.

Section 5.13. Waiver. Nothing in this Agreement shall be deemed to waive any remedy of either Party under California law.

CITY:
CITY OF _______________, CALIFORNIA

By: ___________________________________
Its: ___________________________________

APPROVED AS TO FORM:

By: ________________________________
_____________________, City Attorney

ATTEST:

____
_____________________, City Clerk

DEVELOPER:
By: ___________________________________
Its: ___________________________________

APPENDIX 7

Sample Project School Facilities Agreement (California)

THIS PROJECT SCHOOL FACILITIES AGREEMENT ("**Agreement**") shall be effective as of ____________ ("**Effective Date**"), and is entered into by and between CITY UNIFIED SCHOOL DISTRICT, a public school district in the State of California ("**District**"), on the one hand, and ___________________________ ("**Developer**"), on the other. For purposes of this Agreement, the term "**Party**" shall refer to either the District or Developer, and the term "**Parties**" shall refer to the District and Developer, collectively. Terms capitalized herein are defined in the text where the term appears for the first time or in Article 1 hereof.

RECITALS

A. WHEREAS, Developer is the owner/developer of certain real property located within the District's boundaries, in the City of ______________, State of California, as more particularly described below and in Exhibit A, attached hereto (hereinafter "**Property**") on which Developer is seeking entitlements to construct residential units, commercial space, and other public improvements.

B. WHEREAS, Developer seeks certain development approvals from the City of ______________ to allow construction of a mixed use community on approximately ______ acres of land currently planned to include between ______ and ______ mid and high-rise residential units, together with approximately ______ Million square feet of commercial/retail/

non-residential space which includes hotels, theaters, museums and parks, and may also include a Major League stadium planned to accommodate ______ fans and a ______ acre ______________ Hospital complex (hereinafter "**Project**").

C. WHEREAS, the Parties desire to set forth the terms and conditions under which Developer will (1) provide a school site for and fund a new elementary school within the boundaries of the Property to accommodate students from its Project, (2) fund its proportionate share of the cost of additional elementary school facilities (which may include a second elementary school) to accommodate students from the Project that cannot be housed in the new elementary school or other District facilities, and (3) provide additional funding for costs of interim or permanent facilities to accommodate Project Students.

D. WHEREAS, the Parties acknowledge that the number of students to be generated by the Project is difficult to predict due to the very-high-density and urban nature of the planned residential units in the Project (a development type that does not exist in the District), but that even at lower numbers, students generated by the Project will have an impact on the District's elementary school ("**K–6**") facilities and infrastructure and may require construction of one or more permanent elementary K–6 school facilities (preceded by acquisition of one or more school sites for the permanent elementary K–6 facilities), and provision of interim facilities to accommodate students generated by the Project until permanent new elementary K–6 facilities are complete.

E. WHEREAS, the Parties agree that the statutory development fees on residential and non-residential construction authorized by law, and including, without limitation, Section 53080 of the Government Code, as limited by Section 65995 of the California Government Code, Chapter 4.7 (commencing with Section 65970), Chapter 4.9 (commencing with Section 65995) of Division 1 of Title 7 of the Government Code, and existing court decisions together with State grants offered through the Leroy F. Greene School Facilities Act of 1998 (as amended) may not be adequate to fund permanent elementary K–6 school facilities, and provision of interim facilities, as and when needed to accommodate students generated by the Project.

F. WHEREAS, the Parties wish to provide for quality educational facilities to accommodate students within the Project and to memorialize their agreements and understandings regarding funding and construction of such facilities, statutory school fees, mitigation payments, state funding and other matters pertaining to school facilities mitigation.

AGREEMENT

NOW, THEREFORE, in consideration of the above recitals, the terms and conditions, and mutual covenants and obligations of the Parties set forth herein, District and Developer hereby agree as follows:

ARTICLE I
STATUTORY AUTHORITY AND DEFINITIONS

Section 1.1 Recitals. The recitals stated above are true and correct and are incorporated by reference into this Agreement.

Section 1.2 Authority for this Agreement. This Agreement discharges all obligations of Developer and the Property, statutory or otherwise, to mitigate the impacts of the Project on the District, except as set forth in this Agreement.

Section 1.3 Definitions. All references herein to "Articles," "Sections" and other subdivisions are to the corresponding articles, sections or subdivisions of this Agreement, and the words "herein," "hereof," "hereunder" and other words of similar import refer to this Agreement as a whole and not to any particular Article, Section or subdivision hereof. In addition to the terms defined elsewhere in this Agreement, the following terms have the meaning set forth below:

"**Actual Student Generation Rate**" has the meaning ascribed thereto in Section 2.6(a).

"**Additional Elementary School Facilities**" has the meaning ascribed thereto in Section 2.4(a).

"**Additional Elementary School Project Students**" has the meaning ascribed thereto in Section 2.4(a).

"**Advance Payments**" has the meaning ascribed thereto in Section 2.7(c).

"**Agreement**" has the meaning ascribed thereto in the preamble.

"**Annual Review Meeting**" has the meaning ascribed thereto in Section 2.6(a).

"**Approved List**" has the meaning ascribed thereto in Section 4.2.

"**Architect**" has the meaning ascribed thereto in Section 2.3(b).

"**Assisted Living Unit**" has the meaning ascribed thereto in Section 2.7(a).

"**Audit**" has the meaning ascribed thereto in Section 3.2.

"**Auditing Agency**" has the meaning ascribed thereto in Section 3.2.

"**Calendar Year**" means the period commencing January 1 of any year and ending the following December 31.

"**CDE**" has the meaning ascribed thereto in Section 2.3(b).

"**Certificate of Compliance**" means a certification issued by the District pursuant to Education Code Section 17620(b) acknowledging that the recipient thereof has complied with any fee, charge, dedication, or other requirement levied by the District for the purpose of funding the construction or reconstruction of school facilities or that the fee, charge, dedication, or other requirement does not apply to the referenced development.

"**Chargeable Covered and Enclosed Space**" has the meaning ascribed thereto in Government Code Section 65995(b)(2).

"**City**" has the meaning ascribed thereto in Section 2.2.

"**Closing**" has the meaning ascribed thereto in Section 4.3.

"**Commercial Mitigation Payments**" has the meaning ascribed thereto in Section 2.7(a).

"**Completion Date**" has the meaning ascribed thereto in Section 2.3(d).

"**Construction Ready Condition**" means, unless otherwise agreed in writing by the Parties, that:

(i) the school site being rough graded to pad as verified by a registered civil engineer as described in the plans for development of the school site, including:

(A) one-hundred percent (100%) useable to construct a public school structure including adequate surface drainage without any additional engineering and design costs due to topographic conditions;

(B) utilities stubbed to the property line of the site (and the cost of utility hookups), including water, sewer, power, internet (including fiber optic if available), all sized adequately for the particular designed school facilities called for by this Agreement; and

(C) curbs, gutters, roadways, landscaping and irrigation, signals if required and approved by the City, signage, street lighting in and on two adjacent rights of way and any other improvements necessary to access and serve the school facilities called for by this Agreement.

(ii) In addition, Construction Ready Condition requires the school site to be in accordance with the standards for school site construction, as approved by the Division of State Architect or other applicable approving authority relating to off-site utility services (e.g., water, sewage, gas, electricity, telephone, internet).

(iii) In addition, Construction Ready Condition requires the school site to be in accordance with the standards set by the California Department of Education and the Department of Toxic Substances Control.

"**Construction Requirements**" has the meaning ascribed thereto in Section 2.3(b).

"**Cure Period**" has the meaning ascribed thereto in Section 5.3.

"**Default**" means any material or substantial failure by a Party to perform its obligations or responsibilities under this Agreement. Minor or technical breaches or deviations from the terms of the Agreement that do not materially affect the rights or obligations of the Parties shall not constitute a Default. A Default shall not exist until expiration of the applicable notice and Cure Period under Section 5.3.

"**Default Notice**" has the meaning ascribed thereto in Section 5.3.

"**Defaulting Party**" has the meaning ascribed thereto in Section 5.3.

"**Developer**" has the meaning ascribed thereto in the preamble.

"**District**" has the meaning ascribed thereto in the preamble.

"**District Funded Capacity**" has the meaning ascribed thereto in Section 2.3(h).

"**DTSC**" has the meaning ascribed thereto in Section 4.1.

"**Effective Date**" has the meaning ascribed thereto in the preamble.

"**Elementary School Facilities**" means school facilities serving students in any or all of grades K–6.

"**Elementary School Project Students**" means Project Students in grades K–6.

"**Five-Year Student Projection**" has the meaning ascribed thereto in Section 2.6(c).

"**K–6**" means kindergarten through sixth grade.

"**K–6 School**" has the meaning ascribed thereto in Section 2.3(a).

"**K–6 School Need Determination**" has the meaning ascribed thereto in Section 2.3(d).

"**K–6 School Site**" has the meaning ascribed thereto in Section 4.1.

"**Loss of State Funds**" has the meaning ascribed thereto in Section 3.2.

"**Mitigation Funds**" has the meaning ascribed thereto in Section 2.7(b).

"**Mitigation Payment**" has the meaning ascribed thereto in Section 2.7(a).

"**Non-Defaulting Party**" has the meaning ascribed thereto in Section 5.3.

"**OPSC**" has the meaning ascribed thereto in Section 2.3(b).

"**Originally Identified Site**" has the meaning ascribed thereto in Section 4.1.

"**Other Authorized Uses**" has the meaning ascribed thereto in Section 2.7(d).

"**Outstanding Obligations**" has the meaning ascribed thereto in Section 2.7(d).

"**Party**" or "**Parties**" has the meaning ascribed thereto in the preamble.

"**Percentage Share**" means the percentage figure derived by dividing (i) the number of Additional Elementary School Project Students by (ii) the total student capacity of the facility. Solely by way of example, if 240 Additional Elementary School Project Students are generated by the Project and a new school facility has a capacity of 600 students, Developer's Percentage Share would be 0.40 or 40%.

"**Project**" has the meaning ascribed thereto in the recitals.

"**Project School Facilities**" has the meaning ascribed thereto in Section 2.4(a).

"**Project Students**" means school-age (K–12) students residing within or projected to reside within the Project and the District.

"**Property**" has the meaning ascribed thereto in the recitals.

"**SAB Adjustment**" has the meaning ascribed thereto in Section 2.7(a).

"**School Facility Program**" means the State program established pursuant to the School Facilities Act to provide for funding for new construction and modernization of school facilities, as described in Title 2 of the California Code of Regulations, Section 1859 *et seq.*

"**School Site PSA**" has the meaning ascribed thereto in Section 4.1.

"**Second K–6 School**" has the meaning ascribed thereto in Section 2.4(b).

"**Second K–6 School Need Determination**" has the meaning ascribed thereto in Section 2.4(b).

"**Second K–6 School Site**" has the meaning ascribed thereto in Section 2.4(d).

"**Senior Unit**" has the meaning ascribed thereto in Section 2.7(a).

"**Site Acquisition Cost**" has the meaning ascribed thereto in Section 4.2.

"**State Funds**" has the meaning ascribed thereto in Section 3.1.

"**State Law**" means the applicable laws and/or administrative regulations of the State of California and its agencies.

"**Statutory Fees**" means the fees that may be imposed as a condition of development established by Section 17620 of the Education Code, as limited by Chapter 4.9 (commencing with Section 65995) of Division 1 of Title 7 of the Government Code. Notwithstanding the limitation presently set forth in Section 65995, *et seq.*, of the Government Code, in the event that such sections are rescinded, amended, or otherwise become inoperative, the Statutory Fee shall include the full fee intended to be levied by the District pursuant to Section 17620 of the Education Code or any other provision of law.

"**Third-Party Litigation**" has the meaning ascribed thereto in Section 2.2.

ARTICLE II
FEES, MITIGATION, AND PAYMENT CONDITIONS

Section 2.1 Fees and Credits. It is the intention of this Agreement that all requirements relating to Statutory Fees or other school mitigation by Developer in relation to the Project shall be satisfied by the performance of the obligations set forth in this Agreement and that Developer shall not be required to provide any additional school mitigation payments for the Project.

Section 2.2 Conditions Precedent. The obligations set forth in this Agreement are binding on the Parties as of the Effective Date, but are not subject to enforcement against the Parties until and upon approval of the

Project by the City of ______________ ("**City**"), and after applicable statutes of limitation for challenging entitlements for the Project, including under the California Environmental Quality Act, have expired without any cause of action being brought by a third party ("**Third-Party Litigation**"). In the event of Third-Party Litigation, the obligations set forth herein become enforceable after entry of a final, non-appealable judgment or other resolution allowing the Project to proceed.

Section 2.3 School Facilities.

(a) K–6 School. The Parties agree that, provided the K–6 School Need Determination is made, the Parties shall meet to discuss the timing and cost of planning and construction of a K–6 School. Unless the Parties otherwise agree, the District shall plan, design, install site improvements for, and construct on the K–6 School Site a complete, multi-story, K–6 elementary school sufficient to accommodate 600 students together with new furniture, fixtures, equipment, standard service equipment and enhanced intersection or enhanced crosswalk features as needed to access the joint-use park (all such improvements, together with the K–6 School Site, collectively "**K–6 School**"), to be funded as provided in this Agreement. The District may elect, in its reasonable discretion, to convert the K–6 School to a K–8 school at no additional cost to Developer; provided, however, that the K–6 School Need Determination and all other determinations concerning the type, size, capacity, fixtures, equipment and other elements of the K–6 School shall continue to be predicated on Elementary School Project Students. If the District elects to convert the K–6 School to a K–8 school, all references in this Agreement to the K–6 School shall be deemed to refer to the K–8 school. District shall provide notice of such election to Developer within 90 days after the K–6 School Need Determination. Unless the Parties otherwise agree, the grade configuration of the K–6 School shall not be changed for a period of ten (10) years from the date of opening the K–6 School. The preceding sentence shall not apply to the Second K–6 School.

(b) Architect; Design and Specifications. The architect for the design and ongoing supervision of construction of the K–6 School ("**Architect**") shall be selected by the Parties according to a qualifications-based selection process consistent with State law from a list of District-approved candidates, all of whom are fully licensed and qualified in the manner required by California law for the design and ongoing supervision of construction of a California public school facility. From that list, Developer shall select three candidates, one of which shall be selected by the District as the Architect. The District shall hire the Architect directly, pursuant to a contract whose terms are reasonably approved by Developer, and all fees and costs of the Architect shall be paid from Mitigation Funds. The Parties shall cooperate in good faith and work with the Architect to ensure that the K–6 School (i) is sized to accommodate 75 square feet per student, for 600 students, within a multi-story facility; (ii) is generally compatible with the architectural theme of the community in which the K–6 School will be located; (iii) complies with all applicable provisions of California law, including Title 24, and all regulations of the California Department of Education ("**CDE**"), Division of the State Architect, Office of Public School Construction ("**OPSC**"), and other agencies with jurisdiction; and (iv) maximizes joint use opportunities to the extent possible, including joint use parking, parks and multi-use facilities, each of which shall be suitable for school use as approved by the City of ______________ and CDE (collectively the "**Construction Requirements**"). The furnishings, fixtures, equipment and education technology provided for the K–6 School shall conform to the District's educational specifications, subject to modifications for technological advances or energy-saving incentives or requirements that are necessary to achieve cost savings. Nothing herein shall be construed to limit the education or design specifications of the K–6 School with respect to any changes mandated by State, local or federal law or regulation, which mandated changes shall be included in the design specifications. Subject to compliance with the Construction Requirements, all final decisions relating to the design of the K–6 School shall be made in the District's sole discretion.

(c) Cooperation in Design. Prior to commencement of the design of the K–6 School, the Parties shall meet with the Architect to discuss and reasonably agree upon the K–6 School Construction Requirements and the process of developing and selecting the exterior materials, colors, textures, landscaping and other design elements and features.

(d) K–6 School Need Determination; Completion and Occupancy. The trigger for planning, design and construction of the K–6 School shall be the determination, based on the Five-Year Student Projection, that the Project will generate at least 300 Elementary School Project Students ("**K–6 School Need Determination**"). If the K–6

School Need Determination is made, unless the Parties otherwise agree, the District shall use its best efforts to cause the K–6 School to be complete and ready for occupancy in the fall of the year in which the Five-Year Student Projection shows that the Project will have generated at least 300 Elementary School Project Students ("**Completion Date**").

(e) Furniture, Equipment, Books, Materials and Technology. The K–6 School shall include all furniture, fixtures and equipment, library books and materials, and technology equipment, supplies, and materials necessary for the effective operation of a K–6 elementary school, provided, however, that the total amount to be funded by Mitigation Funds shall not exceed one million dollars ($1,000,000.00), which shall be adjusted annually pursuant to the SAB index applicable to furnishings, fixtures and equipment for schools or, if there is no longer such index, by the California Consumer Price Index, with the first increase applicable on December 1, ____.

(f) Priority Attendance Rights. The attendance boundary for the K–6 School shall be coterminous with the boundary of the Property to the fullest extent permitted by law. District shall provide Developer with at least two years' notice of any proposed changes in the attendance boundary. To the extent consistent with District policy, priority shall be given for enrollment in the K–6 School (and, if applicable, Second K–6 School) to students residing within the attendance boundary.

(g) Additional Amenities or Costs. Nothing in this Agreement shall limit the District's discretion to expand the capacity of or provide additional facilities or amenities for the K–6 School provided that such increased capacity or additional facilities or amenities shall be at the District's sole and separate cost unless otherwise agreed by the Parties.

(h) Adjustment in School Size; Pro Rata Funding Obligation. If, based on the Five-Year Student Projection and other information reviewed by the Parties in conjunction with the Annual Review Meetings, the Project, at build-out, will generate more than 300 Elementary School Project Students but fewer than 500 Elementary School Project Students, the size of the K–6 School shall be reduced to conform to the number of Elementary School Project Students reasonably projected to be generated; provided, however, that under such circumstance, the District may elect to construct a school that is larger than necessary to accommodate Elementary School Project Students if the District funds the pro rata cost of the additional capacity that will be available to house students other than Elementary School Project Students ("**District Funded Capacity**"). Solely by way of illustrative example, if the Project is projected to generate 400 Elementary School Project Students at build-out, but the District elects to construct facilities to accommodate 500 students, the District Funded Capacity would be the facilities necessary to accommodate the additional 100 students. The District Funded Capacity and any payment by District therefor shall not include the cost of the school site acquisition. In the event that Elementary School Project Students actually generated by the Project thereafter exceed the projected number such that some or all of the District Funded Capacity would not have been required, the cost of such District Funded Capacity shall be reimbursed to the District from Mitigation Funds up to the amount commensurate with the number of Elementary School Project Students in excess of the number projected. Under the foregoing example, if the Project actually generated 500 Elementary School Project Students, the District would be reimbursed for the cost of all of the District Funded Capacity from Mitigation Funds; if it actually generated 450 Elementary School Projected Students, the District would be reimbursed for half of the cost of the District Funded Capacity.

(i) Fewer Than 300 Elementary Students; Other Use of Funds. If, based on the Five-Year Student Projection and other information reviewed by the Parties in conjunction with the Annual Review Meetings, the Project, at build-out, will generate fewer than 300 Elementary School Project Students, unless the Parties otherwise agree, the K–6 School shall not be built (and the K–6 School Site shall not be conveyed to the District). If the Parties mutually agree that the K–6 School shall not be built, Mitigation Funds in the ______________ SFE Account shall be available to the District for Other Authorized Uses in the discretion of the District.

Section 2.4 Additional Elementary School Project Students.

(a) Additional Elementary School Facilities. In the event that more than 600 Elementary School Project Students are projected to be generated by the Project (those Elementary School Project Students in excess of 600 being defined as the "**Additional Elementary School Project Students**"), then Developer shall fund its Percentage Share of the cost of any new Elementary School Facilities to accommodate the Additional Elementary School Project Students ("**Additional**

Elementary School Facilities") in the same manner as the funding of the K–6 School described in Section 2.7. The K–6 School and the Additional Elementary School Facilities are collectively referred to as the "**Project School Facilities.**" Depending upon current and projected enrollment, capacity, development projections and other relevant factors, the Additional Elementary School Facilities may include renovation or expansion of then-existing District Elementary School Facilities and/or use of relocatable classrooms or, provided the Second K–6 School Need Determination is made pursuant to Section 2.4(b), acquisition of a school site and construction of the Second K–6 School thereon (as described in Section 2.4(b)). At the first Annual Review Meeting following final completion and occupancy of the K–6 School (and, as applicable, at subsequent Annual Review Meetings), the Parties shall determine, based on the Five-Year Student Projection, whether or not any Additional Elementary School Facilities will be required to accommodate Elementary School Project Students and, if so, the cost of funding of such Additional Elementary School Facilities from the ______________ SFE Account.

(b) Second K–6 School Need Determination. If the Five-Year Student Projection shows that the Project will generate at least 350 Additional Elementary School Project Students ("**Second K–6 School Need Determination**"), the District shall plan, design, install site improvements for, and construct a second K–6 elementary school on the Second K–6 School Site sufficient to accommodate the Additional Elementary School Project Students together with new furniture, fixtures, equipment, and standard service equipment (all such improvements, together with the Second K–6 School Site, collectively "**Second K–6 School**"). The District shall use best efforts to cause the Second K–6 School to be complete and ready for occupancy in the fall of the year in which the Five-Year Student Projection shows that the Project will have generated at least 350 Additional Elementary School Project Students. The Second K–6 School shall be sized to accommodate the number of Additional Elementary School Project Students reasonably projected to be generated; provided, however, that the District may elect to construct a school that is larger than necessary to accommodate the Additional Elementary School Project Students if the District funds the pro rata cost for the additional capacity that will be available to house students from outside the Project.

(c) Design and Specifications; Other Requirements. Except as otherwise expressly provided, the Second K–6 School shall be subject to the same requirements, standards and restrictions pertaining to design, construction, furnishings, fixtures and equipment, books and materials, attendance boundary and priority enrollment, and additional amenities as those for the K–6 School described in Section 2.3(a) through (h). As with the K–6 School, the District may elect, in its reasonable discretion, to convert the Second K–6 School to a K–8 school at no additional cost to Developer and subject to the same requirements and conditions as those for conversion of the K–6 School set forth in Section 2.3(a), except as expressly provided in that section.

(d) Second K–6 School Site. The Parties acknowledge that, as of the date of the Second K–6 School Need Determination, there is a substantial probability that all of the parcels within the Property of a location, size and configuration necessary for the Second K–6 School will have been developed, sold or otherwise committed to other purposes. The Parties shall use commercially reasonable efforts to find a suitable and mutually agreeable school site for the Second K–6 School ("**Second K–6 School Site**") within the Property boundaries. If the Parties are unable to find and/or reasonably agree upon such a site, the Parties shall select a mutually agreeable site outside the boundaries of the Property. The purchase price for the Second K–6 School Site shall be the fair market value of the Second K–6 School Site in a Construction Ready Condition, based upon an appraisal conducted in conformance with the requirements of Section 4.2 by an appraiser selected in the same manner as the appraiser for the K–6 School. The Second K–6 School Site shall be funded in the same manner as the K–6 School Site, as described in Article IV.

Section 2.5 Middle School and High School Facilities. Middle school (grades 7–8) and high school (grades 9–12) Project Students shall be accommodated in the District's existing middle schools and high schools, or in such additional, expanded, renovated and/or temporary school facilities as the District may elect to fund with proceeds of the Commercial Mitigation Payments.

Section 2.6 Coordination of Parties.

(a) Annual Meeting. The Parties acknowledge that enrollment, capacity, timing, cost and other assumptions underlying this Agreement may change over time. Accordingly, the Parties shall meet at least annually, on or about November 1 of each year, and no later than December 1 ("**Annual Review Meeting**"), and more often if requested by a Party, to review the status of development of the Project and the then-current projection of anticipated Elementary School Project Students to be served by the District. The student generation rates will be calculated and revised on an annual basis by the District based upon actual generation of Elementary School Project Students from the Project applied to the then-current development plan of the Developer ("**Actual Student Generation Rate**"), as further described below. The Parties will also communicate regarding timing for acquisition, preparation and conveyance of the K–6 School and, if applicable, the Additional Elementary School Facilities. Each Party will use its best efforts to cooperate in good faith and avoid interference with the other Party in the satisfaction of its obligations relating to this Agreement.

(b) Development Projections. At least 30 days prior to each Annual Review Meeting, the Developer will provide the District with updated information on the status of the Project's development plans, including but not limited to: (i) modifications to the timing and product phasing of future construction; (ii) modifications to the housing type (i.e., multi-family, high density condominiums, active adult, senior living, etc.) and products offered ("for sale," apartment rental units, etc.); (iii) a summary of the housing types and products to be constructed, including square footage and number of bedrooms; and (iv) anticipated timing of development and build-out of the Project.

(c) Student Enrollment and Projections. Prior to each Annual Review Meeting, the District shall prepare and provide to Developer a report (the cost of which shall be paid from Mitigation Funds) in which the District shall (i) determine its district-wide K–6 enrollment (separately identifying the number and grade levels of students enrolled in the District but not residing within District's boundaries), based on the most recent CBEDS report and residency information and other relevant data; (ii) determine the number of Elementary School Project Students in each grade level based on the most recent CBEDS report and other relevant information; and (iii) estimate, based on the Actual Student

Generation Rate, the number of Elementary School Project Students reasonably expected to be generated from projected new development within the Property over each of the next five Calendar Years, inclusive of the Calendar Year in which the report is being prepared, based on the number and mix of new Project units anticipated to be constructed and occupied during such time period (the "**Five-Year Student Projection**"). The Annual Review Meeting shall include enrollment planning for the K–6 School (or Second K–6 School) based on Elementary School Project Students anticipated to be generated by the Project and discussion of any potential changes in grade configuration of the K–6 School.

Section 2.7 Mitigation Funds; SFE Account.

(a) Mitigation Funds. For the purpose of funding the Project School Facilities, Developer shall pay to the District the sum of $4.50 per square foot for each new residential unit constructed within the Project ("**Mitigation Payment**") at the time of issuance of a certificate of occupancy for each such unit (or equivalent approval or certification that the unit is ready for occupancy). Developer shall ensure that District receives notice of the issuance of a building permit and advance notice of the intent to issue a certificate of occupancy for each such unit. At the time of issuance of a building permit for any commercial or industrial development or any Assisted Living Unit or Senior Unit constructed on the Property, Developer shall pay to the District the sum of $0.56 per square foot of Chargeable Covered and Enclosed Space of such development ("**Commercial Mitigation Payment**"). The Mitigation Payment and Commercial Mitigation Payment shall be adjusted for inflation according to the adjustment for inflation set forth in the statewide cost index for class B construction, as determined by the State Allocation Board ("**SAB Adjustment**"), which increase shall be effective as of the date of the meeting at which the adjustment is approved by the State Allocation Board. If the SAB Adjustment is no longer available, the adjustment shall be pursuant to the RS Means Construction Cost Index. As used herein, "**Assisted Living Unit**" means any unit which is a part of a residential care facility for the elderly as described in Health & Safety Code Section 1569.2(k) or a multilevel facility for the elderly as described in Health & Safety Code Section 15432(d)(9); and "**Senior Unit**" means a unit within the Property developed for senior citizen housing as described in Civil Code Section 51.3.

(b) Use of Payment Proceeds. All Mitigation Payments (including all interest earned thereon) shall be deposited in a separate, interest-bearing account denominated the ______________ School Facilities Escrow Account ("______________ **SFE Account**") and applied by the District solely to fund Project School Facilities, to reimburse Developer for Advance Payments (including, without limitation, any portion of the Site Acquisition Cost treated as an Advance Payment), as provided below, or to reimburse District pursuant to Section 2.3(h) until all such Project School Facilities have been fully funded. Funds in the ______________ SFE Account, including interest earned thereon, are referred to as "**Mitigation Funds**." Proceeds of Commercial Mitigation Payments shall not be deposited in the ______________ SFE Account, but shall be deposited in the District's existing capital facilities accounts and used to fund interim school facilities and/or additional, expanded, renovated and/or temporary middle school or high school facilities that will serve Project Students and for bussing necessary to transport Project Students to school facilities.

(c) Advance Payment of Elementary School Costs. The Parties recognize that, at times, there may not be sufficient Mitigation Funds in the ______________ SFE Account to pay the costs of the K–6 School (including, without limitation, the balance of the Site Acquisition Cost) or the Additional Elementary School Facilities (including, if applicable, the Second K–6 School) as and when required under this Agreement. If sufficient Mitigation Funds are not available in the ______________ SFE Account as and when needed to pay for such costs, Developer shall advance to the District such amounts as are reasonably required to fund the Project School Facilities costs ("**Advance Payments**"). The District shall provide Developer with 60 days' written notice of a request for the Advance Payment. All Advance Payments shall be deposited in the ______________ SFE Account and shall be treated as an advance to the District and promptly reimbursed to Developer at such time as there are sufficient funds, net of the Advance Payments, in the ______________ SFE Account to pay ongoing Project School Facilities costs. Alternatively, in its discretion, Developer may take credits against future Mitigation Payments until such credits equal the amount of Advance Payments to be reimbursed. The credits shall be reflected in a certificate issued by the District, which shall be assignable to merchant builders or other Parties constructing residential units on the Property with prior notice of the assignment by Developer to District.

(d) Full Funding; Other Authorized Uses. Upon the mutual determination of the Parties that sufficient funds exist in the ____________ SFE Account to reimburse Developer for all Advance Payments and pay all outstanding and projected costs of the Project School Facilities (all such reimbursement and cost amounts, collectively, "**Outstanding Obligations**"), the balance of Mitigation Funds in the ____________ SFE Account over and above the amount of the Outstanding Obligations shall be available to the District to fund construction, expansion, renovation or modernization of other interim or permanent school facilities that will serve Project Students ("**Other Authorized Uses**"). If the Parties are unable to agree that release of Mitigation Funds to the District has been triggered under this Section 2.7(d), and provided Developer has been fully reimbursed for all Advance Payments, the District shall have the option, in its discretion, to send written confirmation to Developer that its obligations under this Agreement have been fully satisfied, whereupon the balance of the Mitigation Funds shall be released to the District.

(e) Increases in Mitigation Payment Amount. The Parties acknowledge and agree that in light of Developer's obligation to make Advance Payments to the District in amounts reasonably required to fund current Project School Facilities costs, and to be reimbursed for such Advance Payments from the ____________ SFE Account, Developer shall have the right to determine whether the Mitigation Payment should be increased, in addition to the inflationary increases required by Section 2.7(a), in order to reflect changes in assumptions regarding the density of the Project, the number of Project Students, the availability of State Funds, the needed Project School Facilities, and other variables. Accordingly, at the first Annual Review Meeting, and no more than annually thereafter, Developer, in its sole and absolute discretion, shall have the option of increasing (but not reducing) the amount of the required Mitigation Payment for Project residential units for which a certificate of occupancy has not yet been issued. Except for inflationary increases as provided in Section 2.7(a), nothing in this Agreement shall be construed to require Developer at any time to increase the amount of the Mitigation Payment.

Section 2.8 State Funds and Local Match Obligation. The Parties intend and agree that the Mitigation Payments and Advance Payments by Developer under this Agreement shall be used to fund the equivalent of the District's local match obligation under the School Facility Program for the K–6 School Site, the K–6 School, the Second K–6 School Site, the Second K–6 School, and/or the other Additional Elementary School Facilities and that the balance of the costs of these school facilities should be funded by State Funds under the School Facility Program. However, the Parties acknowledge that all or part of the State Funds for which the Project School Facilities are eligible may not be available as and when needed to fund these facilities. Accordingly, Developer agrees that the Mitigation Payments and Advance Payments shall be used as and when needed to fund the Project School Facilities, and that any State Funds received for the Project School Facilities, whether before or after such facilities are funded, shall be paid to Developer upon receipt by the District (provided, however, that State Funds received for the K–6 School Site or the Second K–6 School Site, as applicable, shall be paid to Developer no earlier than close of escrow of the conveyance of the K–6 School Site or the Second K–6 School Site as applicable, to the District). Consistent with this understanding, Developer shall bear the risk that no such State Funds will be received by the District, despite the best efforts of both Parties under Article III to secure such funds, either before or after the K–6 School Site or the Second K–6 School Site as applicable, is conveyed or Project School Facilities are funded through the ______________ SFE Account. Developer shall be entitled only to State Funds actually received by the District for property conveyed or school facilities (or portion thereof) funded by Developer. The Parties acknowledge and agree that this Agreement and/or the School Site PSA shall be used by the District as evidence that it has secured funding for the 50% local matching funds required under the School Facility Program and as part of the certification to the SAB that the District will fund its local match share of each school facilities project.

ARTICLE III
OTHER SOURCES OF FUNDING FOR SCHOOL FACILITIES

Section 3.1 State Funds. The District shall diligently apply for and use its best effort to obtain State Funds for the Project School Facilities (including, without limitation, acquisition of the K–6 School Site and, as applicable, the Second K–6 School site) to the extent that eligibility for such funds results from tentative map approval of the Project. As used herein, "**State Funds**" means funds available to or obtained by the District from the State of California under all school funding programs including, without limitation, the Leroy F. Greene School Facilities Act of 1998, as amended, or any other law related to funding of school facilities, and are either (a) designated by the State for the Project School Facilities, or (b) in the event such funds are not specifically designated by the State for the Project School Facilities, applied by the District to such Project School Facilities. Notwithstanding the foregoing, "State Funds" shall not include any funds available to or obtained by District from the State exclusively for enhancements to such facilities beyond the size, scope, design and education specifications of the facilities contemplated by this Agreement (including, without limitation, State Funds obtained by the District for District Funded Capacity). The District shall, in cooperation with a District-selected school facilities consultant (to be paid from Mitigation Funds) and a consultant retained by Developer, in good faith, use its best efforts to establish the District's eligibility for and obtain an apportionment from the State Allocation Board (SAB) of the maximum allowable amount of State Funds available for site acquisition, site development and new construction (including, without limitation, new construction grants, grants for site acquisition, site utilities, off-site improvements, service site development costs and other supplemental grants and/or enhancements, such as energy allowances) for the Project School Facilities; provided, however, that nothing in this Agreement requires the District to file applications under the State Financial Hardship Program, or to utilize eligibility for State Funds that is generated by other new development in the District. In so doing, the District's obligation shall include, but not be limited to, promptly submitting to the CDE, OPSC, SAB, and any other state or local agency as may be desirable or necessary, any and all properly completed forms, documents, reports, studies or information of any kind that may be required or advisable during the term of this Agreement for apportionment and release of State Funds to the District. All State Funds obtained by the District for Project School Facilities shall be paid to Developer in accordance with Section 2.8.

Section 3.2 Audit. The Parties acknowledge that the use of State Funds received by District pursuant to Section 3.1 herein may give rise to an audit by the OPSC, SAB or other state agency (any or all such entities, "**Auditing Agency**") pursuant to Title 2, Section 1859.106 of the California Code of Regulations or other applicable law ("**Audit**"). Upon receipt of notice that an Auditing Agency intends to conduct an Audit, District shall immediately notify Developer, whereupon Developer and District shall reasonably cooperate with and assist each other in connection with the Audit with the aim of ensuring that the Audit does not result in adjustment of the apportionment of State Funds, collection or reimbursement procedures, or any other actions or determinations that may require District to surrender or reimburse any or all such State Funds to the State, to forego future State Funds allocations, to have funds deducted from future State Funds allocations, or otherwise to lose all or any part of the State Funds allocated (any or all such results, collectively, "**Loss of State Funds**"). If the District is compelled to surrender or reimburse all or any portion of the State Funds actually received and paid to Developer in connection with acquisition or construction of the Project School Facilities, Developer shall reimburse the District for the Loss of State Funds.

ARTICLE IV
K–6 SCHOOL SITE

Section 4.1 K–6 School Site. Developer has identified a site within the Project, depicted in Exhibit "B" hereto ("**Originally Identified Site**"), that is acceptable to the District to serve as the site for the K–6 School ("**K–6 School Site**"). The K–6 School Site shall be free and clear of encumbrances that would affect the District's ability to use the site for its intended purposes. Developer shall convey the K–6 School Site no later than 18 months prior to the Completion Date for the K–6 School. The Parties shall in good faith negotiate a purchase and sale agreement ("**School Site PSA**") for the K–6 School Site. Failure to agree on the terms of the School Site PSA shall not relieve Developer of its obligations to convey the K–6 School Site to the District. Further, the K–6 School Site shall be subject to final approval by CDE, the Department of Toxic Substances Control ("**DTSC**"), and the District Board of Education pursuant to Education Code Section 17211, and the District shall not be required to acquire the K–6 School Site if CDE and/or DTSC determines the K–6 School Site is unacceptable or the K–6 School Site otherwise fails to meet State-mandated site selection standards. If CDE and/or DTSC does not approve the Originally Identified Site or the Originally Identified Site otherwise fails to meet State-mandated site selection standards, Developer and District shall act promptly to take all further actions reasonably necessary to obtain CDE and DTSC approval of the Originally Identified Site and satisfy State selection standards or shall identify to District an alternate to the Originally Identified Site of the approximate size, access, and use as a school site for the District that is acceptable to CDE and DTSC and meets State site selection standards. Developer shall use commercially reasonable efforts to identify an alternate site with proximity to a public park available for joint use. All costs relating to obtaining the necessary State approvals for the K–6 School Site (including, without limitation, costs of a Phase 1 site assessment and geological and soil engineering investigations) shall be paid from Mitigation Funds.

Section 4.2 Site Acquisition Cost; Appraisal. The purchase price for the K–6 School Site or, as applicable, the Second K–6 School Site ("**Site Acquisition Cost**") shall be the fair market value of the K–6 School Site in a Construction Ready Condition, based upon an appraisal. The Parties shall jointly select a certified MAI appraiser from a list of four qualified appraisers selected by the District with the reasonable approval of Developer ("**Approved List**"). If the Parties cannot agree on a single appraiser, each Party shall select one appraiser from the Approved List to prepare an independent opinion of value of the applicable school site, and the purchase price shall be the average of the two. The appraiser shall conduct an appraisal of the applicable school site according to its highest and best use without regard to its proposed use for school purposes using the Uniform Standards of Professional Appraisal Practice, and in accordance with all applicable requirements for appraisal of property to be acquired for school purposes. If close of escrow of the conveyance of the applicable school site does not occur within six months of the date of the appraisal determining the purchase price, the appraisal shall be updated, such that the appraised fair market value of the applicable school site shall always be established as of a date not more than six months prior to the date of acquisition of the applicable school site by District. Costs of the appraisal shall be paid from Mitigation Funds.

Section 4.3 Payment of Site Acquisition Cost. The Site Acquisition Cost shall be paid to Developer at close of escrow for the applicable school site ("**Closing**") from a combination of the State Funds received by the District for site acquisition (anticipated to fund 50% of the Site Acquisition Cost) and Mitigation Funds from the ______________ SFE Account (anticipated to fund the balance of the Site Acquisition Cost); provided, however, that in the event the District does not have sufficient funds (in the form of the State Funds and Mitigation Funds) available at Closing to pay the full Site Acquisition Cost, the Closing shall nonetheless proceed and any unfunded amount shall be treated as an Advance Payment to the District, the repayment of which shall be made at such time as there are sufficient funds in the ______________ SFE Account, in combination with any State

Funds received by the District for site acquisition, to repay the unfunded amount to Developer. Solely by way of illustrative example, if the Site Acquisition Cost is $5 million and, at Closing, no State Funds have been received, but there are $1.5 million in Mitigation Funds, Developer will be paid $1.5 million through escrow and the $3.5 million unfunded amount shall be treated as an Advance Payment. If State Funds of $2.5 million are subsequently received by the District, these shall be paid to Developer, and Developer shall be paid $1 million in Mitigation Funds when those funds become available in the ____________ SFE Account. If, under this example, no State Funds for site acquisition are received, Developer shall be paid, post-Closing, $3.5 million from the ____________ SFE Account when such funds are available. In the event State Funds received after Closing, together with Mitigation Funds previously paid to Developer for the Site Acquisition Cost, exceed the Site Acquisition Cost, the amount in excess of the Site Acquisition Cost shall be deposited in the ____________ SFE Account. (As used in this example, "State Funds" means State Funds received for site acquisition).

ARTICLE V
MISCELLANEOUS PROVISIONS

Section 5.1 Support of the Developer and the Project. So long as Developer is not in Default under this Agreement, the District shall:

(a) Not object to or in any manner impede the processing of applications for any land use entitlements with respect to the Project.

(b) Not oppose development of the Project as herein described (including but not limited to commercial, industrial or residential development) or challenge the entitlements for the Project on the basis of inadequate school facilities or any other grounds or seek other forms of mitigation with respect to the adequacy of school facilities, including but not limited to the establishment of developer fees, the payment of money by Developer, the dedication of land, or the application of an assessment or requirement of any nature against Developer or the Project;

(c) Not oppose development on the basis of the City's or Developer's compliance or alleged non-compliance with the California Environmental Quality Act (commencing with Section 21000 of the Public Resources Code) or any regulations implemented with respect thereto, whether or not such opposition relates to potential environmental impacts upon schools;

(d) Except as herein provided, not exercise any power or authority (under Section 65995 of the California Government Code or any other provision of applicable law) to levy a Statutory School Fee, charge, dedication, special tax or other form of requirement against any development of the Property for the purpose of funding or financing any school facilities; and

(e) Not require the City or any other governmental entity to exercise, or cooperate with the City or any other governmental entity in the exercise of, the power under Title 7, Division 1, Chapter 4.7 of the California Government Code (commencing with Section 65970) or any other provision of applicable law to require the dedication of land, the payment of fees or special taxes in lieu thereof, or both for classroom or related facilities for school facilities as a condition to the approval of the Project (including but not limited to any commercial, industrial or residential project).

No action taken by the District prior to the execution of this Agreement shall be construed as a violation of this Section.

Section 5.2 Certificates of Compliance. Provided Developer is not in Default under this Agreement, the District authorizes the Superintendent or designee to issue Certificates of Compliance and execute letters or other written materials, as reasonably requested by Developer, describing this Agreement and confirming that adequate provision for school facilities to house the Project Students has been made in connection with development of the Property. Developer acknowledges that, pursuant to Section 2.9 of its Development Agreement with the City of _______________ and further pursuant to the City of _______________'s special conditions of approval for the Project, the City may refuse to issue building permits if the District provides written notice to the City that Developer is in default of this Agreement or has failed to pay Mitigation Payments required under this Agreement.

Section 5.3 Breach, Default and Cure. Before either Party may declare a Default and take any action based thereon (including, without limitation, commencing any administrative or judicial proceeding), the procedures in this Section 5.3 must be followed. The Party asserting a Default ("**Non-Defaulting Party**") may elect to do so by providing written notice to the Party alleged to be in Default ("**Defaulting Party**") specifying the nature of the Default and the actions, if any, to be taken by the Defaulting

Party to cure or remedy the Default ("**Default Notice**"). The Defaulting Party shall have 45 days from receipt of the Default Notice within which to cure the Default (the "**Cure Period**") and, if it fails to do so within that period, it shall be deemed in Default, and the Non-Defaulting Party may exercise any rights or remedies available under this Agreement or by law; provided, however, that if the nature of the Default is such that it cannot reasonably be cured within 45 days, the Defaulting Party shall be afforded reasonable additional time so long as it commences such cure within the Cure Period and diligently pursues such cure to completion.

Section 5.4 Future Owners of the Property.

(a) Covenant Running with Land. This Agreement is created for the benefit of Developer, District, and the Property. Subject to the limitations set forth herein, the covenants of this Agreement shall run with the land constituting the Property. Developer agrees for the benefit of District that the Property shall be held, transferred, and encumbered subject to the provisions of this Agreement which are for the use and benefit of the District, the Developer, the Property and of each and every person who now or in the future owns any portion or portions of the Property (except as provided below). After execution of this Agreement, the Parties shall execute a Memorandum of Agreement in a form substantially conforming to Exhibit "C." For any portion of the Property not yet owned by Developer, upon acquisition by Developer, the Parties shall execute such a Memorandum of Agreement as to that portion of the Property. Developer shall provide the District with notice of the recordation of the final map for the Property or any portion thereof, whereupon either Party to this Agreement may cause the applicable Memorandum of Agreement to be recorded with the Recorder's Office of ________________ County, and shall reasonably cooperate to prepare or provide any further documents and signatures necessary for the recording of the terms of this Agreement. This Agreement is not intended to and shall not apply to any agreement between Developer and a member of the home-buying public pursuant to which such home buyer has agreed to purchase a residential unit, to the sale or conveyance of such a unit or to any subsequent sale or conveyance of such a unit. This Agreement shall automatically terminate on a unit-by-unit basis upon the conveyance of each such completed dwelling unit to a member of the home-buying public.

(b) Right to Reimbursement. Any right of Developer to receive any payment or reimbursement under this Agreement, including, without limitation, payments of State Funds or reimbursements for Advance Payments, shall be (i) a benefit personal to Developer and shall not run with the land or be assigned by virtue of transfer of any interest in the Property or Project unless expressly so provided in a written instrument executed by Developer; and (ii) assignable by Developer whether or not accompanied by transfer of an interest in the Property or the Project.

Section 5.5 Disputes. If a dispute arises relating to the interpretation of, enforcement of, or compliance with the terms of this Agreement, the Parties shall first attempt to resolve such dispute through informal discussions or other alternative means. Any Party may convene such discussions by written notice, and shall reasonably accommodate the other Party with respect to scheduling any such discussion. If the dispute is not resolved in this manner within thirty (30) days of such written notice, it shall be referred to mediation upon the request of either Party for a period not to exceed an additional thirty (30) days. This dispute resolution process shall be undertaken in good faith and exhausted prior to judicial review. However, compliance with this process does not waive any Party's obligation to comply with, or right to assert as a defense, any applicable statutes of limitation. The Parties may agree in writing to toll any applicable statutes of limitation for such period as may reasonably be necessary to complete the dispute resolution process outlined in this section.

Section 5.6 Enforceability. Either Party may, following the dispute resolution process set forth in Section 5.5 herein, take such legal action as is necessary to enforce the terms of this Agreement, including but not limited to an action for specific performance.

Section 5.7 Successors and Assignees. Except as otherwise provided in this Agreement, all terms and conditions of this Agreement shall be binding upon all successors-in-interest, including without limitation purchasers of all or any part of the Property. Prior to any such transfer or assignment, Developer shall also notify the District in writing of the name of the successor or assign and all appropriate contact information for the District's records.

Section 5.8 Headings. The headings of this Agreement are for convenience purposes only and shall not limit or define the meaning of the provisions of this Agreement.

Section 5.9 Governing Law and Venue. This Agreement shall be construed in accordance with, and governed by, the laws of the State of California applicable to contracts to be performed wholly within this State. Any dispute arising from the terms and conditions of this Agreement shall be heard by a court of competent jurisdiction located within _______________ County.

Section 5.10 Attorneys' Fees and Costs. In the event of any legal proceeding or alternative dispute resolution proceeding, including any lawsuit, action, or proceeding in law or equity, arising out of or relating to this Agreement, the prevailing Party shall be entitled to recover its reasonable attorneys' fees and costs arising from the proceeding, including expert witness fees. The prevailing Party on any appeal shall also be entitled to recover its reasonable attorneys' fees and costs arising out of any such appeal. In addition to the foregoing attorneys' fees and costs, the prevailing Party shall be entitled to its attorneys' fees and costs incurred in any post-judgment proceedings to collect or enforce the judgment. This provision is separate and several and shall survive the merger of this Agreement into any judgment on this Agreement.

Section 5.11 Construction. The singular includes the plural, "shall" is mandatory, and "may" is permissive. The Parties acknowledge and agree each of the Parties and each of the Parties' attorneys have participated fully in the negotiation and drafting of this Agreement. In cases of uncertainty as to the meaning, intent or interpretation of any provision of this Agreement, the Agreement shall be construed without regard to which of the Parties caused, or may have caused, the uncertainty to exist. No presumption shall arise from the fact that particular provisions were or may have been drafted by a specific Party, and prior versions or drafts of this Agreement may not be used to interpret the meaning or intent of this Agreement or any provision thereof.

Section 5.12 Notices. Any notice to be given hereunder to either Party shall be in writing and shall be given either by personal delivery (including express or courier service), by receipt-confirmed facsimile, or by registered or certified mail, with return receipt requested and postage prepaid (excluding electronic messaging) and addressed as follows:

To District:	CITY UNIFIED SCHOOL DISTRICT Attn: Superintendent _______________________ _______________________ Fax: ___________________

With a copy to Legal Counsel:

____
____
____
____
Email: ______________________
Fax: ________________________

To Developer:

____
____
____
____
Email: ______________________
Fax: ________________________

With a copy to Legal Counsel:

____
____
____
____
Email: ______________________
Fax: ________________________

Section 5.13 No Joint Venture. The relationship of the Parties to this Agreement is determined solely by the provisions of this Agreement. This Agreement does not create and shall not be construed to create any agency, partnership, joint venture, trust or other relationship with duties or incidents different from those of Parties to an arm's-length contract.

Section 5.14 No Third-Party Beneficiaries. Nothing in this Agreement, whether express or implied, is intended to or shall do any of the following: (a) confer any benefits, rights or remedies under or by reason of this Agreement on any persons or entities other than the express Parties to this Agreement; (b) relieve or discharge the obligation or liability of any person not an express Party to this Agreement; or (c) give any person not an express Party to this Agreement any right of subrogation or action against any Party to this Agreement.

Section 5.15 Time Is of the Essence. Time is of the essence in the performance of each Party's respective obligations under this Agreement.

Section 5.16 Amendments and Waivers. No amendment of, supplement to, or waiver of any obligations under this Agreement shall be enforceable or admissible unless set forth in writing signed by the Party against which enforcement or admission is sought. No delay or failure to require performance of any provision of this Agreement shall constitute a waiver of that provision as to that or any other instance. Any waiver granted shall apply solely to the specific instance expressly stated in a writing signed by the Parties.

Section 5.17 Entire Agreement. This Agreement sets forth the entire understanding of the Parties relating to the transactions it contemplates, and supersedes all prior understandings relating to them, whether written or oral. There are no obligations, commitments, representations, or warranties relating to them except those expressly set forth in this Agreement.

Section 5.18 Severability. If any provision of this Agreement is held invalid, void or unenforceable by a court of competent jurisdiction, but the remainder of the Agreement can be enforced without failure of material consideration to either Party, then this Agreement shall not be affected and it shall remain in full force and effect, unless amended or modified by mutual consent of the Parties.

Section 5.19 Execution in Counterparts. This Agreement may be executed in multiple counterparts, each of which shall be deemed an original, and counterpart signature pages may be assembled to form a single document which shall be deemed an original document. Consolidated signature pages shall be compiled by District and forwarded to Developer to constitute the Developer's executed copy of the Agreement.

Section 5.20 Signatures. By signing below, each of the signatories represents and warrants that he or she has been duly authorized to execute this Agreement on behalf of the Party on whose behalf he or she is signing.

Section 5.21 Eminent Domain. Nothing in the Agreement shall prevent the District from exercising its rights of eminent domain pursuant to law.

Section 5.22 Represented by Counsel. Each Party hereto acknowledges that it has been represented by legal counsel, or had the opportunity to obtain legal counsel and consciously chose not to obtain it, in the negotiation, drafting, and execution of this Agreement.

Section 5.23 Force Majeure. Neither Party shall be deemed to be in default where failure or delay in performance of any of its obligations under this Agreement is caused by earthquakes, other Acts of God, fires, wars, riots or similar hostilities, strikes and other labor difficulties beyond the Party's control (including the Party's employment force), governmental regulations beyond the Party's reasonable control, court actions (such as restraining orders or injunctions), or other causes beyond the Party's reasonable control.

IN WITNESS WHEREOF, this Agreement has been entered into by and between the District and Developer as of the Effective Date.

CITY UNIFIED SCHOOL DISTRICT

By: ______________________________

__________, Superintendent

Dated: __________________

CITY UNIFIED SCHOOL DISTRICT

__________________________, a Delaware limited liability company
By: ______________________, a California limited liability company
Its: Manager
By: ______________________
Its: Member

By: ______________________
Name: __________________________
Title: Manager
Dated:

[Exhibits A, B & C Omitted]

APPENDIX 8

Sample Subdivision Improvement Agreement (California)

RECORDING REQUESTED BY
AND WHEN RECORDED MAIL TO:

____
____
____
____
____

SPACE ABOVE THIS LINE FOR RECORDER'S USE

SUBDIVISION IMPROVEMENT AGREEMENT

(Project Name)

THIS SUBDIVISION IMPROVEMENT AGREEMENT FOR ________________________ (Project Name) between ________________ and _________________ (Agreement) is made and entered into as of ___________, 20__ by and between the COUNTY OF ________________, a political subdivision of the State of California, hereafter referred to as "County," and______________, a California Limited Partnership as "Subdivider."

WITNESSETH:

WHEREAS, the conditions of approval for Major Subdivision Application _____________ approved and effective on _____________, by the ____________ County Board of Supervisors as "_______________ _______________," Tract No. ____, Subdivisions of ____________ County, California, located at ____________, require various public improvements to be installed; and,

WHEREAS, Subdivider has requested approval of the final map prior to the completion and acceptance of the required public improvements; and,

WHEREAS, the Subdivision Map Act (Government Code Section 66410 *et seq.*) requires that if, at the time of the filing of the final map, any public improvements required to be installed have not been completed and accepted, County, as a condition precedent to the approval of the final map, shall require the Subdivider to enter into an Agreement to complete the improvements at Subdivider's expense (see Government Code Section 66462); and,

WHEREAS, the same statute requires that performance of such improvement Agreement be guaranteed by the posting of security.

NOW, THEREFORE, IT IS MUTUALLY AGREED AS FOLLOWS:

1. PERFORMANCE OF WORK

Subdivider shall construct or cause to be constructed, at no cost to the County, the public improvements listed in Table 1 below pursuant to the conditions of approval for County Major Subdivision Application ____________ for "__________________________," Tract No. ____, Subdivisions of ____________ County, California, hereinafter referred to as "Improvements."

Table 1

Title	Date
Phase 1 of ___________ (the Improvements secured herein appear on Sheet 7 of said plans)	___________

Said Improvements shall be constructed in accordance with the improvement plans and specifications approved by the ____________ Community Services District ("CSD") General Manager ("General Manager"), together with any changes required or ordered by the General Manager, or their designee, which, in their opinion, are necessary or required to complete the work, and in accordance with the CSD Improvement Standards and Specifications and applicable ordinances of ____________ County.

Except during an emergency, as determined by the General Manager, all work shall be performed within the hours specified in the CSD Standards or as may be extended subject to the General Manager's approval.

The CSD may require Subdivider to furnish a licensed soils engineer to test and certify that all cuts, fills and trench backfill conform to the requirements of the CSD and State codes.

2. WORK: PLACES AND GRADES TO BE FIXED BY ENGINEER

All of said work to construct Improvements is to be done as shown upon the approved plans and specifications on file in the office of the Director of Public Works (Director) and the CSD. Subdivider warrants that construction of Improvements will not adversely affect any portion of adjacent properties.

3. TIMING OF IMPROVEMENTS

The Improvements shall be completed within twenty-four (24) months of the effective date of this Agreement subject to extension by the Director as described in Section 4.

4. TIME IS OF THE ESSENCE: EXTENSION

Time is of the essence for this Agreement.

The date for completion of the required improvements may not be extended, except as provided in this paragraph. The Director may extend the date for a maximum of three hundred sixty-five (365) days due to delays in the work actually caused by inclement weather, riots, strikes, lockouts, fires, earthquakes, floods and conditions resulting therefrom, or for other reason beyond the control of the Subdivider. Extension of the date for any other cause or beyond three hundred sixty-five (365) days shall be made only by the Board of Supervisors. Extensions shall be considered only upon a showing of good cause by the Subdivider. The Board of Supervisors or the Director, as appropriate, shall be the sole and final judge as to whether good cause has been shown to entitle the Subdivider to an extension.

Requests for extension of the completion date shall be in writing and delivered to County in the manner hereinafter specified for service of notices at least forty-five (45) days prior to the due date for completion of the improvements as specified in this agreement and approved amendments thereto. An extension of time, if any, shall be granted only in writing, and an oral extension shall not be valid or binding on County.

In the event County extends the time of completion of the required improvements, such extension may be granted without notice by County to the Subdivider's surety and shall in no way release any guarantee or security given by the Subdivider pursuant to this Agreement, or relieve or release those providing an improvement security pursuant to this Agreement. The surety or sureties, if any, in executing the securities shall be deemed to have expressly agreed to any such extension of time.

In granting any extension of time, County may require new or amended improvement security in amounts increased to reflect increases in the costs of constructing the required improvements or impose other conditions to protect its interests and ensure the timely completion of the required improvements.

5. REPAIRS AND REPLACEMENTS

Subdivider shall replace, or have replaced, or repair or have repaired, as the case may be, all pipes and monuments shown on the map which have been destroyed or damaged by reason of any work done hereunder, and Subdivider shall replace or have replaced, repair or have repaired, as the case may be, or pay the owner, the entire cost of replacement or repairs, of any and all property damaged or destroyed by reason of any work done hereunder, whether such property be owned by the United States or any agency thereof, or the State of California or any agency or political subdivision thereof, or by the CSD or by any public or private corporation, or by any combination of such owners. Any such repair or replacement shall be to the specifications and standards of the CSD.

6. UTILITY DEPOSITS: STATEMENT

Subdivider shall make all deposits legally required by each public utility corporation for the connection of any and all public utilities to be supplied by such public utility corporation within the Subdivision.

7. PERMITS: COMPLIANCE WITH LAW

Subdivider shall, at Subdivider's expense, obtain all necessary permits and licenses for the construction of Improvements, give all necessary notices and pay all fees and taxes required by law. Necessary permits include encroachment permits for any and all work conducted within a right-of-way or connection to any and all utilities or other improvements.

8. SUPERINTENDENCE BY SUBDIVIDER

Subdivider shall give personal superintendence to the work on said Improvement, or have a competent foreman or superintendent on the work at all times during progress, with authority to act for Subdivider.

9. INSPECTION

Subdivider shall at all times maintain proper facilities, and provide safe access for inspection to all parts of the work.

10. CONTRACT SECURITY

Concurrently with the execution hereof, Subdivider shall furnish:

A. A cash bond guaranteeing payment for placing monuments in the amount of .... $__________

B. For Performance: Security in the amount of $__________, which totals one hundred percent (100%) of the County approved estimated cost to complete the Improvements. Such security shall be presented in the form of a surety bond issued by a California admitted surety or other security acceptable to County.

C. With this security, Subdivider guarantees performance under this Agreement. If Subdivider fails to perform its obligations under this Agreement and the form of performance security provided is a surety bond, it shall be the issuing surety's responsibility to complete, or cause completion of, such outstanding obligations, unless County agrees to complete the outstanding obligations using funds provided by the surety.

D. For Laborers and Materialmen: Security in the amount of $___________, which totals one hundred percent (100%) of the County approved estimated cost of the Improvements. Such security shall be presented in the form of a surety bond issued by a California admitted surety or other security acceptable to County.

E. The above bonds may be combined.

See Exhibit A for Engineers Bond Estimate prepared by the engineer of record.

11. RELEASE OF CONTRACT SECURITY

All of the Securities posted for the Improvements, referenced in Section 10 above, shall be released as follows with the exception of item 17 in this agreement, and subject to Government Code Section 66499.7.

A. Security given for faithful performance (Section 10.B above) shall be released after acceptance of the work and a warranty bond in the amount of twenty percent (20%) of the said work is provided for a term of not less than one (1) year following the date of such acceptance of the work. If a significant repair to a certain improvement is required during the one (1) year warranty period, the warranty period for that repair work, and any facility related to the repair work, shall be extended for one (1) year from the date the significant repair is completed and approved.

B. Security securing the payment to the contractor, the subcontractors of the contractor, and to persons furnishing labor, materials and equipment shall be released sixty (60) days or as otherwise required by the State Code after recording the Notice of Completion provided that the work has been accepted and provided no claims or liens have been filed. If claims of lien have been filed, an amount of security at least equal to the claims shall be retained pending the outcome of the claims.
C. The security guaranteeing that the completed work remains operational and free of defect during the required 1-year warranty period shall be released upon correction, by Subdivider, of any defects in the work existing at the end of the warranty period. The warranty shall be extended for one (1) year after any major repairs.
D. In the event that Improvements do not conform to the plans and specifications or defects are not corrected within the time limit specified by the County, the County shall have the authority to order the necessary work done and to recover the actual costs of such work as well as any costs of enforcing such obligation, including attorney fees, from the Subdivider and the Subdivider's surety or the financial institution providing the instrument of credit.

12. HOLD HARMLESS AGREEMENT

Subdivider hereby agrees to, and shall hold the County, its elective and appointive boards, commissions, officers, agents, and employees, harmless from any liability for damage or claims for damage for personal injury, including death, as well as from claims for property damage which may arise from Subdivider's or Subdivider's contractors', subcontractors', agents' or employees' operations under this Agreement, whether such operations be by Subdivider or by any Subdivider's contractors, subcontractors, or by any one or more persons directly or indirectly employed by, or acting as agent for Subdivider or any of Subdivider's contractors or subcontractors. Subdivider agrees to, and shall indemnify and defend the County and its elective and appointive boards, commissions, officers, agents and employees from any suits or actions at law or in equity for damages caused, or alleged to have been caused, by reason of any of the aforesaid operations and Subdivider shall pay all reasonable attorney's fees and costs that the County may incur.

The aforesaid hold harmless agreement by Subdivider shall apply to all damages and claims for damages of every kind suffered, or alleged to have been suffered, by reason of any of the aforesaid operations referred to in this paragraph, regardless of whether or not the County has prepared, supplied or approved of, plans and/or specifications for the Subdivision.

The Subdivider shall, during the life of this Agreement take out and maintain insurance coverage with an insurance carrier authorized to transact business in the State of California as will protect the Subdivider or any Contractor or any Subcontractor or anyone directly or indirectly employed by any of them or by anyone for whose acts any of them may be liable, from claims for damages because of bodily injury, sickness, disease, or death of their employees or any person other than their employees, or for damages because of injury to or destruction of tangible property, including loss of use resulting there from.

The minimum limits of liability for such insurance coverage which shall include comprehensive general and automobile liability, including contractual liability assumed under this Agreement, shall be as follows:

A. Limit of Liability for Injury or Accidental Death
   Per Occurrence............................$1,000,000
B. Limit of Liability for Property Damage
   Aggregate Liability for Loss........$1,000,000

Such liability insurance policies shall name the County as an additional insured, by separate endorsement, and shall agree to defend and indemnify the County against loss arising from operations performed under this Agreement and before permitting any Contractor or Subcontractors to perform work under this Agreement, the Subdivider shall require Contractor or Subcontractors to furnish satisfactory proof that insurance has been taken out and is maintained similar to that provided by the Subdivider as it may be applied to the contractor's or subcontractor's work. Said policy limits shall not be reduced without the prior written notification to the County.

13. ASSIGNMENT

Subdivider may assign this Agreement and its rights and obligations with the prior written approval of the Director, which approval shall not be unreasonably withheld, provided that such assignee expressly assumes the obligations of Subdivider hereunder. Upon any such assignment by Subdivider, Subdivider shall be fully relieved from any further liability hereunder. This Agreement shall be binding upon and shall inure to the benefit of the successors and permitted assigns of the parties to this Agreement.

County may assign this Agreement in its sole and absolute discretion to CSD, provided that CSD agrees to accept title to all improvements contemplated hereunder upon Subdivider's completion of said improvements pursuant to the terms of this Agreement. In the event of such an assignment, Subdivider's obligations hereunder shall be owed to CSD, with any references to the "Director" being deemed to refer to the General Manager and any references to the Board of Supervisors being deemed to refer to the CSD Board of Directors. Moreover, in the event of an assignment to the CSD, County will release the security by Subdivider under Section 10, and Subdivider shall provide replacement security in favor of the CSD in an amount necessary to ensure completion of any outstanding improvements and to ensure any remaining warranty obligations.

14. REPAIR OR RECONSTRUCTION OF DEFECTIVE WORK

If, within a period of one (1) year after final acceptance of the Improvements performed under this Agreement, any structure or part of any structure furnished and/or installed or constructed, or caused to be installed or constructed by Subdivider, or any of the work done under this Agreement, fails to fulfill any of the requirements of this Agreement or the specifications referred to herein, Subdivider shall without delay and without any cost to the County, repair or replace or reconstruct any defective or otherwise unsatisfactory part or parts of the work or structure. Should Subdivider fail to act within thirty (30) days after written notice or in case of emergency, the County may, at its option, make the necessary repairs or replacements or perform the necessary work and Subdivider shall pay to the County the actual cost of such repairs plus twenty-five (25) percent as administrative costs.

15. REPAIR OR RECONSTRUCTION OF DAMAGED WORK

A. Repair of Public Improvements Constructed by Subdivider but Not Yet Accepted:

Public improvements that do not meet applicable specifications and standards for public improvements because of damages or defects that have arisen after construction, but before Subdivider seeks acceptance shall not be accepted. Subdivider agrees that for any such improvements, Subdivider shall, as may be necessary to return those improvements to the condition in which they were when constructed, repair or re-construct, at Subdivider's own expense, in a good and workmanlike manner within 15 working days of Subdivider's receipt of a deficiency list.

B. Public Improvements Constructed by Subdivider and Accepted:

Subdivider agrees to repair and restore any public improvements within the Subdivision that have been accepted but are subsequently damaged by Subdivider's homebuilding activities within the Subdivision, until such time as all homes within the Subdivision are complete. Subdivider shall complete such repair or construction at its cost, and in a good and workmanlike manner to the applicable construction specifications. Subdivider shall repair or reconstruct said Improvements as necessary within 15 working days from receipt of a deficiency list.

16. REPAIRS AND REPLACEMENTS OF DAMAGE BY HOME BUILDER ACTIVITIES

Subdivider shall replace, or have replaced, or repair or have repaired, as the case may be, all pipes and monuments shown on the map which have been destroyed or damaged by home building activities, and Subdivider shall replace or have replaced, repair or have repaired, as the case may be, or pay the affected entity, the entire cost of replacement or repairs, of any and all property damaged or destroyed by reason of any work done hereunder, whether such property be owned by the United States or any agency thereof, or the State of California or any agency or political subdivision thereof, or by the County, the CSD or by any public or private corporation, or by any combination of such owners. Any such repair or replacement shall be to the published specifications and standards of the CSD and/or agencies as needed.

17. FULL RELEASE OF SECURITY; MAINTENANCE PRIOR TO ACCEPTANCE

Existing bond(s) in place by Subdivider cannot be fully released until all covenants of this agreement have been satisfied. Subject to Government Code 66499.7, the bonds will be released only upon completion of all the obligations of the development including the acceptance of all improvements and meeting of all other obligations in this agreement. Subdivider shall be responsible for maintenance and upkeep of all improvements during a partial acceptance until building construction is completed or the developer is specifically released from this responsibility in writing at the final and full acceptance of all the Improvements. If there are any conflicts between this Section 17 and Section 11, Section 11 shall prevail.

18. SUBDIVIDER NOT AGENT OF THE COUNTY

Neither Subdivider nor any of Subdivider's agents or contractors are or shall be considered to be agents of the County in connection with the performance of Subdivider's obligations under this Agreement.

19. COST OF ENGINEERING AND INSPECTION

All plan check or inspection charges shall be billed to, and paid by, Subdivider pursuant to the terms of the applicable fee schedule.

20. NOTICE OF BREACH AND DEFAULT

If Subdivider refuses or fails to obtain prosecution of the work, or any severable part thereof, with such diligence as will insure its completion within the time specified, or any extensions thereof, or fails to obtain completion of said work within such time, or if the Subdivider should be adjudged a bankrupt, or Subdivider should make a general assignment for the benefit of Subdivider's creditors, or if a receiver should be appointed in the event of Subdivider insolvency, or if Subdivider, or any of Subdivider's contractors, subcontractors, agents, or employees should violate any of the provisions of this Agreement, the County may serve written notice upon Subdivider and Subdivider's surety of breach of this Agreement or of any portion thereof and default of Subdivider.

21. BREACH OF AGREEMENT: PERFORMANCE BY SURETY OR THE COUNTY

In the event of any such notice, Subdivider's surety shall have the duty to take over and complete the work and the improvements herein specified; provided, however, that if the surety, within ten (10) days after the serving upon it of such notice of breach does not give the County written notice of its intention to take over the performance of the contract, and does not commence performance thereof within ten (10) days after notice to the County of such election, the County may take over the work and prosecute the same to completion, by contract or by any other method the County may deem advisable, for the account and at the expense of Subdivider, and Subdivider's surety shall be liable to the County for the cost and damages occasioned by the County thereby; and, in such event, the County without liability for so doing may take possession of, and utilize in completing the work, such materials, appliances, plant and other property belonging to Subdivider as may be on the site of the work and necessary therefore. The County reserves to itself all remedies available to it at law or in equity for breach of Subdivider's obligations under this Agreement. The right of the County to draw upon or utilize the security is additional to and not in lieu of any other remedy available to the County. In the event that Subdivider fails to perform any obligations hereunder, Subdivider agrees to pay all costs and expenses incurred by the County in securing performance of such obligations, including costs of suit and reasonable attorney fees.

22. NOTICES

All notices herein required shall be in writing, and delivered in person or sent by registered mail, postage prepaid.

Notices required to be given to the County shall be addressed as follows:

Director

____________________ County Public Works Department

____

____

Notices required to be given to Subdivider shall be addressed as follows:

____

____

____

Attn: _______________

Notices required to be given to surety of Subdivider shall be addressed as follows:

____

____

____

Attn: _______________

Provided that any party or the surety may change such address by notice in writing to the other party and, thereafter, notices shall be addressed and transmitted to the new address.

23. FIRE PROTECTION

No building permits will be issued in this Subdivision until the water system has been completed and tested and all access streets installed and made serviceable. This provision may be modified or waived if an alternate method of providing fire protection is provided and approved by the Director.

24. STREETLIGHTS

The Subdivider is installing specialized streetlights and poles in the Subdivision. For every 15 streetlights and poles or fraction thereof installed by Subdivider, Subdivider shall, upon request, provide one additional streetlight and pole. This shall be delivered when requested anytime at or after the acceptance of the improvements.

25. STREET NAME SIGNS

The Subdivider is installing specialized street signs and poles in the Subdivision. For every 10 street name signs and poles or fraction thereof installed by Subdivider, Subdivider shall, upon request provide one additional street pole and sign bracket and extension.

26. SLURRY SEAL

The Subdivider shall install a slurry seal to the paved surface of the Subdivision upon completion of homebuilding activities in the Subdivision. Slurry seal shall be installed as described in the CSD Standard Specifications and Details. All streets constructed as part of this subdivision and shown on this map shall be included in the slurry seal project by the developer or builder who is performing this requirement regardless of whether buildings are built on those streets or not, including arterial and collector streets.

27. STREET STRIPING

The Subdivider shall install permanent street striping and markings with "Hot Applied Thermoplastic" as described in the CSD Standard Specifications and Details. Subdivider shall apply thermoplastic striping and signage to all streets within the Final Map including arterial and collector streets adjacent to the subdivision.

28. BEST MANAGEMENT PRACTICES—STORM WATER MANAGEMENT

The Subdivider shall purchase, install and maintain catch basin filters and/or other source control Best Management Practices (BMPs) for urban runoff as determined by the CSD consistent with any of CSD's published standards. CSD-approved catch basin filters must be installed in all streets and on the abutting arterial streets prior to home construction and acceptance. The filters shall be properly maintained and filters replaced if damaged or filled with debris prior to acceptance.

29. LANDSCAPE PLANS

The Subdivider shall install full landscaping and irrigation on both sides of ________ Avenue. The Subdivider shall pay for three (3) years of calculated water usage for both the north and south landscaped areas to the CSD upon the County's direction.

[Signatures on next page]

IN WITNESS WHEREOF, the parties hereto have executed this Agreement on the day and year first written above.

<table>
<tr><td>COUNTY OF _____________, a
Political subdivision of the State
of California</td><td>_________________________,
a California limited partnership</td></tr>
<tr><td>By: _________________________
__________, Chair
Board of Supervisors</td><td>By: _________________________
Name: _______________________
Title: _______________________</td></tr>
<tr><td>ATTEST: __________
Clerk of the Board of Supervisors
of the County of __________
State of California</td><td>By: _________________________
Name: _______________________
Title: _______________________</td></tr>
</table>

By______________________(SEAL)
Deputy Clerk

"SUBDIVIDER"
"COUNTY"
APPROVED AS TO CONTENT:

By: ___________________________

____
Director of Public Works

APPROVED AS TO FORM:

By ____________________________

____
Deputy County Counsel

Attachments: Exhibit A – BOND ESTIMATE

APPENDIX 9

Sample Parkland Dedication Agreement

This Agreement is dated _______________, _____, and is between the _______________________ ("**DEVELOPER**"), the **City of** _____________ ("**CITY**"), and the _____________ **Park District** ("**DISTRICT**").

WHEREAS, the DISTRICT has proposed to redevelop parcels located at [ADDRESS] as a residential subdivision (the "**Development**"); and

WHEREAS, the Development will consist of [_____] acres of land and will include [______] number of residential units; and

WHEREAS, the Development is subject to parkland dedication as required by [CITE CITY ORDINANCE]; and

WHEREAS, the DEVELOPER is proposing a [______] square foot park on the land described in Exhibit A, with the buildout of the park depicted in Exhibit B, as a part of the overall Development. The DEVELOPER estimates that the value of the land and improvements for the park conveyed under this Agreement ("**Improvements**") will exceed [$____________] and will be in excess of 10% of the total area being improved by the Development; and

WHEREAS, as part of the Development, the DEVELOPER proposes to convey the parkland and project Improvements in fulfillment of the land dedication requirements for the Development under the CITY ordinances. The conveyance of the land and Improvements will take place at the substantial completion of the Development or by [DATE] whichever occurs first; and

WHEREAS, the DISTRICT has determined the conveyance of the park property and related Improvements described in this Agreement will satisfy the parkland dedication criteria of CITY ordinances; and

WHEREAS, through the conveyance, the park would become dedicated parkland, with the DISTRICT holding fee simple ownership of the park property; and

WHEREAS, the DISTRICT has authorized this Parkland Dedication Agreement to facilitate the dedication of land and other commitments by the DEVELOPER as described herein; and

WHEREAS, the CITY has approved execution of this Parkland Dedication Agreement; and

WHEREAS, the DEVELOPER, the CITY and the DISTRICT wish to enter into this Parkland Dedication Agreement to convey the park property for parkland use and waive park impact fees for future phases of the Development.

The parties agree as follows:

ARTICLE I

PROPERTY CONVEYANCE

1. Conveyance of Park Property. The DEVELOPER will grant to the DISTRICT at no cost, all right, title and interest in the following real property for park use the property described in Exhibit A.

2. Closing. The closing and conveyance contemplated by this Agreement ("Closing") will occur on a date mutually acceptable to the DEVELOPER and DISTRICT, at the time of substantial completion of the Improvements, but no later than [DATE]. Except for specific commitments made herein, the site will be conveyed "as-is," "where-is" and "with all faults" and such sale shall be without representation or warranty of any kind, express or implied, as to the condition of the Property.

At the time of Closing, the DEVELOPER will assign to the DISTRICT any warranties related to the construction of the Improvements. The DEVELOPER must consult with the DISTRICT on the construction documents for the Improvements.

The DEVELOPER must include the DISTRICT in reviews of systems and features to be incorporated into the Improvements at the time those reviews occur in the construction sequence. The DEVELOPER must provide to the DISTRICT all operations manuals, as built drawings, material and equipment logs and descriptions, and other items typical of project closeout.

The DEVELOPER will warrant that all costs of the construction of the park have been paid and will demonstrate the project to be free from liens and other encumbrances. This provision will survive termination of this Agreement.

3. Intended Use. The Property will be used for park purposes on a permanent basis.

4. Title. On the Closing date, DEVELOPER will deliver to DISTRICT a quit-claim deed conveying the Property to DISTRICT.

5. Prorations. DEVELOPER and DISTRICT agree to the following prorations and allocation of costs regarding the Agreement.

   a. Deed Tax. DEVELOPER must pay the state deed tax on the Deed to be delivered by DEVELOPER under this Agreement.

   b. Real Estate Taxes and Special Assessments. n/a

   c. Recording Costs. DEVELOPER will pay the cost of recording the Deed.

6. Release. By accepting ownership of the Property at no cost and by accepting the funds described in Article II below, DISTRICT assumes sole responsibility for the Property and Improvements, including ongoing maintenance required for future uses.

ARTICLE II

PARKLAND DEDICATION FEES

1. This Agreement will commence upon execution and terminate on the Closing date or when the Development has been completed, whichever is later.

2. In recognition of the dedication of and improvement of the Property, the CITY and the DISTRICT agree that the conveyance of the Property and Improvements will satisfy parkland dedication requirements associated with the Development Agreement between the CITY and the DEVELOPER.

3. If for some reason the DEVELOPER fails to convey to the DISTRICT on behalf of the CITY the Property and Improvements by [DATE], the DEVELOPER will immediately pay the CITY all the fees that would have otherwise been due under the CITY and DISTRICT ordinances for the entire Development. This provision will survive termination of this Agreement.

ARTICLE III

GENERAL TERMS

1. Records—Availability/Access. The CITY will have access to and the right to examine, audit, excerpt, and transcribe any books, documents, papers, records, etc., which are pertinent to the accounting practices and procedures of the DEVELOPER or DISTRICT and involve transactions relating to this Agreement. The DEVELOPER and DISTRICT must maintain these materials and allow access during the period of the Agreement and for six (6) years after its expiration or cancellation or termination.

2. Notices. Any notice required or permitted to be given by any party upon the other is given in accordance with this Agreement if it is directed to DEVELOPER by delivering it personally to an officer of DEVELOPER; or if it is directed to DISTRICT, by delivering it personally to an officer of DISTRICT; or if mailed by United States registered or certified mail, return receipt requested, postage prepaid; or if transmitted by facsimile copy followed by mailed notice as above required; or if deposited cost paid with a nationally recognized, reputable overnight courier, properly addressed as follows:

If to the CITY:

If to DISTRICT:

If to DEVELOPER:

Notices will be deemed effective on the earlier of the date of receipt or the date of deposit as aforesaid; provided, however, that if notice is given by deposit, that the time for response to any notice by the other party will commence to run two (2) business days after any such deposit. Any party may change its address for the service of notice by giving written notice of such change to the other party, in any manner above specified.

3. Default and Cancellation/Termination. If DISTRICT fails to perform any of the provisions of this Agreement or fails to ensure the performance of the Agreement, it will be in default. Unless DISTRICT's default is excused in writing by the DEVELOPER, the DEVELOPER may, in its discretion, upon written notice immediately demand specific performance by DISTRICT.

If DEVELOPER fails to perform any of the provisions of this Agreement or fails to administer the work so as to endanger the performance of the Agreement and fails to cure such performance or administration after 30 days' notice by the CITY or DISTRICT, it will be in default. Unless

DEVELOPER's default is excused in writing by the CITY and DISTRICT, the DISTRICT may, in its discretion, upon written notice immediately demand specific performance by DEVELOPER.

4. Survival of Provisions. Provisions that by their nature are intended to survive the term, cancellation, or termination of this Agreement do survive the term, cancellation, or termination.

5. Assignment. This Cooperative Agreement may not be assigned, pledged, or transferred without the prior written consent of all parties.

[SIGNATURE BLOCKS]

APPENDIX 10

Sample Economic Development and Tax Sharing Agreement

This Economic Development and Tax Sharing Agreement ("**Agreement**") is entered into by and between the COUNTY OF ____________, State of California (the "**County**"), and ___________ ("**Developer**"). The County and Developer are sometimes referred to individually herein as a "Party" and collectively as the "Parties."

RECITALS

This Agreement is entered into on the basis of the following facts, understandings, and intentions of the Parties. The following recitals are a substantive part of this Agreement.

A. On ____________, the Board of Supervisors of the County (the "**Board**"), pursuant to Resolution No. ___________ and Ordinance No. ______, approved, among other things, (i) necessary California Environmental Quality Act ("**CEQA**") findings to certify the Environmental Impact Report related to State Clearinghouse No. ___________ (the "**EIR**"), (ii) a Mitigation Monitoring and Reporting Program in connection with the EIR (the "**MMRP**"), (iii) an amendment to the County's General Plan to change the land use designation of the site of the project (the "**Site**") from Agriculture to Highway Commercial, (iv) a rezoning of the Site from Exclusive Agriculture to General Commercial, (v) a Development Agreement between the County and ____________ (later recorded in the Official Records of the County as Document No. ____________) (the "**Development Agreement**") (collectively, the "**Entitlements**").

B. The 2022 Entitlements allow for, among other things, the development of a _____ room Hotel on the Site (the "**Hotel Project**").

C. The Parties anticipate that the Hotel Project will generate substantial economic and fiscal benefits for the County including revenue from transient occupancy taxes, property taxes, sales taxes, and other economic activity including approximately 1,200 construction jobs and approximately 500 full and part time permanent jobs.

D. To assist with the significant investment associated with development of the Hotel Project, the County has agreed to share with Developer a portion of transient occupancy tax revenues that are generated solely by the Hotel Project that will be used to recover, defray, and/or defer construction and other investment costs that include County fees, other agency fees, and land acquisition costs.

E. The Board adopted Resolution No. ______ approving this Agreement; following required notice and a hearing.

F. This Agreement is advantageous to and benefits the County; is consistent with the County's General Plan and the Entitlements; will promote the public convenience, general welfare, and good land use practice; will not be detrimental to the public's health, safety, or general welfare; will not adversely affect the orderly development of the Hotel Project; and will promote and encourage the development of the Hotel Project by providing economic incentives and a greater degree of requisite certainty.

G. The County and Developer have reached mutual agreement and desire to voluntarily enter into this Agreement to facilitate development of the Hotel Project subject to the conditions and requirements set forth herein.

AGREEMENT

NOW, THEREFORE, in consideration of the covenants set forth herein and for other good and valuable consideration, the receipt and sufficiency of which are hereby acknowledged and approved, the Parties agree as follows:
Article I. HOTEL PROJECT, SITE, EFFECTIVE DATE, TERM.

Section 1.01 Property. This Agreement applies to the Hotel Project to be built on the Site.

Section 1.02 Effective Date. The rights, duties, and obligations under this Agreement shall become effective on the "Effective Date," which shall be the date that this Agreement is fully executed by the Parties.

Section 1.03 Term. The term ("**Term**") of this Agreement shall commence on the Effective Date and shall expire 180 days following the last quarterly payment of TOT Revenue (defined in Section 2.01 below) to Developer under Section 2.02, unless sooner terminated in accordance with this Agreement.

Article II. TRANSIENT OCCUPANCY TAXES.

Section 2.01 Transient Occupancy Tax Revenue Sharing and Deferred Impact Fees. Provided that the Hotel Project has been constructed with a minimum of 450 rooms, the County shall allocate, beginning on the date that transient occupancy taxes are first received from the Hotel Project ("**TOT Revenue**") and continuing for 15 years thereafter, TOT Revenue in the following order of priority as TOT Revenue is received by the County:

(a) First, pay the County its Deferred County Fees (defined in Section 2.03 below), amortized over 5 years, without interest from year 1 to year 5.

(b) Next, pay the remaining TOT Revenue 100 percent to Developer from year 1 to year 5.

(c) Next, pay TOT Revenue 25 percent to the County and 75 percent to Developer from year 6 to year 10.

(d) Next, pay TOT Revenue 50 percent to the County and 50 percent to Developer from year 11 to year 15.

An illustrative example of TOT Revenue sharing between the County and Developer described in this Section 2.01 is attached hereto as Exhibit C.

Section 2.02 Quarterly Payments and Accounting. TOT Revenue shall be paid and accounted for on a calendar quarterly basis (*i.e.*, the quarters ending on March 31, June 30, September 30, and December 31 of each calendar year) beginning with the first quarter in which the Hotel Project is open and continuing for the remainder of the Term. Developer shall pay to the County the TOT Revenue generated during each quarter no later than 30 days after the end of each such quarter, and the County shall pay Developer its share of TOT Revenue for each such quarter in accordance with and subject to Section 2.01 within 10 business days thereafter. The County also shall provide Developer with a quarterly written accounting of the TOT Revenue received and allocated concurrent with each quarterly payment of TOT Revenue to Developer.

Section 2.03 Deferred County Fees. All development fees otherwise due to the County by Developer in connection with development of the Hotel Project ("**Deferred County Fees**") shall be deferred until paid with TOT

Revenue pursuant to Section 2.01(a). An illustrative example of Deferred County Fees for the Hotel Project is attached hereto as Exhibit D.

Article III. DEFAULT, LEGAL ACTION, REMEDIES AND DISPUTE RESOLUTION.

Section 3.01 Default. Failure by either Party to perform any term or condition of this Agreement shall constitute a default ("**Default**"). In the event of an alleged Default of any term, condition, or obligation of this Agreement, the Party alleging such Default shall give the Party in Default notice in writing specifying the nature of the alleged Default and the manner in which the Default may be satisfactorily cured ("**Notice of Breach**"). The Party in Default shall cure the Default within 30 days following receipt of the Notice of Breach. However, if such cure cannot be accomplished within such 30-day period, then the Party in Default will be deemed to have cured the default upon the commencement of a cure within the 30-day period and diligent subsequent completion thereof. If the alleged failure is cured within the time provided above, then no Default shall exist, and the noticing Party shall take no further action to exercise any remedies available hereunder. If the alleged failure is not cured, then a Default shall exist under this Agreement and the Party not in Default may exercise any of the remedies available under this Agreement.

Section 3.02 Legal Actions. Following completion of the dispute resolution processes provided for in Section 3.03 below, in addition to any other rights or remedies, a Party may institute legal action to cure, correct, or remedy any Default, to enforce any covenants or agreements herein, to enjoin any threatened or attempted violation thereof, or to obtain any other remedies consistent with the purpose of this Agreement, including without limitation specific performance. Any such legal action shall be brought in the Superior Court for _________ County.

Section 3.03 Resolution of Disputes.

(a) With regard to any dispute involving the Hotel Project, a Party shall, at the written request of another Party, meet and confer with designated representatives of the requesting Party promptly following its written request. The written request shall specify the nature of the dispute and the manner in which the dispute may be satisfactorily resolved ("**Notice of Dispute**"). The Parties to any such meeting(s) shall attempt in good faith to resolve any such disputes. Nothing in this Section 3.03 shall in any way be interpreted as requiring that any Party reach agreement with regard to such dispute, nor shall the outcome of these meeting(s) be binding in any way on any Party unless expressly agreed to in writing by both Parties.

(b) The Parties agree that the meet and confer, including proceedings or discussions concerning the proposed meet and confer, is to be considered a confidential settlement negotiation for the purpose of all state and federal rules protecting disclosures made during such conferences from later discovery or use in evidence. All conduct, statements, promises, offers, views and opinions, oral or written, made during a meet and confer by any Party or a Party's agent, employee, or attorney shall be deemed to be confidential and shall not be subject to discovery or be admissible for any purpose, including impeachment, in any litigation or other proceeding, including mediation, involving the Parties; provided, however, that evidence otherwise subject to discovery or otherwise admissible is not excluded from discovery or admission into evidence simply as a result of it having been used in connection with the meet and confer.

(c) If the dispute is not resolved to the satisfaction of the Parties within thirty (30) days after the first meeting (or such other time period as the Parties may agree upon), then upon the written request of either Party, the dispute may be submitted to non-binding mediation in accordance with Subsection (d) below ("**Mediation Request**").

(d) **Mediation**. (i) In the event a dispute arising under this Agreement is not resolved through the above-described meet and confer process, then within 30 days after notice is provided through a Mediation Request, the Parties agree to participate in non-binding mediation administered by a mediator to help mediate and settle the dispute as soon as practicable. The non-binding mediation shall be held at a mutually agreeable location in _________ County, California. The Parties must mutually select the mediator, but in case of disagreement, then the Parties will select the mediator by lot from among two nominations provided by each Party. The Parties will split equally all costs and fees required by the mediator; otherwise, each Party will bear its own costs of mediation. If mediation fails to resolve the dispute within 30 days (or such other time period as the Parties may agree upon), then either Party may pursue litigation to resolve the dispute.

(ii) Mediation will be conducted consistent with California Evidence Code Sections 1115-1129, this Section 3.03, and, to the extent practicable, the Commercial Mediation Procedures of the

American Arbitration Association ("**AAA**"). The Mediator shall owe a professional duty to both Parties and shall be barred from testifying in any litigation concerning any information obtained or disclosed in the course of the mediation.

(iii) The Mediator's recommendations shall not be binding on or admissible against either Party. The Parties agree that the mediation, including proceedings or discussions concerning the mediation, is to be considered a confidential settlement negotiation for the purpose of all state and federal rules protecting disclosures made during such conferences from later discovery or use in evidence. All conduct, statements, promises, offers, views and opinions, oral or written, made during the mediation by any Party or a Party's agent, employee, or attorney shall be deemed to be confidential and shall not be subject to discovery or admissible for any purpose, including impeachment, in any litigation or other proceeding involving the Parties; provided, however, that evidence otherwise subject to discovery or admissible is not excluded from discovery or admission into evidence simply as a result of it having been used in connection with the mediation.

Section 3.04 Rights and Remedies Are Cumulative. The rights and remedies of the Parties are cumulative, and the exercise by a Party of one or more of such rights or remedies shall not preclude the exercise by it, at the same or different times, of any other rights or remedies for the same Default or any other Default by the other Party, except as otherwise expressly provided herein.

Article IV. COOPERATION IN DEVELOPMENT OF HOTEL PROJECT.

Section 4.01 Future County Approvals. County approvals and permits will be necessary or desirable for development of the Hotel Project ("**Future County Approvals**"). Future County Approvals may include, without limitation: amendments to the Entitlements, use permits, grading permits, building permits, sewer and water connection permits, certificates of occupancy, lot line adjustments, site plans, development plans, land use plans, building plans and specifications, and any amendments to, or repealing of, any of the foregoing. Upon submission by Developer of complete applications for Future County Approvals, including payment of all applicable processing fees, the County shall promptly and diligently cooperate with Developer and take all steps necessary to process and act upon such applications.

Section 4.02 Other Government Approvals. The County shall cooperate with Developer in Developer's efforts to obtain any future approvals and permits from other governmental or quasi-governmental entities that may be required for development of the Hotel Project and shall use its best efforts to enter into binding agreements with such entities as may be necessary to ensure the timely availability of such permits and approvals for development of the Hotel Project.

Article V. AMENDMENT.

Section 5.01 Amendment. This Agreement may be amended from time to time, in whole or in part, only by mutual written consent of the Parties. Except as otherwise provided herein, County's consent to such amendment will require formal written approval from the County Board of Supervisors.

Article VI. ASSIGNMENT.

Section 6.01 Assignment. Developer shall have the right to sell, transfer, or ground lease (each, an "**Assignment**") its interests in the Property to any person, partnership, joint venture, firm, company, corporation, or other entity (any of the foregoing, an "**Assignee**") provided that an Assignee continues to operate the Hotel Project or contracts with Developer, or another resort operator with similar experience and qualifications, to operate the Hotel Project with operational and quality standards substantially similar to those of Developer as of the Effective Date, subject to the written consent of the County, which consent shall not unreasonably be withheld, conditioned, or delayed; provided that Developer may assign its rights under this Agreement without the consent of the County to any affiliate of Developer. Developer shall provide the County with written notice of any proposed Assignment at least 30 days prior to such Assignment. Notwithstanding the foregoing, Developer may assign this Agreement as security to the holder of any deed of trust or other security instrument encumbering Developer's interest in the Property and/or the Hotel Project ("**Holder**") and any such Holder may foreclose its interest in this Agreement or otherwise assume this Agreement and be deemed a permitted Assignee; in such event, Holder may further assign this Agreement without the County's consent.

Article VII. NOTICES.

All notices and demands required by this Agreement shall be given in writing by certified mail, postage prepaid, and return receipt requested, or by reputable overnight messenger. Notices shall be considered given upon the earlier of (a) one business day following deposit or delivery with a nationally recognized overnight courier delivery charges prepaid, or (b) three business days following the date of mailing if given by certified mail. Notices shall be addressed as provided below for the respective Party; provided that if any Party gives notice in writing of a change of name or address, notices to such Party shall thereafter be given as demanded in that notice:

The County: County of ____________
Attn: County Administrative Officer
____
____

With copies to:

County Counsel
County of ___________
____
____

Developer: ____________________
____
____
____

With copies to:
____
____
____
____

Article VIII. MISCELLANEOUS.

Section 8.01 Counterparts. This Agreement may be executed in one or more counterparts, each of which shall be deemed an original, but all of which together shall constitute one and the same instrument. A signed copy or signed counterpart of this Agreement delivered by facsimile, email, or other means of electronic transmission shall be deemed to have the same legal effect as delivery of a signed original or signed copy of this Agreement.

Section 8.02 Manual or Electronic Signatures. The Parties may sign this Agreement by means of manual or electronic signatures. The Parties agree that the electronic signature of a Party, whether digital or encrypted, is intended to authenticate this Agreement and to have the same force and effect as a manual signature. For purposes of this Agreement, the term "electronic signature" means any electronic sound, symbol, or process attached to or logically associated with this Agreement and executed and adopted by a Party with the intent to sign this Agreement, including facsimile, portable document format, or email electronic signatures, pursuant to the California Uniform Electronic Transactions Act (Cal. Civ. Code §§ 1633.1 to 1633.17), as it may be amended from time to time.

Section 8.03 Waivers. Notwithstanding any other provision in this Agreement, any failure or delay by any Party in asserting any of its rights and remedies under this Agreement shall not operate as a waiver of any such rights or remedies or deprive any such Party of its right to institute and maintain any actions or proceedings which it may deem necessary to protect, assert or enforce any such rights or remedies. A Party may specifically and expressly waive in writing any condition or breach of this Agreement by the other Party, but no such waiver shall constitute a further or continuing waiver of any preceding or succeeding breach of the same or any other provision. Consent by one Party to any act by the other Party shall not be deemed to imply consent or waiver of the necessity of obtaining such consent for the same or similar acts in the future.

Section 8.04 Construction of Agreement. All Parties have been represented by counsel in the preparation and negotiation of this Agreement and this Agreement shall be construed according to the fair meaning of its language. The rule of construction to the effect that ambiguities are to be resolved against the drafting party shall not be employed in interpreting this Agreement. Unless the context clearly requires otherwise, (a) the plural and singular numbers shall each be deemed to include the other; (b) the masculine, feminine, and neuter genders shall each be deemed to include the others; (c) "shall," "will," or "agrees" are mandatory, and "may" is permissive; (d) "or" is not exclusive; (e) "includes" and "including" are not limiting; and (f) "days" means calendar days unless specifically provided otherwise.

Section 8.05 Headings. Section headings in this Agreement are for convenience only and are not intended to be used in interpreting or construing the terms, covenants, or conditions of this Agreement.

Section 8.06 Severability. Each and every provision of this Agreement is, and shall be construed to be, a separate and independent covenant and agreement. If any term or provision of this Agreement or the application thereof shall to any extent be held to be invalid or unenforceable, the remainder of this Agreement, or the application of such term or provision to circumstances other than those to which it is invalid or unenforceable, shall not be affected hereby, and each term and provision of this Agreement shall be valid and shall be enforced to the extent permitted by law.

Section 8.07 Time Is of the Essence. Time is of the essence of each and every provision of this Agreement in which time is a factor.

Section 8.08 Extension of Time Limits. The time limits set forth in this Agreement may be extended by mutual consent in writing of the Parties in accordance with the provisions of this Agreement.

Section 8.09 Signatures. Developer and the County represent and warrant that the individuals executing this Agreement have the right, power, legal capacity, and authority to enter into and to execute this Agreement on behalf of the respective legal entities of Developer and the County.

Section 8.10 Entire Agreement. This Agreement constitutes the entire understanding and agreement of the Parties, integrates all of the terms and conditions mentioned herein and therein or incidental hereto and thereto, and supersede all negotiations or previous agreements between the Parties with respect to the subject matter hereof and thereof. No subsequent agreement, representation or promise made by either Party, or by or to any employee, officer, agent or representative of either Party, shall be of any effect unless it is in writing and executed by the Party to be bound thereby.

Section 8.11 Estoppel Certificate. Developer or any Holder may, at any time, and from time to time, deliver written notice to the County requesting the County to certify in writing that: (a) this Agreement is in full force and effect; (b) this Agreement has not been amended or modified or, if so amended or modified, identifying the amendments or modifications; (c) Developer is not in Default of the performance of its obligations, or if in Default, to describe therein the nature and extent of any such Defaults;

and (d) such other certifications that Developer may reasonably request. The County Administrative Officer or his or her designee shall execute and return such certificate within 30 days following Developer's written request therefor. Developer and the County acknowledge that a certificate hereunder may be relied upon by tenants, transferees, investors, partners, bond counsel, underwriters, bond holders and Holders. The failure to deliver such a statement, or to explain in writing why such notice cannot be provided, within such time shall constitute a conclusive presumption against the County that this Agreement is in full force and effect without modification (except as may be asserted by Developer) and that there are no uncured defaults in the performance of Developer.

Section 8.12 County Approvals and Actions. Whenever a reference is made herein to an action or approval to be undertaken by the County, the County Administrative Officer or his or her designee is authorized to act on behalf of the County, unless specifically provided otherwise or the context requires otherwise.

Section 8.13 Negation of Partnership. The Parties specifically acknowledge that the Hotel Project is a private development, that no Party to this Agreement is acting as the agent of any other in any respect hereunder, and that each Party is an independent contracting entity with respect to the terms, covenants and conditions contained in this Agreement. None of the terms or provisions of this Agreement shall be deemed to create a partnership between or among the Parties in the businesses of Developer, the affairs of the County, or otherwise, or cause them to be considered joint venturers or members of any joint enterprise.

Section 8.14 No Third-Party Beneficiaries. This Agreement is made and entered into for the sole protection and benefit of the signatory Parties and their successors and assigns, including Holders. No other person, agency, or entity shall have any right of action based upon any provision in this Agreement.

Section 8.15 Governing Law. This Agreement shall be construed in accordance with the laws of the State of California, without reference to its choice of law provisions.

Section 8.16 Exhibits. The following exhibits are attached to this Agreement and are incorporated herein as though set forth in full for all purposes except as provided below:

Exhibit A	Description/Depiction of the Site
Exhibit B	Description/Depiction of the Hotel Project

Exhibit C	Illustrative Example of TOT Revenue Distribution
Exhibit D	Illustrative Example of Deferred County Fees for the Hotel Project

"THE COUNTY"	"DEVELOPER"
COUNTY OF ____________________,	______________________,
State of California	______________________,
By:____________________________	______________________,
Chair, Board of Supervisors	______________________,
Date:__________________________	

ATTEST: ______________________
County Administrative Officer/Clerk
of the Board of Supervisors of the County
of ____________________________

____
Deputy Clerk

APPROVED AS TO FORM:
County Counsel

By:____________________________

Print Name: ______________________

TABLE OF CASES

INDEX